T0318458

Caribbean Public Policy

Caribbean Public Policy

Regional, Cultural, and Socioeconomic Issues for the 21st Century

EDITED BY

Jacqueline Anne Braveboy-Wagner and Dennis J. Gayle

Routledge
Taylor & Francis Group
New York London

First published 1998 by Westview Press

Published 2018 by Routledge
605 Third Avenue, New York, NY 10017
2 Park Square, Milton Park, Abingdon, Oxon OX14 4RN

Routledge is an imprint of the Taylor & Francis Group, an informa business

Library of Congress Cataloging-in-Publication Data
Caribbean public policy : regional, cultural, and socioeconomic
    issues for the 21st century / edited by Jacqueline Anne Braveboy-Wagner
    and Dennis J. Gayle.
        p.   cm.
    Includes index.
    ISBN 0-8133-3627-9
    1. Caribbean Area—Economic conditions.   2. Caribbean Area—
Economic integration.   3. Caribbean Area—Cultural policy.
4.   Education and state—Caribbean Area.   5. Caribbean Area—Social
policy.   I. Braveboy-Wagner, Jacqueline Anne.   II. Gayle, Dennis
John, 1949–   .
HC151.C344   1997
338.9729—dc21   97-25026
                                                                                            CIP

Typeset by Letra Libre

ISBN 13: 978-0-8133-3627-5 (pbk)

To Justin and Jeremy

To Jean-Pierre and Sophia

Contents

Part Three
The Caribbean Public Policy Agenda:
Human Development Issues

Acknowledgments

The editors would like to acknowledge the role played by the Caribbean Studies Association (CSA) in the genesis of this work. In 1993 while the editors were serving, respectively, as president of the CSA and co-chair of the CSA's annual conference, the theme of Caribbean public policy was explored thoroughly by conference participants meeting in Jamaica. We came away from these discussions surprised that so few publications existed on the subject of public policy in the Caribbean and convinced that in this era of global change a lasting contribution on the subject was warranted. A relatively comprehensive book-length manuscript was our preferred option, although we were aware that publication would not be as timely as a dedicated journal issue.

In addition to acknowledging the role of the CSA, we would like to thank all the contributors to this volume for the patience they have displayed while the work was in progress. Moreover, we thank all who sent us submissions that could not be included due to space or theme limitations. Finally, we offer special thanks to Bamijoko Smith, editor of the *Century Policy Review,* for granting us permission to reprint the article that became Chapter 15 of this book, and to Rosemary Barba and the Instructional Resource Center of Florida International University for preparing the two maps included.

J. Braveboy-Wagner
Dennis J. Gayle

Map of the Caribbean Basin

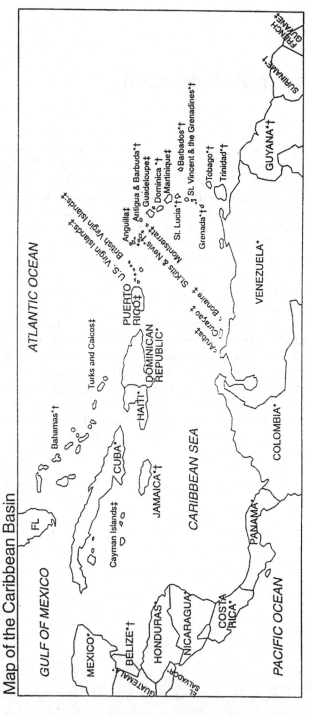

LEGEND:

* Member countries of the Association of Caribbean States

† CARICOM Member States

‡ States, countries and territories eligible for membership in the Association of Caribbean States

France, the U.K., and the Netherlands became associate members in 1995

Bermuda is also eligible for membership in the Association of Caribbean States

1

Introduction: Caribbean Public Policy Issues in the 1990s

Jacqueline Anne Braveboy-Wagner

The Public Policy Environment of the 1990s

In the mid-1990s, the main characteristics of the post–Cold War era, endorsed in theory by the global community, are reasonably well-defined. They include, in the civic sphere, the primacy of democratic procedures, norms and values; and in the economic sphere, endorsement of liberal policies designed to remove national barriers to trade and investment, to expand regional integration, and to further global free trade. In this era, a concentration on military-ideological issues has given way to a more diffuse distribution of global attention so that even as the global community agonizes over civil conflict in Bosnia, Rwanda, or Chechnya, its attention is diverted to the oft-heated trade battles between Japan and the United States, the global implications of the economic woes of Mexico, and the conclusion of a financial services agreement among the members of the World Trade Organization (WTO). Moreover, nagging social problems ranging from depletion of the ozone layer to the intractability of the narcotics problem provide a backdrop to more immediate political and economic issues.

For the developing countries, however, the new order has posed a number of problems. Despite efforts to keep development issues on the global agenda (see for example, United Nations 1994), decision-making in international fora has tended to be dominated by conflict resolution and peacekeeping/peacemaking issues. Moreover, the conception of development as a matter of social justice and correction of economic and social imbalances and inequities, a dominant conception in the 1970s and early 1980s, has been subordinated to the conservative paradigm of development as growth and self-help.[1] The last can be contrasted to the much-advocated "self-reliant" development of the 1970s. Self-reliance among the developing countries involved "de-linking" from certain unfavorable aspects of the international economic and financial system; self-help, on the other hand, refers to internally generated, if externally assisted, structural change.

For developing countries, what this means is that they can no longer expect development assistance by virtue of appeals to social justice. This is compounded by their loss of leverage resulting from the demise of communism. Thus, as global capital becomes scarcer, given the need of industrial nations to sustain democratic transitions in Russia, the former Soviet republics, and Eastern Europe, developing countries have been forced to reassess earlier policies and stances. From deeply nationalist policies and structures, including culturally or politically rationalized autocratic systems and protectionist economic regimes, developing countries have, however reluctantly and however pressured by their industrial colleagues, turned to more open political structures and liberal economic regimes. In the new spirit of self-help, fresh lessons about managerial efficiency and economic competitiveness have had to be learned, new worries about preserving old sources and finding new sources of external capital and aid have preoccupied policy-makers, and new leadership challenges have presented themselves as governments seek to rationalize a decline in social humanism and to reconcile economic reform with growing social inequities.

Policy Dilemmas for the Caribbean

The Caribbean region both embodies the policy dilemmas of the developing countries in the new era and presents the opportunity to assess developing country *possibilities* for successful coping and survival in this new order. That is to say, if adaptability, a moderate level of development, and basic democratic values give a region a "leg up" in the new era, the English-speaking Caribbean at least has an advantage over other areas of the developing south. Africa, for example, risks greater marginalization in the new era due to its relative geographic isolation and the persistence of old structures and ideas. On a tour of Central Africa in 1995, U.N. Secretary-General Boutros Boutros-Ghali expressed this concern quite clearly, as reported wryly in one major newspaper: "The poorest continent, he said in one crumbling city after another, risks being further marginalized and devastated by its own politicians. The world is not going to help, he said, until Africans demonstrate the 'political will and imagination' to help themselves" (*New York Times*, July 23, 1995: 3).

On the other hand, the relatively modernized structures and economies of the Caribbean give the region an advantage in the race to adapt to new global norms. The Caribbean also benefits from geographic proximity, history, and social links—via migration—with the United States. These characteristics continue to give the region a certain degree of visibility to U.S. policy-makers. Clearly also, U.S. and global attention continues to be residually focused on political problems in Haiti, and this country can therefore count on some level of development assistance for the rest of the 1990s. Cuba, too, is in no danger of being forgotten. Moreover, the Spanish-speaking mainland states of the "Basin" (South America and Central America) maintain some leverage in the 1990s either because their democracies are still transitional (as in Central America) or their size and economic relationships are hemispherically significant (Mexico, Colombia, and Venezuela).

But even if the Caribbean countries are not as much at risk of marginalization as African countries, adaptation to the new era is not easy. First, there is the fragility of the emerging democracies and the uneasiness of the older ones in the face of new challenges. Second, for the many small states of the region, there is the heightened difficulty of achieving economies of scale and production efficiencies in a highly competitive economic era. Third, all the region's countries must also deal with the logistical, political, and social difficulties that arise from the dismantling of protectionist structures, the divestment of inefficient state enterprises, the implementation of effective incentives to foreign investment, and other measures intended to restructure their economies. Fourth, externally, they are presented with a number of strategies for countering marginalization, but each strategy in turn presents its own difficulties. Among the strategies being espoused are:

- enhanced regional integration (but this has proven to be a painfully slow and somewhat contentious process);
- pursuit of possible membership in the North American Free Trade Area or NAFTA (a proposition subject to the vagaries of public and governmental opinion in the United States, and whose benefits may be rather dubious);
- active lobbying for preservation of privileges under the Caribbean Basin Initiative (CBI) and the European Union—African-Caribbean-Pacific (ACP) accords (a temporary reprieve at best);
- and diversification of trade and aid ties (long on the agenda of developing countries as a whole but very difficult to implement).

The problems of adaptation form the backdrop of public policy formulation in the 1990s and into the next century. In actuality, the details of national policy have a more complex sectoral focus. Whereas the policy superstructure is defined in terms of the broad strokes of liberalization, export promotion, regionalism, and diversification, the details of policy formulation and implementation address many technical issues. Among them are such questions as how to make the agricultural, manufacturing, and banking sectors efficient and competitive; how to retool the educational sector to facilitate technological literacy; how to deal with the increasing levels of poverty and unemployment that are the result of economic restructuring; and what to do about increased crime and drug abuse, arising to a large degree from the stresses of modernization and structural reform. Other key issues are how to foster economic growth without significant environmental damage, environmental awareness being now not only a global norm but also a condition of external aid and a lightning rod for pressure from an ever-increasing number of non-governmental groups; how to provide educational and work opportunities for disadvantaged groups and for women, the latter representing more than half of the population; how to appease labor in the midst of policies that have eroded hard-won social and monetary gains; and in general how to ensure the country's economic survival and growth and how to make life bearable for the bulk of the populace.

Changes in the Policy-Making Process

As the global order and policy strategies have changed, so too has the policy-making process in the Caribbean. Policy-making involves goal setting, problem solving, prioritization in the allocation of resources, decision taking, and implementation or action. In the past, analysts contrasted the "first world" policy and decision process characterized by interest group lobbying, multiplicity of actors, significant legislative debate, varying degrees of bureaucratic neutrality, and incremental decision-making or "satisficing" (March and Simon 1993; also Braybrooke and Lindblom 1963; Heisler 1974) with the impulsive, unrealistically comprehensive planning of developing states (Hirschman 1988, 1993; Clark 1982). Such planning has often been undertaken in an atmosphere of suppression of dissent and "groupthink," the term coined by Janis (1982) to refer to harmonized, closed decision taking. First-world Weberian rational-legal analysis has also been contrasted with third world personalistic decision-making.

But in the late 1980s and 1990s, there have been substantive changes in the decision-making environment of the developing world, including the Caribbean. The demise of old charismatic leaders has brought in a new technocratic and pragmatic ruling elite (see Braveboy-Wagner 1992). In the past, the ruling elites were the sole formulators or dictators of policy, given the long-standing weakness of the political opposition both within the modified Westminster systems characteristic of the English-speaking Caribbean, and the oligarchic systems of the Spanish Caribbean and Suriname. Now democratization has brought a greater concern for accountability and a new emphasis on effectiveness, backed by greater popular restiveness. In this atmosphere, although the organized opposition remains weak in many countries, governments are being forced to democratize policy-making somewhat, at least to the extent of reaching out to involve and placate certain societal groups, in particular labor, business, and an increasingly vigilant media.

At another level, the *scope* of policy-making has also changed. Very few countries maintain the comprehensive five-year goals of the past; most have since moved to sectoral planning and, in many instances, planning is so short-term as to be based primarily on the year's budget projections and other interim analyses. In today's difficult economic climate, leaders who promise major achievements within specified time frames are apt to be derided by a jaded electorate.

The planning process in the Caribbean is still weakened by many of the factors observed in the past by third world analysts. Clark, for example, speaks of incorrect goal setting based on unreliable information, lack of trained experts in crucial areas, lack of funds, political corruption, and the tendency to import foreign solutions (Clark 1982: 124–131). The last is particularly problematic today as governments struggle to weigh the persistent demands of the international institutions (primarily the World Bank and International Monetary Fund) and the perceived need to conform to the global orthodoxy of liberalization, against their own cultural and social inclinations and the hostility of domestic sectors to liberal reform.

Academic Influence on Policy

Sidney Verba, well-recognized as a theorist of rationality in foreign policy decision-making, once noted that, although actual decision-making does not conform to a rational means-ends model, the distinction "suggests the importance of decision-making, or, at least, decision-recommending outside of a bureaucratic context." Verba continued:

> Means-ends rationality as a process of decision-making is more closely approximated in research and in decisions that are "unattached" rather than bureaucratic. The search for policy alternatives by unattached intellectuals is less inhibited by organizational coalitions. A wider range of alternatives is likely to be considered, and the values invoked are likely to be more explicit and consistent. And, because of the over-all norms of loyalty

to the system, the more explicit the values operative in a particular decision situation, the more they will tend to be non-parochial. Unattached intellectual research, therefore, can introduce a higher level of means-ends rationality into foreign-policy decision-making (Verba 1969: 230).

Verba went on to warn, however, that it is precisely this means-ends research, which makes values explicit and calculates the consequences of alternative policies, that arouses opposition among members of the foreign policy coalition whose value preferences are different.

Verba's classic analysis remains true today and applicable to domestic as well as foreign policy decision-making. The approach of the intellectual, even the policy-oriented intellectual, is usually very different methodologically from that of the bureaucrat or decision-maker intimately involved in the decision. On the specific matter of rationality, the researcher should normally be able to look at alternatives relatively objectively and offer suggestions from that perspective. That perspective, however, is rarely acceptable to value-conscious decision-makers.

Although Verba speaks primarily about decision-making in the industrialized countries, the problem of intellectual or academic participation in public policy is compounded in the developing world where traditionally academics have been viewed as (and many have indeed been) ideologues opposed to existing political elites and structures. "Rationality" has been a rare commodity on either side. In these developing societies, often polarized between elites and masses, academics have traditionally championed the cause of the dispossessed, and both their intellectual and practical involvement in social and political activities have tended to alienate policy-makers. Their advice has generally been automatically rejected by government elites as either self-serving or serving a hidden agenda. Although to some extent these ideological differences are common to the policy-maker—academic debate in all countries, pure hostility has often characterized the relationship between the two forces in developing countries.

The mistrust of academics in the Caribbean and developing world usually also permeated academic—bureaucrat relations. Unlike the "neutral" bureaucrats of the first world, third world bureaucrats, often owing their jobs to patronage, have tended to be extremely sensitive to the political winds, and overly cautious about what information they give to researchers. Often, in the Caribbean, bureaucrats have been more receptive to researchers coming from abroad than to those, presumably the ones with "hidden" agendas, residing in their own country. The chief exception to the rule has been, of course, the disgruntled or disenchanted bureaucrat, eager to "blow the whistle" anonymously. As in all such situations, in any country, a wealth of information can be had in those circumstances with very little effort. But for the third world academic seeking to exercise some influence rather than write a seminal, ground-breaking analysis, the mistrust exhibited by bureaucrats has been a major obstacle. The unfortunate cycle of distrust has left bureaucrats fearful for their jobs, governments suspicious of the bureaucracy and the intellectual, and academics distrustful of and alienated from both government elites and bureaucrats.

The global changes of the 1990s have also changed the chances for influence of the academic in the third world. Today the left-wing third world academic is as scarce as the left-wing policy-maker. Conditions would seemingly be ripe for greater collaboration between the two sides, certainly in the Caribbean. Caribbean academics can presumably contribute effectively to public policy debate at a time when both creativity and technical knowledge, the supposed hallmarks of the intellectual, are sorely needed. And indeed, in the region today, anecdotal evidence suggests that the circulation of elites between academia and government, quite common in many industrial countries, has increased in many countries. It used to be that academics were only invited to serve, or felt comfortable serving in, "radical" regimes. Now, in the English-speaking Caribbean, for example, non-elected appointments to government positions are becoming more common, and many of these non-elected persons are drawn from the academic community. Academics are also serving as consultants and advisors to policy-makers at both formal and informal levels.

On the other hand, the issue of credibility remains a major barrier to greater academic—policy-maker collaboration. Almost everywhere in the world, academics tend to be viewed as "ivory tower" theorists who do not understand the "real" world of policy-making. When added to the ideological differences traditionally apparent between academics and policy-makers in the third world, the credibility gap is bound to be even more acute.

John Lewis Gaddis made a pertinent comment in the introduction to his well-received analysis of why prevailing international relations theories could not predict the end of the Cold War. He noted that "princes have always sought out soothsayers of one kind or another for the purposes of learning what the future holds. These hired visionaries have found portents in the configurations of stars, the entrails of animals, and most indicators in between. The results, on the whole, have been disappointing" (Gaddis 1992/1993: 5).

Among today's soothsayers, according to Gaddis, are "historians, political scientists, economists, psychologists, and even mathematicians" who "have claimed the power to detect patterns in the behavior of nations and the individuals who lead them; an awareness of these, they have assured us, will better equip statesmen—and states—to deal with the uncertainties that lie ahead" (Gaddis, pp. 5–6). Gaddis goes on to analyze the nature of and reasons for the failure of academic theory. Given this record of failure, perhaps it is not surprising that a 1994 study by the Carnegie Foundation for the Advancement of Teaching found that the majority of faculty in the United States and many other countries feel they are not among the most influential opinion leaders in their countries and that respect for professors is declining. Yet they overwhelmingly believe that they have an obligation to apply their knowledge to solving problems in society (Boyer 1994).[2]

The credibility gap, whether in the developed or the developing world, can only be overcome by the sharing of ideas between policy-makers and academics through conferences, working groups, and meaningful published public policy contributions, as well as the circulation of elites so that academics can have hands-on experience in government and government elites can be given opportunities to speak to academic audiences.

In 1958, Gordon K. Lewis, recognized as one of the Caribbean's most respected intellectuals, suggested: "We must see the social sciences, not as arid accountants of the way we live now, but as the way we might live, as the handmaiden of power over the material environment . . . private research is a sterile ivory tower unless it is translated into public policy (in Williams 1969: 273). Although Lewis was speaking at the dawn of the nationalist era in the English-speaking Caribbean, the words remain as pertinent today as then. In the United States, the pure research of the behavioral era in social science has long given way to a more policy-oriented focus that blends positivism and advocacy. The new global era presents Caribbean academics with the opportunity to move in the other direction, away from pure *advocacy* and toward that same blend.

Scope of Contributions

The contributions that follow represent an attempt by leading Caribbean academics to initiate the process of interchange of ideas with policy-makers. For this reason, contributions from persons with policy experience have been specifically solicited to complement the academic contributions. The book does not seek to deal with the technical aspects of policy formulation and decision-making in the region. Rather, its focus is on public policy issues, the aim being to evaluate current policy and suggest realistic improvements and alternatives.

The contributors to this book, and the contributions themselves, are representative of all the various cultural areas that comprise the Caribbean. In the past, the Caribbean tended to be conceptualized by both the region's academics and policy-makers as culturally separate and unique sub-units of countries. Except for strategic collaboration in various international and regional fora, policy-makers of each cultural sub-region—Spanish, English, Dutch, and French—devised their public policy without particular reference to what was being done by their neighbors. Today, the risk of marginalization is bringing about closer regional collaboration. Acknowledging that small countries maximize their chances of survival through collaboration, Caribbean countries have crossed the cultural divide in establishing in 1994 the Association of Caribbean States (ACS), an association of Caribbean Basin countries. Ironically, the Caribbean is moving in the direction of the foreign conception of the region in that U.S., European, Japanese, and other external policy-makers have long dealt with the Caribbean programmatically as a seamless, if culturally diverse, unit. Regional academics and policy-makers, however, depart from this programmatic view in recognizing that certain aspects of sub-group uniqueness must still be maintained. For example, the existing Caribbean Community (CARICOM) integration area will for the foreseeable future co-exist with the ACS. Moreover, the unit's viability is being enhanced by cautious widening. In 1995 Dutch-speaking Suriname became the first non-English-speaking country to become a full member of CARICOM and the first new member since the movement's inception. Venezuela and Colombia already have formal linkages to CARICOM and the participation of other non-English speaking countries is contemplated.

In this volume, the new regional reality is recognized by the scope of both the contributions and contributors. While each contributor emphasizes his or her own sub-regional strengths, the range of contributions encompass all the cultural areas of the Caribbean: the island Caribbean (including Cuba, Puerto Rico, Dominican Republic, the French and Dutch Antilles, Aruba, and the English-speaking islands of Antigua and Barbuda, Barbados, Dominica, Grenada, Jamaica, Montserrat, St. Kitts/Nevis, Saint Lucia, St. Vincent and the Grenadines, and Trinidad and Tobago); and the circum-Caribbean countries of Mexico, Venezuela, Colombia, and Suriname as well as Belize and Guyana which are integral parts of the English-speaking Caribbean. On the other hand, because of the large number of published works that deal separately with Central American countries, Central America (apart from Belize) is discussed only in terms of its incipient economic relationships with the rest of the Caribbean region.

The book aims to be fairly comprehensive in the range of issues discussed. However, given the large number of sectors for which policy is formulated in any country, some selectivity has of necessity been exercised. The following sectors have been chosen as particularly important for policy analysis at this point in time: global, regional, and hemispheric affairs (Part One); culture, education, and training (Part Two); and human development issues, including social issues (narcotics, gender, labor, and migration), and "sustainability" issues, specifically information and environment (Part Three). A mix of practitioner and academic perspectives inform these discussions.

In Part One, Denis Benn of the United Nations Development Program (UNDP) seeks to assess the effect of global trends on Caribbean development. He suggests that despite liberalization, governmental and public sector intervention is still desirable in certain economic areas. In the related, key policy area of regionalism and integration, Ransford Palmer presents a concise analysis of the effects of the North American Free Trade Area (NAFTA) on Caribbean industry, particularly textiles, suggesting areas where the Caribbean is not competitive. Jean-Pierre Chardon interjects a note on the possible impact of NAFTA on the oft-forgotten French Antilles, and discusses the move by the *départments d'outremer* (DOM) to forge closer relationships with the independent Caribbean. The discussion of NAFTA is followed by Venezuelan Andrés Serbín's critical analysis of the prospects for closer relations between the "Grupo de los Tres" (Mexico, Venezuela, and Colombia) and the Caribbean. In addition, Damián Fernández and Olga Nazarío speak to Cuba's evolving relations with the Caribbean Community (CARICOM). This section is completed by Roderick Rainford, former CARICOM Secretary-General, who puts these evolving relationships into context, commenting on their viability and their impact on the core CARICOM area.

In Part Two, contributors suggest needs in the areas of culture and training. Cultural policy is discussed by Rex Nettleford, well known in Caribbean circles as both an academic and founder of the Jamaica National Dance Theater. Nettleford offers a philosophical commentary on Caribbean identity and diversity, and focuses on the need to erase ethno-cultural barriers to cooperation. Fred Constant, a French cultural specialist, endorses Nettleford's call to erase cultural barriers and adds a concrete appeal for more official recognition of the arts. Rosemarijn Hoefte notes that, notwithstanding Nettleford's call for national integration, there are special difficulties inherent in integrating the Indian population of Suriname.

On the matter of training needs in today's new competitive era, Dennis Gayle and Bhoendradatt Tewarie, a former government minister, seek to specify the type of new manager needed in the Caribbean, given the evolving business environment, and suggest changes in education to meet the new management demands. In another important emerging area, environmental education, LaVerne Ragster offers some specific proposals with regard to marine resource management. Finally, Cora Christian, a medical doctor, pinpoints urgent needs with respect to the treatment of Acquired Immune Deficiency (AIDS) patients in the Caribbean.

Four chapters in Part Three deal with social issues. Ivelaw Griffith discusses criminal justice limitations in the key area of narco-trafficking. Rita Giacalone details the structure of female economic and political participation in the region and suggests several strategies that can be used by state, private sector, and women's organizations to enhance the participation of women in Caribbean development. Migration has long played an important role in the Caribbean, easing the burden of unemployment and under-employment. Mario Trajtenberg of the International Labor Organization (ILO) outlines the international legislative agenda that seeks to protect migrants. Monica Gordon summarizes prevailing patterns of Caribbean migration and important changes in the immigration laws of the United States.

Part Three also addresses some technical issues phrased within the debate about sustainable development. Informatics is a high priority area for Caribbean policy-makers today. Felipe Noguera of the Caribbean Association of National Telecommunications Organizations (CANTO) details various regulatory issues arising from the Caribbean's recent rush to privatize telecommunications, and Ewart Skinner discusses the telecommunications issue within a sociological context while offering specific suggestions that would permit the region to take advantage of the much-touted information super-highway. In the environmental area, Alfredo César Dachary and Stella Maris Arnaíz provide details of land use along the Mexican Caribbean coasts, emphasizing the adverse impact of tourism and mega-development on Mexico's coastal areas.

Finally, three appendices are included. In a speech given while still in office and while chairman of CARICOM (1993–1994), former Prime Minister Patrick Manning of Trinidad and Tobago outlines his view of the regional agenda of the 1990s: liberalization, efficiency, and competitiveness; CARICOM's current secretary-general Edwin Carrington offers some views as to the survival of CARICOM in an era of broader integration initiatives; and useful excerpts from the U.N. report of the 1994 conference on Sustainable Development of Small Island Developing States are reproduced.

The hope is that this volume will offer insights, first to Caribbean researchers and policy-makers at this time of global and regional change, and second, to persons who work and do research in other areas of the developing world. As globalization proceeds, traditional national boundary lines are disappearing and we are experiencing truly what it means to live in Marshall McLuhan's "global village." The problems being experienced in the Caribbean today are not very different from those elsewhere in the developing South. The suggestions made here for coping with global change are therefore generalizable and should find an audience beyond the boundaries of the Caribbean.

Notes

1. There are so many works dealing with conceptions of development that it is difficult to single out one for purposes of illustration. However, two books that can be recommended on the basis of their comprehensiveness and precise analyses are: Charles K. Wilber (1992) and Seligson and Passé-Smith (1993).

2. The countries surveyed in the Carnegie report were Australia, Brazil, Hong Kong, Germany, Israel, Japan, Korea, Mexico, the Netherlands, Russia, Sweden, the United Kingdom and the United States. In all, 20,000 faculty were interviewed for the study.

Bibliography

Boyer, Ernest L. 1994. *The Academic Profession: An International Perspective.* A Carnegie Foundation Report. Princeton N.J.: Carnegie Foundation for the Advancement of Teaching.

Braveboy-Wagner, Jacqueline A. 1992. "Winds of Change." *Hemisfile* 3(6), November/December: 6–7.

Braybrooke, David and Charles E. Lindblom. 1963. *A Strategy of Decision: Policy Evaluation as a Social Process.* New York: Free Press.

Clark, Robert. 1982. *Power and Policy in The Third World.* New York: Wiley.

Gaddis, John Lewis. 1992/93. "International Relations Theory and the End of the Cold War." *International Security* 17(3), Winter: 5–58.

Heisler, Martin O., ed. 1974. *Politics in Europe: Structures and Processes in Some Postindustrial Democracies.* New York: David Kay.

Hirschman, Albert O. 1988. *The Strategy of Economic Development.* Boulder, CO: Westview.

———. 1993. *Journeys Toward Progress: Studies of Economic Policy Making in Latin America.* Boulder, CO: Westview.

Janis, Irving. 1982. *Victims of Groupthink.* Boston: Houghton Mifflin.

March, James G. and Herbert Simon, with the collaboration of Harold Guetzkow. 1993. *Organizations.* Cambridge, MA: Blackwell.

New York Times. July 23, 1995.

Seligson, Mitchell and John Passé-Smith, eds. 1993. *Development and Underdevelopment.* Boulder, CO: Lynne Rienner.

United Nations. 1994. *Agenda for Development.* Report of the Secretary-General, May 6, 1994. U.N. Document A/48/935.

Verba, Sidney. 1969. "Assumptions of Rationality and Non-Rationality in Models of the International System." Pp. 217–231 in James N. Rosenau, ed., *International Politics and Foreign Policy.* New York: Free Press, 1969.

Wilber, Charles K., ed. 1992. *The Political Economy of Development and Underdevelopment.* New York: McGraw-Hill.

Williams, Eric. 1969. *Inward Hunger: The Education of a Prime Minister.* London: André Deutsch.

PART ONE

Global, Hemispheric, and Regional Trends: Impact on Caribbean Public Policy

We are in the present, contemplating how to respond to the future. And we are a knit of sub-groupings which are emerging in Latin America and of course there is the whole issue of a deepening of relationships in the Caribbean. There is indeed an irresistible trend toward regional economic groupings and other means of meeting the challenges to competitiveness, in order to survive in the new world order.

—Former foreign minister of Jamaica Paul Robertson
to the Caribbean Studies Association, May 1993

2

Global and Regional Trends: Impact on Caribbean Development

Denis Benn

Global and Regional Development Trends[1]

The Caribbean stands at a critical juncture in its historical evolution. Five hundred years after the "discovery," the countries of the region, by an almost perverse twist of fate, are confronted with the need to make a number of fundamental choices both in their domestic economic policy and in their external economic relations. These choices are a basic precondition for future economic prosperity (in some cases, economic survival) as Caribbean states prepare to enter the twenty-first century. In order to appreciate their significance, it is necessary first to sketch briefly the changes in the global environment that have affected the development choices and strategies being espoused today.

In the 1960s and 1970s, most developing countries, in attempting to counter the persistent imbalance in trade between the countries of the industrial "north" and those of the "south," adopted economic strategies that included negotiation of preferential access to industrial markets, regional integration, and import-substitution industrialization (ISI), later succeeded by export promotion strategies. Caribbean countries were no exception. For example, the English-speaking Caribbean, historically dependent on the export of primary commodities, most notably sugar and bananas, to metropolitan markets, negotiated a series of preferential arrangements that are still in effect, specifically the European Community's Lomé Convention governing arrangements with the African, Caribbean, and Pacific countries (EEC-ACP); the Caribbean Basin Initiative (CBI) through which preferences are offered by the United States; and the Caribbean/Canada preferential accord, CARIBCAN. Meanwhile, they complemented export-oriented primary commodity production for external markets with an inward-looking manufacturing strategy based on import substitution. Regionally, they formed the Caribbean Free Trade Area (CARIFTA) in 1967, and subsequently the Caribbean Community (CARICOM) in 1973, which enlarged the possibilities for an expansion of intra-Caribbean trade and the opportunities for collective action, even while leaving the structure of metropolitan preferences essentially intact.

The oil crisis of the 1970s severely affected non-oil developing countries, including those of the Caribbean. The gains achieved by some countries during the 1960s and 1970s in the wake of political independence were reversed, or at least partially lost as a result of the dual impact of the increase in oil prices and imported manufactured goods and the relative decline in the price of a number of primary commodities on which the countries of the region remain heavily dependent.

Against the background of these developments, a number of countries in the region, as elsewhere in the developing south, embarked in the 1980s on International Monetary Fund (IMF)/World Bank-sponsored economic stabilization and structural adjustment programs designed to restore economic stability and to lay the foundations for economic growth. In the region, Jamaica became the most notable example of this process, having adopted a series of adjustment programs beginning in the early 1980s. In fact, Jamaica became a virtual test case for early experiments in structural adjustment.

The economic prescriptions embodied in these programs were influenced to a large extent by the assumptions of the new conservative economics[2] that emerged in the early 1980s, most notably in the United States and Britain, that sought to counter the focus of the developing countries on the external constraints to development. It emphasized instead the need for an appropriate domestic policy framework as a necessary condition for the promotion of sustained economic progress.

At the heart of the new economic orthodoxy was an emphasis on the need to promote greater economic liberalization, the stimulation of increased private sector involvement, a corresponding reduction in the role of government, and an increased reliance on market forces in the regulation of economic activity. An appropriate policy stimulus deriving from the adoption of a suitable exchange rate policy and the establishment of appropriate interest rates was an essential element of the overall theoretical equation. In other words, the new economic orthodoxy rejected a fundamental premise of traditional development economics, which argued not only that the economic structures of the developing countries reflected characteristics that required special governmental interventions, but that the assumption of an active developmental role for the state was an indispensable element in the development process. In contrast, the new conservative economics argued that all countries—developed and developing—were susceptible to the same laws of economic analysis and therefore could be developed by adopting market-based economic solutions to their problems.

A fundamental intellectual underpinning of the model of adjustment being applied in the 1990s is the financial programming approach, which is influenced to a significant degree by the writings of J. J. Polak (1990, 1994). Polak established a critical equation between money and its value, on the one hand, and inflation and the balance of payments on the other hand. This initial theoretical framework, with the several modifications that have been introduced by IMF and World Bank staff as well as other academic economists over the years, has exercised a major influence on the content and orientation of structural adjustment programs.

The adjustment programs that have been implemented in the Caribbean have produced mixed results. While public sector deficits have been reduced in many cases and private sector investment has been stimulated both in terms of the divestment of public enterprises and new investment, the social costs of adjustment have been significant. Statistics suggest that, in spite of compensatory measures that have been put in place by governments in the form of food stamp programs and increased social sector investment in health and education, a significant proportion of the region's population lives below the poverty line. This is particularly true in the case of Jamaica and Guyana. In Jamaica, for example, some 30 percent of the population is thought to live below the poverty line. The persistence of poverty in the midst of marked disparities in income distribution has given rise to an increase in crime and has created the potential for social instability that could negate efforts to stimulate private sector investment.

The economic situation in the Caribbean has been complicated by the significant changes that have occurred in recent years in international relations. The creation of a number of new states out of the former Soviet Union and the increasing "balkanization" that is taking place in other parts of Europe, coupled with the difficult economic circumstances in which these countries find themselves, have created new demands for international aid. Similarly, the humanitarian and security needs evident in places such as Bosnia-Herzegovina have also put increased pressure on international development assistance. The Caribbean, having lost its geopolitical significance, is therefore likely to face increasing competition for scarce aid resources, particularly in light of budgetary and trade deficits in the United States. In fact U.S. assistance to the Caribbean has already declined in recent years and is likely to continue to do so in the future.

Furthermore, as U.S. global economic hegemony has declined, new economic power centers have emerged in the form of the European Community (now European Union) and Japan and the East Asian Newly Industrializing Countries (NICs). This has set up a fierce trade rivalry between power centers. Whatever the cultural and political considerations involved, the prospect of economic gain was a powerful stimulus to European integration. The U.S. initiative to promote the North American Free Trade Area (NAFTA), initially linking the United States, Canada, and Mexico in a combined market of some 360 million, represented a calculated response to European integration and indeed foreshadowed the possible emergence—now expected by the year 2005 (see Summit of the Americas 1994)—of a hemispheric economic system of considerable importance. In a sense, both the European and the U.S. initiative were also motivated by the growing economic ascendancy of Japan and the East Asian NICs.

What is significant as far as the Caribbean is concerned is that the regionalization of the global economy and the emergence of these trade blocs in Europe, North America, and East Asia threaten to undermine the trade preferences traditionally enjoyed by the Caribbean under the EEC-ACP Lomé Convention, the CBI, and CARIBCAN. In terms of the European Community, the expansion of membership to include Spain and Portugal has generated increased pressure to grant the Central American countries similar preferences enjoyed by the Caribbean, particularly in bananas. This would put the Caribbean countries at a significant disadvantage vis-à-vis the low-cost producers in Central America. Similarly, the NAFTA and the extension of CBI preferences to the Andean countries have also threatened to undercut the preferences granted to the Caribbean countries under the CBI.

The NAFTA option actually presents the Caribbean with a major dilemma. Whereas, on the one hand, the region's economic viability, or even survival, may depend on favorable access to NAFTA, some of the conditions for accession impose significant constraints on the development options available to these countries. For example, it is clear that Caribbean countries would need to subscribe to market-oriented policies sanctioned by the IMF and the World Bank, and demonstrate commitment to a liberalized international trading system. Despite governmental statements of commitment to liberalization, it will be difficult for Caribbean countries to succeed in putting their economies on a firmer footing that would enable them to compete on the basis of reciprocity instead of preferential arrangements. Since this is unlikely in the short term, Caribbean countries have been forced to lobby hard, and fortunately, successfully, to preserve some form of preference as a transitional measure.

Strategies to Meet New Challenges

Confronted with these developments, the Caribbean faces the dual challenge of fashioning an economic strategy consistent with its long-term development needs while at the same time seeking to shape the contours of the newly emerging structure of international economic relations.

New Economic Strategies

On the first challenge, it is clear that the Caribbean countries would need to engage in a fundamental re-thinking of their development strategies in order to enable them to become viable economic entities in the twenty-first century. While the Caribbean countries cannot abandon overnight their traditional reliance on sugar, bananas, bauxite and, in some cases, tourism and light manufacturing, it would be important for them to identify new areas of production of goods and services in terms of niche manufacturing and other knowledge-based services utilizing modern technology. This would in turn require the articulation of an industrial strategy or, more appropriately, a production policy identifying strategic areas of investment to be pursued by the private sector with appropriate government support.

On this point, it should be noted that economists such as Michael Porter (1980; 1985; 1990) of the Harvard Business School have built on the growth accounting models advanced by Solow (1957) and Denison (1962) that link technical change to economic growth, and the insights of Kuznets (1930) into the role of product innovation in the development process. Porter and others have argued that the advent of technology has created new possibilities for the development of competitive advantages quite distinct from the traditional Ricardian notion of comparative advantage based on natural resource endowments. The logic of this proposition is that developing countries such as those in the Caribbean should seek to expand the parameters of production beyond traditional areas such as sugar, bananas, bauxite/alumina, manufacturing, and tourism by exploring new technological options for the production of goods and services. This would require the articulation of strategies geared to the identification of new forms of production that could attract private sector investment with the support of suitable government incentives. It is worth mentioning that this emphasis has not featured sufficiently in the existing model of adjustment, largely because of an overly optimistic reliance on policy incentives to stimulate investment instead of focusing on new and non-conventional investment opportunities. In fact, what is needed is a conscious modification of the existing adjustment model to include a dynamic theory of production that is conspicuously absent in current approaches to adjustment.

In pursuing such a strategy, it is critical to forge a creative partnership between government and the private sector in the context of a private sector-led development effort. In fact, while it would be undesirable for the government to compete with the private sector in productive sector activities, a much larger involvement for government would need to be conceded in support of the private sector-led development effort than was evident in the conservative economics of the 1980s which actually sought to marginalize the role of government.

It is true that the collapse of the socialist model in the former Soviet Union and in Eastern Europe has served to accentuate the emphasis on free market solutions and has thus created much uncertainty regarding the role of government in the economy. In fact, some minimalist theories of government associated with a *laissez-faire* conception of economics advocate the radical retrenchment of the functions of government in the economy, and assert a virtually unfettered role for the private sector, responding to the stimulus of market forces. However, it is clear that such a proposition is too simplistic and indeed quite inappropriate to the reality and circumstances of developing countries such as those in the Caribbean. In these countries, the production structure in many areas is still not fully developed and the private sector would need to overcome a number of problems if it is to become genuinely export-oriented and competitive in external markets.

Given the development challenges facing the Caribbean countries, and based on the foregoing analysis, at least three functions could be identified for government in the context of a liberalized economic system that relies on increased private sector participation and the stimulus of market forces. First, a primary responsibility of government is to provide the broad policy framework to guide economic activity. In this sense, the government should provide a broad regulatory and supportive framework with a minimum of red tape, instead of a controlling framework in which bureaucratic procedures frustrate or detract from the efficiency of genuine private sector operations. Second, in light of the existence of significant levels of poverty and social deprivation that exist in the society, the government has a major responsibility to guarantee welfare objectives at an acceptable level. It is urgently necessary for governments to supplement macro-economic policy and social sector investment by adopting creative poverty alleviation strategies aimed at stimulating increased income as well as employment generation activities in specially targeted socially-deprived communities. Such strategies should also encompass activities aimed at effecting improvements in the physical infrastructure of these communities, with special reference to improved housing, water, and sanitation. Thus a creative link between poverty alleviation and environmental management can be forged as a basis for promoting a genuine pattern of sustainable development. Programs in this area will therefore need to be effectively coordinated in order to increase their efficiency and overall impact. The third area in which the government can play a critical role is in the definition of future strategic production possibilities, although such a function should be carried out in close cooperation or, preferably, jointly, with the private sector.

In reality there is still some reservation with respect to this type of government involvement, largely because of a residual ideological debate on the role of government in the new dispensation. However, in a liberalized market-oriented economic system, the function of government would be clearly different from what it would have been in a centralized planning model, and therefore it has different implications. This conception of the role of the government in the economy is consistent with the experience of Japan and the so-called Newly Industrializing countries (NICs) which, as is well known, have achieved spectacular economic growth during the past two decades.[3] In fact, World Bank analysis has suggested that the economic prosperity of Korea is not attributable merely to a private sector-led development effort but also to the strategic role of the government in stimulating and supporting such activities. What should be actively encouraged, therefore, is the development of a strategic planning capability in government geared, among other things, to encouraging new patterns of investment based on the creative application of technology. Such a program should be carried out in close collaboration with the private sector.

This analysis suggests the need to effect a further modification of the existing model of adjustment in at least two essential respects: first, by incorporating a specific strategy for the expansion of the production parameters of the economy as a necessary complement to the adoption of overall macro-economic policy measures (in other words, the macro-economic policy framework is a necessary but not a sufficient condition for development); and second, by defining a new strategic role for government which would work in close collaboration with the private sector in identifying new investment possibilities geared to a major expansion in output. In this way, the basis would be laid for a long-term and more sustainable development effort that would take Caribbean countries beyond the shorter-term perspectives of the adjustment process. These measures would complement the previous modification in the model that explicitly recognized the need for the introduction of compensatory social measures in order to guarantee welfare objectives and thus ensure the political viability of the process.

The analysis also implies that the abandonment of certain assumptions of traditional development economics, which recognized that the particular structural characteristics of the developing countries necessitated special measures to overcome them, may have been premature, since the argument presented by the new conservative economics to the effect that all economies are susceptible to the same laws of economic analysis may be somewhat misleading. What is needed instead is a new conceptual synthesis incorporating some of the assumptions of traditional development economics together with free-market economic principles, in order to arrive at a viable and sustainable strategy for development.

New External Strategies

With regard to the second challenge of responding to the changed external environment, the Caribbean needs to devise strategic alliances to pursue diplomatic initiatives designed to influence the contours of the newly emerging system, and also to determine the most appropriate form of their integration into that system. It is obvious that in seeking to respond to this challenge the CARICOM countries would need both to consolidate their internal unity and to establish suitable alliances with other states in the wider Caribbean and in Central America and the rest of Latin America vis-à-vis the trading blocs that have emerged in the wake of the regionalization of the global economy. However, this effort would also require the resolution of residual differences between CARICOM and Central America and also the rest of Latin America. It would also be necessary for CARICOM countries to reconcile the potential contradictions that might arise between their relationship with the European Union and their future participation in NAFTA.

The Caribbean would therefore need to engage in what may be described as a policy of "concentric diplomacy" that would seek to reconcile its relationships with a number of economic and trading groups, including the countries of the wider Caribbean, Central America, Latin America as a whole, the hemispheric system, the European Union, and, ultimately, the global system. In all of this, a word needs to be said about CARICOM itself which has been the main instrument for collective action on the part of the English-speaking Caribbean countries. Despite solemn agreements contained in the Treaty of Chaguaramas, which was amplified by subsequent agreements and declarations such as the Nassau Understanding and the Grande Anse Declaration adopted by the Heads of Government of the Community, it is generally conceded that CARICOM is not yet a genuine common market. A number of commentators have argued that the community would need to move rapidly from trade integration to production integration in order to rationalize the use of resources within an integrated economic framework and thus to optimize the development potential of its individual member countries. In 1992 the West Indian Commission strongly recommended an intensification of the CARICOM integration process as a means of promoting the economic viability of the region in the context of a rapidly changing global economic and trading system (West Indian Commission 1992). However, in the 1990s, this intensification has occurred much too slowly.

While this deepening of integration has been the dominant assumption in the analysis of the economic prospects of the region, there is evidence of some ambivalence on the part of some member states about putting, as the saying goes, "all their eggs in one (CARICOM) basket," that is to say, seeing CARICOM as their ultimate salvation. It is well known, for example, that although formally a part of CARICOM, the members of the Organization of Eastern Caribbean States (OECS) constitute a separate economic grouping, and that they have been seeking to formulate an economic strategy suitable to their particular needs and circumstances as very small island states. In fact, the initiative on the part of some of these countries to establish links with territories such as Martinique and Guadeloupe indicates an interest in exploring other economic relationships that may or may not affect their interests in CARICOM, depending on the manner in which these relations evolve. Similarly, it would be difficult for Jamaica, by virtue of the fact that it has virtually half of the population of CARICOM, to see its future economic possibilities exclusively within the CARICOM framework. Indeed, Jamaica, as well as Trinidad and Tobago, have advanced individual initiatives to join the NAFTA. Finally, even within the framework of CARICOM, some of the member states have been exploring the possibility of forming smaller groupings as was the case with the "Manning Initiative," a proposal made in 1992 by Trinidad and Tobago's prime minister Patrick Manning for closer links between Barbados, Guyana, and Trinidad and Tobago.[4] These initiatives point to a continuing search on the part of CARICOM member countries, acting either singly or as sub-groups, to explore economic options that go beyond CARICOM.

Despite these apparently contradictory initiatives, the Caribbean countries do have a vested interest in maintaining CARICOM as a framework for functional and economic cooperation. Whether this means it should be increasingly structured as a mechanism for joint negotiations with other economic groupings on behalf of its members, as some commentators have suggested, or as a tighter economic integration arrangement, as the report of the West Indian Commission advocated, is likely to be a subject of continuing debate. It would seem, however, that CARICOM would need to demonstrate an increased capacity for adaptation to the needs of a changing regional and global economic environment. The real challenge is to reconcile CARICOM obligations with the new opportunities deriving from a series of concentric economic and trade linkages within the wider Caribbean, Latin America, the wider hemispheric system, and the global economic community.

In brief, the challenges facing the Caribbean in the late 1990s would require a fundamental re-thinking of development options and the fashioning of a new development paradigm. Such a paradigm would seek to forge a conceptual synthesis between some of the assumptions of traditional development economics and the premises of a market-based economics, in order to enable the Caribbean to pursue a viable strategy of economic development. This effort would need to be nurtured and sustained by a significant intellectual effort on the part of the academic community, aimed at arriving at a fundamental understanding of existing economic realities and possibilities, and on this basis formulating a strategy for optimizing the development possibilities of the region. There has, unfortunately, been little significant theorizing about the macro-policy dimension of Caribbean economic reality. The time is ripe for Caribbean scholars and policy-makers to articulate new and creative development insights if the region is to prosper economically in the twenty-first century.

Notes

1. This article was originally prepared for presentation to the University of the West Indies Gathering of Graduates, April 14–18, 1993. The views expressed as not those of the United Nations Development Program or any other United Nations agency.

2. Moseley, Harrigan, and Toye (1991) have referred to the phenomenon as the "new political economy (NPE) of development" utilizing classical micro-economic assumptions.

3. Skousen (1981: 199) has characterized the Japanese and NIC model as "small but strong government."

4. *Editors' Note.* The Manning initiative was viewed as promising one but the process of collaboration has been hampered by differences in policy approaches between Guyana and the other countries. In 1995, Guyana's president Dr. Cheddi Jagan noted that the initiative "is not dead but it's not getting anywhere fast. . . . I don't think the powers that be—and I'm not talking only about at [sic] the government level—share my thinking [on continuing state involvement in the economy]" (*Trinidad Express,* August 20, 1995: 11).

Bibliography

Denison, Edward. 1962. *The Source of Economic Growth in the U.S.* New York: Committee for Economic Development.

Kuznets, S. 1930. *Secular Movements in Production and Prices.* Boston: Houghton Mifflin.

Moseley, Paul, Jane Harrigan and John Toye. 1991. *Aid and Power: The World Bank and Policy- Based Lending.* Volumes 1 and 2. New York: Routledge.

Polak, J. J. 1990. *Financial Policies and Development.* San Francisco, CA: ICS Press.

———. 1994. *Economic Theory and Financial Policy: The Selected Essays of Jacques J. Polak.* Brookfield, VT: E. Elgar

Porter, Michael. 1980. *Competitive Strategy: Techniques for Analyzing Industries and Competitors.* New York: Macmillan.

———. 1985. *Competitive Advantage: Creating and Sustaining Superior Performance.* New York: Free Press.

———. 1990. *The Competitive Advantage of Nations.* New York: The Free Press.

Skousen, Mark. 1991. *Economics on Trial: Lies, Myths and Realities.* Homewood, Ill: Business One, Irwin.

Solow, Robert. 1957. "Technical Change and the Aggregate Production Function." *Review of Economics and Statistics* 39(3), August: 312–320.

Summit of the Americas. *Declaration of Principles and Plan of Action.* Miami, Florida, December 11, 1994.

Trinidad Express. August 20, 1995.

West Indian Commission. 1992. *Time for Action.* Barbados: West Indian Commission.

3

Hemispheric Trends: Regional Impact of the North American Free Trade Area

Ransford W. Palmer

Introduction

The accession of Mexico to the North American Free Trade Area (NAFTA) has raised an issue of prime importance to Caribbean states: What effect does/will NAFTA have on Caribbean trade with the United States? The following assessment addresses both the macro-economic and micro-economic levels. The latter is particularly important because it is not possible to assess the impact of the NAFTA without knowing what industries in the Caribbean are most likely to be affected. Because of the special treatment given to agriculture and textiles in the NAFTA accord, these will provide the focus of this discussion. It is also in these areas that Mexico and the Caribbean countries are most in competition.

NAFTA and the United States

The United States is both Mexico's leading trading partner and the major export market for the Caribbean; yet there is relatively little trade between Mexico and the Caribbean. This means that any Caribbean gains from NAFTA would in all probability be transmitted through the United States. At the theoretical level, an increase in U.S. exports to Mexico as a result of NAFTA could eventually expand incomes in the United States. Given some U.S. propensity to import Caribbean goods and services, this increase in U.S. income would induce greater imports from the Caribbean. This in turn would have a positive impact on Caribbean incomes.

Among the analyses done before the agreement with Mexico was concluded, all the econometric models of the impact of NAFTA predicted significant gains for the United States because of the expected increased flow of U.S. exports to Mexico and the returns on increased U.S. direct investment there (see, for example, Brown, Deardoff, and Stern 1992: 1507–1517). However, the models also predicted that the major beneficiary of the agreement would be Mexico, where real income was expected to rise anywhere from 0.3 percent to 11 percent. These gains would arise from greater exports to the United States and from greater U.S. investment in Mexico. The change in U.S. real income predicted by the models varied from .02 percent to 2.6 percent. Even if in actuality the realized gain falls somewhere in the middle of this range, it would be substantial for an economy as large as the United States.

Over the years, an increase in U.S. income has induced an increase in the demand for those Caribbean goods and services that are income elastic, such as tourism and certain specialty products. It has also induced a demand for Caribbean labor, thereby increasing the migratory flow to the United States. The magnitude of future flows will depend on the extent to which Mexican imports are substituted for Caribbean imports, and the extent to which U.S. gains are transmitted to the Caribbean through increased imports from the region.

Agriculture and Textiles

The substitution effect, if any does occur, of Mexican exports for Caribbean exports will be felt primarily in the areas of agriculture and textile products. To examine these areas, it is important to look at the particular provisions in the NAFTA agreement that deal with them. Under the agreement, the United States, Canada, and Mexico promised to phase out over ten years their customs duties on textile and apparel goods manufactured in North America that meet the NAFTA rules of origin. The United States agreed to immediately remove all quotas on such goods produced in Mexico and to gradually phase out import quotas on Mexican textile and apparel goods that do not meet such rules. Certain safeguards built into this agreement allow a country to impose quotas on imports temporarily to provide relief to a domestic industry. In the case of those sensitive goods that satisfy the NAFTA rules of origin, the importing country may resort only to tariff increases.

It was agreed that the tariff phase-out on most agricultural products would occur over ten years. But on such "highly sensitive products" as corn and dried beans for Mexico, and orange juice and sugar for the United States, the tariff phase-out would take another five years. Both Mexico and the United States agreed to apply tariff rate quotas (TRQ) of equivalent effect on third country sugar by the sixth year after the agreement came into effect. All restrictions on trade in sugar between the two countries would be eliminated by the end of a fifteen-year transition period.

Potential Impact on the Caribbean

To assess the impact of any potential substitution by the United States of Mexican sugar and textile products for similar Caribbean products, it is necessary to disaggregate these imports. Sugar does not lend itself to disaggregation, however, since it is primarily raw cane sugar. Textile and apparel goods, on the other hand, are highly differentiated and under the harmonized trade system code (HTSUSA) are broken down into hundreds of categories.

For the purpose of this chapter, a small sample of some thirty three categories of U.S. textile and apparel goods imports from the Caribbean and Mexico was chosen. Imports from other countries were not considered here because the focus is on Mexico and the Caribbean. The objective here is two-fold: first to identify those categories in which the Caribbean is in competition with Mexico as well as those in which it is not; and second, to compare the landed prices of those imports in which they are in competition. This comparison will permit some conclusions about the relative competitive strength of each country and the possible effect that NAFTA might have on their trade. It will also allow the countries affected to formulate their own strategy for maintaining their share of the U.S. market. Such a strategy might not only involve steps to improve productivity in the affected industries but also an effort to differentiate their products in order to remain competitive. The long tariff phase-out period provided in the agreement should provide the Caribbean countries with enough lead time to improve their competitive position. Part of the strategy of improving their competitiveness may require continuing diplomatic effort to maintain short-term trade concessions that help the adjustment process.

Sugar.   Sugar remains a major export for many Caribbean countries, and the U.S. market has grown more important for the English-speaking Caribbean over the past three decades because of the U.S. trade embargo on Cuba. Although the phase-out of restrictions on sugar imports from Mexico will take fifteen years, the expectation of this phase-out will affect investment decisions much earlier, especially in countries that are high-cost producers.

Table 3.1 shows that the Dominican Republic is the largest western hemisphere supplier of raw sugar to the United States, exporting 120,155 metric tons in 1991 compared to only 8,000 tons for Mexico, 12,212 tons for Jamaica, and 8,030 tons for Haiti. Jamaica had the lowest landed price

Table 3.1   U.S. Imports of Raw Cane Sugar from Mexico and the Caribbean, 1991

Country	Volume (Metric Tons)	Customs Value ($'000)	Customs Value ($ Per Ton)
Mexico	8,000	3,401	425
Jamaica	12,212	4,840	396
Haiti	8,030	3,258	405
Dominican Republic	120,155	52,249	435

Source: U.S. Bureau of the Census. Report FT247/91-A: U.S. Imports for Consumption. Washington, D.C.: U.S. Government Printing Office, 1992.

per ton and the Dominican Republic the highest. On the surface, it does appear that Jamaica has some competitive advantage. However, this may be due more to the sharp depreciation of the value of the Jamaican dollar since 1990 than to production efficiency.

The volume of sugar exported to the United States is governed by quotas, so that price does not affect demand and supply as is the case with other exports. A removal of all restrictions on sugar imports from Mexico, however, would reduce the price of Mexican sugar and stimulate greater production. Jamaica could hold its own in this market if productivity increases were substantial. The old issue of whether to put more capital resources into sugar may arise again, but if the industry is privately owned, that decision would have to made by the owners. Complete mechanization of harvesting and the modernization of old factories would certainly have to occur. However, this might come at the expense of jobs, and labor unions are likely oppose it. If, however, the loss of jobs in this industry is offset by the creation of jobs in other industries positively affected by U.S. gains from NAFTA, labor union opposition may be muted. In an important way, the reaction of labor unions to this restructuring will depend upon the leadership role of the government. It seems inevitable that over the fifteen-year phase-out period, NAFTA will force substantial restructuring of the sugar industry in Jamaica and the rest of the Caribbean.

Textiles and Apparel.   The potential impact of NAFTA on textile and apparel goods is more difficult to assess than the impact on sugar. Textile and apparel firms are more mobile than sugar-producing firms. Sugar production is both labor and land intensive whereas textile and apparel production is labor intensive and most of the raw materials needed are imported. It is also much easier to enter the textile industry than the sugar industry. Consequently, changes in prices and profitability are likely to have a greater impact on the location of textile and apparel production than on sugar production. Moreover, because the textile and apparel industry is highly differentiated, the demand for the output of any one firm is highly elastic. It follows, therefore, that the complete removal of trade restrictions on the import of Mexican textile and apparel goods might trigger wholesale relocation of the industry over the ten year phase-out period provided by the NAFTA.

To understand how this restructuring might occur, a sample of 33 categories of U.S. textile and apparel goods imported from Mexico, Jamaica, the Dominican Republic, Haiti, and Saint Lucia was examined. A pattern of three ranges of imports emerges from the data in Table 3.2. One is a range of imports in which all countries compete; a second is a range of imports in which only the Caribbean countries compete; and a third is a range of imports in which one country is the sole supplier. It may be expected that the exports in which only the Caribbean countries compete and those for which there is a sole Caribbean supplier would not be affected by NAFTA, unless Mexico subsequently decides to enter these markets. The more interesting problem, then, concerns those exports in which Mexico and the Caribbean are in competition. These exports generate the major share of foreign exchange earned by the Caribbean textile and apparel industry. This means that a substitution of Mexican exports for Caribbean exports could have a profound effect on Caribbean export-led development strategy.

Since the demand for each country's output is price-elastic, it is important to examine the landed price of each unit of import from these countries. Table 3.3 shows the landed price per dozen of a range of cotton apparel exported by all the countries. Jamaican exports had the highest landed price of all the countries. The Dominican Republic and Haiti had consistently lower prices than all the others. Therefore, Jamaica and Saint Lucia are potentially more at risk of losing some of their textile industries to Mexico than are the Dominican Republic and Haiti.

In the case of women's trousers, the landed price of Jamaica's exports is almost three times those of Haiti and the Dominican Republic. Jamaica appears to be most competitive with Mexico in boys' tee-shirts and most competitive with the Caribbean countries in women's undergarments. Saint Lucia appears to have a competitive advantage in both boys' and men's tee-shirts. If we assume that the quality of these products is the same for all countries, then the impact of NAFTA may change the composition of their textile exports.

In both Jamaica and the Dominican Republic, the major portion of the textile and apparel exports are produced in free trade zones. This means that the manufacturers pay no tariffs on imported raw materials and no income tax on profits. The only people who pay taxes are the employees. Because wage rates in the free trade zones are low, price differences

Table 3.2 Selected U.S. Imports of Textiles and Apparel from Mexico and the Caribbean by Customs Value, 1991 (Thousands of U.S. Dollars)

HTSUSA Category	Mexico	Jamaica	Dominican Republic	Haiti	St. Lucia
W. Overcoat (MMF)	178	102	479	—	—
G. Overcoat (MMF)	—	—	92	213	—
B. Trousers (C)	140	118	111	83	—
M. Shorts (C)	593	57	2,393	—	—
B. Shorts (C)	—	107	672	70	—
M. Trousers (SF)	—	1,223	261	124	—
B. Trousers (SF)	—	401	2,981	2,045	151
M. Shorts (SF)	—	1,756	1,153	—	—
B. Shorts (SF)	—	—	158	226	—
W/G. Ensemble of shorts (C)	—	—	—	53	—
W/G. Ensemble of blouses/ tops (C)	—	—	—	53	—
W/G. Ensemble of blouses/ tops (SF)	—	—	—	67	—
W/G. Suit-type jackets/blazers	—	—	106	—	—
W/G. Suit-type jackets (SF)	—	—	99	50	—
Dresses (C)	2,009	2,149	269	105	—
G. Dresses (C)	—	—	228	186	—
W. Dresses (SF)	1,107	—	104	156	—
G. Dresses (SF)	365	—	88	500	—
W. Skirts & divided skts (C)	90	379	1,044	—	—
W. Skirts (SF)	852	—	1,165	55	—
W. Trousers (C)	4,783	5,755	2,885	180	543
G. Trousers (C)	1,050	—	331	—	1,071
W. Shorts (C)	702	1,663	1,485	1,061	—
W. Trousers (SF)	2,431	1,027	1,838	—	243
M. Shirts (C)	1,936	12,779	13,280	841	127
W. Blouses & shirts (C)	9,070	4,100	6,211	272	639
B. Night shirts & pajamas (MMF)	2,350	519	13,902	—	—
W. Brief & panties (C)	9,337	17,549	18,826	925	148
M/B. T shirts, all white underwear (C)	508	25,450	6,788	98	—
M. T shirts (C)	685	5,748	4,251	854	656
B. T shirts (C)	85	841	867	675	145
W. Tank tops (C)	169	269	567	1,447	89
W/G. T shirts & tank tops (C)	—	2,929	582	52	—

Note: W = Women; G = Girls; M = Men; C = Cotton; SF = Synthetic Fiber; MMF = Man-made fiber.

Source: U.S. Bureau of the Census. *Report FT247/91-A: U.S. Imports for Consumption.* Washington, D.C.: U.S. Government Printing Office, 1992.

Table 3.3   Customs Value Per Dozen of Selected U.S. Imports from Mexico and
the Caribbean, 1991 ($US)

HTSUSA Category	Mexico	Jamaica	Dominican Republic	Haiti	St. Lucia
W. Trousers (C)	72.46	126.43	44.55	44.15	73.60
M. Shirts (C)	60.62	71.61	78.22	47.19	56.85
W. Blouses & shirts (C)	56.41	65.72	41.96	24.09	59.90
W. Briefs & panties (C)	7.27	9.50	8.34	9.35	12.34
M. T shirts (C)	22.34	28.26	20.33	22.87	10.49
B. T shirts (C)	35.01	32.78	14.17	14.04	13.04
W. Tank tops (C)	34.82	55.52	21.90	22.07	31.52

Note: W = Women; M = Men; B = Boys; C = Cotton.
Source: U.S. Bureau of the Census. *Report FT247/91-A: U.S. Imports for Consumption.*
Washington, D.C.: U.S. Government Printing Office, 1992.

cannot be attributed to the cost of labor but must rather be attributed to the cost of raw materials, electric power, and other inputs, as well as low worker productivity. Whatever the factors accounting for differences in the landed price, the removal of trade restrictions on Mexican exports will eventually tend to widen those differences, forcing Jamaica to differentiate its exports from Mexico's in order to maintain its share of the U.S. market.

When we take transportation costs into account, Mexico's competitive advantage tends to improve because most of Mexico's exports to the United States are manufactured in the *maquiladora* factories along the U.S.-Mexican border and are shipped by land. Caribbean manufactured exports must go by sea or air, which is more costly than land transportation because of the smaller volume shipped.

Scenarios for the Future

The impact of the NAFTA on the Caribbean will for a time be softened by existing trade concessions under the Caribbean Basin Initiative (CBI), Canada-Caribbean preferential agreement (CARIBCAN), and Caribbean-European Union arrangements under the Lomé Convention. It will also be softened by the general tariff reduction agreed under the Uruguay Round of the General Agreement on Tariffs and Trade (GATT). Mexico joined the GATT (now, of course, transformed into the World Trade Organization) in 1985 and, like the other NAFTA countries, is obligated to lower its tariff barriers to non-NAFTA countries. It has been argued that some of the Asian "tigers" that have been graduated from tariff concessions under the U.S generalized system of preferences (GSP) might attempt to use the Caribbean as an export platform into the U.S. market. While NAFTA's rules of origin would prevent this development in the NAFTA countries, it could not prevent it in the Caribbean. If we assume that worker productivity is similar in these Asian countries and the Caribbean, then it would seem that the biggest benefit to the Asian investors would be lower transportation costs.

The inflow of Asian capital into the Caribbean would have a beneficial impact on the region, creating employment and generating foreign exchange. It would facilitate the shift into the production of non-traditional exports. But even if Asian capital inflows are not significant, the potential impact of NAFTA is likely to force a restructuring of Caribbean economies toward greater specialization. This suggests that by the turn of the century the Caribbean may very well become a chain of boutique economies, each country producing a set of highly specialized products for export in order to maintain its competitive advantage with Mexico.

Bibliography

Brown, D. K., A. V. Deardoff, and R. M. Stern. 1992. "North American Integration." The *Economic Journal 77* (3): 1507–1518.

Feinberg, Richard E. 1992. *Testimony Before the Joint Economic Committee, Congress of the United States.* Washington, D.C.: April 29.

Hakim, Peter. 1992. "The United States and Latin America: Good Neighbors Again?" *Current History.* February: 49–53.

Report of the Administration on the North American Free Trade Agreement. 1992. Washington D.C.: U.S. Government Printing Office.

U.S. Bureau of the Census. 1992. *Report FT247/91-A: U.S. Imports for Consumption.* Washington, D.C.: U.S. Government Printing Office.

U.S. House of Representatives. 1993. *A Bill: Caribbean Basin Free Trade Agreement Act, HR 1403.* Washington, D.C.: March.

World Bank. 1988. The *Caribbean: Export Preferences and Performance.* Washington, D.C. : World Bank.

4

Hemispheric Trends: The Impact of Free Trade on the Dependent Caribbean— The Case of the French Overseas Departments

Jean-Pierre Chardon

Introduction

The French Overseas Departments in the Americas (*départments d'outre mer* or DOM), integrated as they are with France, tend to be neglected in consideration of policy matters in the Caribbean. The creation of the North American Free Trade Area (NAFTA) and the Association of Caribbean States (ACS) offer the analyst a good opportunity to discuss the role of the DOM in the region. Certainly, it is not possible for the DOM to ignore such a major global, American, and Caribbean development as NAFTA represents. In the following pages, the significance of new free trade arrangements, particularly NAFTA, is reviewed, and a case is made for including the French territories in policy considerations on free trade issues.

Relevant Trade Issues

The creation of NAFTA was an unprecedented event for various reasons. NAFTA stands as the actual implementation of the first north-south integration movement in the world, and as such it is in keeping with the current world drive towards establishing mega-blocs. It is meant to be the American counterpart of the mega-blocs constituted by the European Union (EU) on the one hand, and the Asian sphere of influence, under Japanese control, on the other hand. NAFTA is the core of the process to be carried forward in the Free Trade Area of the Americas (FTAA) scheduled to be implemented by 2005.

NAFTA aims at bypassing an artificial frontier in the Americas, the frontier that separates a wholly Anglo-Saxon North America from Latin America. It is also the first time ever that an economic power, in fact the major world power, has integrated its economy with a newly industrializing economy that still bears the features of underdevelopment, notwithstanding its admission to the Organization of Economic Cooperation and Development (OECD). Indeed, although Mexico is the second most important Latin American power after Brazil, it is also the first supplier of migrant labor to its powerful northern neighbor. NAFTA is therefore, unlike the European Community in its initial stages, not a relatively homogeneous entity. It stands more like a cluster, or agglutinated mass, than an actual association. Because the binding element is the United States surrounded by what appears to be its two satellites, NAFTA highlights the continuing U.S. hegemony over the American continent. In fact, for some, NAFTA is but the revival of the age-old pan-American lure, revisited and refurbished to fit into the global context of world mega-blocs.

With NAFTA the cornerstone of a much wider construction of continental scope, U.S. primacy in the Americas is likely to go unchallenged, especially since there is no real remaining alternative. Thus, for example, at the economic level, the principles of a market economy seem now to have been accepted by all states of the hemisphere, even if the very tenets of market capitalism are not always mastered by those who advocate or reluctantly apply them. In sum, the American continent has now, in the wake of the removal of the East-West axis (Cuba's isolationist persistence notwithstanding) and the weakening of the North-South axis, reorganized itself along meridian lines.

Fears of marginalization stemming from the creation of NAFTA have helped Caribbean states to forge an unprecedented alliance between the English-speaking Caribbean Community (CARICOM) states and the Spanish-speaking Caribbean and circum-Caribbean countries. The Association of Caribbean States (ACS) encompasses 200 million (plus) inhabitants of the region and, along with free trade arrangements between CARICOM and Venezuela, Colombia, and the Southern Cone countries, represents the consolidation of a Caribbean strategy to participate as fully as possible in the movement toward hemispheric free trade.

Implications of NAFTA for the Caribbean

The countries most impacted by NAFTA have been the members of CARICOM and the African-Caribbean-Pacific (ACP) countries. Other Caribbean countries have remained on the fringes of policy-making on the NAFTA issue. For example, Cuba for now remains relatively isolated from the United States, with no decisive support in Latin America, although it is seeking closer ties with the other islands of the Caribbean. Nevertheless, its potential both at the level of agriculture and tourism is a source of anxiety to the archipelago, with implications for hemispheric free trade in the future. Among the dependent territories, those under British control feel no real involvement in NAFTA, geared as they are towards stay-over tourism, cruise, yachting, and offshore banking rather than trade. The Dutch territories have been preoccupied with constitutional changes, and Aruba, now separated from the five other islands, has opted against independence, seeking instead to develop its potential as a service exporter. Among the American islands, Puerto Rico has indeed shown concern about NAFTA, viewing its creation as a potential threat to the advantages gained by the implementation of Article 936 of the U.S. Code which encourages the relocation of American firms to Puerto Rico. The French Antilles, as detailed in the next section, also share some concerns about NAFTA within the context of European Union-U.S.-Caribbean relations.

The foremost source of worry for the independent Caribbean has been NAFTA's threat to preferences extended by the United States to the region under the Caribbean Basin Initiative (CBI). These preferences are in jeopardy at two levels. First, it is clear that NAFTA and CBI have totally different foci. NAFTA is an international trade treaty among three sovereign states. The CBI is the economic manifestation of U.S. strategic concern about the spread of Marxist ideas in the Caribbean during the seventies. It was also intended to halt the decline of Caribbean exports (in particular, sugar, hydrocarbons, bauxite, and aluminum) to the North American market. The CBI is therefore much easier to reshuffle if needed, with no prior consent of the recipient countries. Second, Caribbean states have been concerned that an unfair competition could be initiated by Mexico, undercutting the advantages given to CBI-eligible member countries. The threat lies in the fact that both the Caribbean and Mexico have similar assets—an attractive pool of cheap labor in an area adjoining the United States, and identical products to offer, such as clothing and electronic equipment. (See Chapter 3 for an analysis of NAFTA's impact on the garment, as well as the agricultural, sectors in Caribbean states.) Mexico, however, has an economic breadth and flexibility that is unrivaled by any of the insular Caribbean countries.

Added to these two concerns about the future of the CBI is the fact that NAFTA exacerbates, and may well challenge in time, the awkwardness of Caribbean dependence on both the United States and Europe. The very nature of the links between Caribbean countries and their two historical protectors has allowed them to benefit from various exceptions and advantages with no reciprocal compensation. In terms of Europe, the Lomé agreements have opened up European markets to Caribbean produce through specific arrangements governing sugar, rum, and bananas. However, with free trade having become the prevailing philosophy governing internationally-traded goods and services, the fairness of those privileges is now being called into question. As the Lomé partners meet to review the operational aspects of the agreement, halfway through the ten-year term of Lomé IV, the rationale behind the creation of the original agreement thirty years ago seems seriously weakened. Moreover, within the African-Caribbean-Pacific (ACP) countries, the worsening of the situation in Africa may well cause the provisions of Lomé to be readjusted to provide further relief to Africa at the expense of the Caribbean.

Existing Europe-Caribbean advantages and exceptions are also threatened by the harsher tone of economic relations between the United States and the European Union (EU). The negotiations on global free trade included some difficult debates between the two parties. As long as the Caribbean countries could associate agreeably with both the United States and Europe, they were in a position to derive maximum benefit from both. Today, despite their desire to preserve traditional links with both partners, they may be forced, as hemispheric integration proceeds, to take sides and choose between Europe and North America.

The Role of the ACS

The ACS, formalized in 1994, institutionalizes for the first time relations between the Antilles archipelago, organized along instruments and principles that are mostly British, and the Spanish-speaking Central American isthmus. If ACS projections are realized, two common markets—Central American Common Market and CARICOM—would be combined, with Panama completing the picture in partnership with Central America. Belize, a member of CARICOM but part of the isthmus, has re-established relations with its neighbors and could well become the gateway between the two groups. Though they are competitors in areas such as banana production, the Central American and island Caribbean countries share the structural problems arising from small size and open economies, as well as certain painful historical experiences.

On the other hand, the decision to open the ACS to the "Group of Three" (G-3, namely Colombia, Mexico, and Venezuela) presents certain problems. These three regional powers have extended their economic alliances in recent times: For example, Venezuela and Colombia have free trade arrangements with CARICOM; Mexico and Colombia with the Central American Common Market; and Venezuela and Colombia with the Andean Pact. Mexico's case is particularly interesting, given that it is a member of NAFTA, the OECD, and the new ACS as well as the G-3. While such plural membership may consolidate alliances and facilitate broader contacts, the participation of the G-3 in the ACS could create an imbalance much too great for the island and isthmian states to overcome. The likely effect could be contrary to the prime goal of the ACS: that is, the union of small states for purposes of reinforcement of their position vis-à-vis the major powers of the hemisphere.

The Role of the French Antilles

Analysts may wonder whether the position of the three French Caribbean territories should be taken into account in discussing the impact of regional and hemispheric free trade. The specific status of these territories and level of economic and cultural integration with Europe tend to give them more of a European than Caribbean identity. But although administratively they are integral parts of France, their economies remain precarious in view of the growing gap between their productive abilities and their level of consumption.

The DOM have been seeking market openings in the rest of the Caribbean, using the tool of regional cooperation, whether directly initiated by France using the DOM, or by the DOM themselves using the latest French framework for regional decentralization. The creation of NAFTA as well as the ACS impacts this type of cooperative outreach. The DOM also share the English-speaking Caribbean's concerns about preserving preferential access to the EU market. In this respect, the DOM have a particular concern about the market for bananas. This issue is above all a French problem, as the overall purpose is to do away with a system, originally set up in 1962, which allocated two-thirds of the French market for bananas to the French Antilles. It is a Caribbean issue because not only French Antillean bananas but also the bananas produced in the English-speaking Antilles (Saint Lucia, Dominica, St. Vincent, Grenada, and Jamaica), which formerly enjoyed a priority status on the British market, are at stake. The bananas from the French departments do have a European status, and are therefore theoretically eligible for preferential community provisions, but as tropical fruits they are governed by the provisions of the General Agreement on Tariffs and Trade (GATT).

The United States has supported the Central American countries, which initially opposed the maintenance of favorable quotas for bananas coming from the Caribbean. Although these countries later reconciled with the English-speaking Caribbean countries, the issue remains a contentious one, pitting the U.S.- supported fruit companies that dominate production in Central America, against the European Union.

The banana issue suggests the extent to which free trade can be detrimental to the smallest producers. For the Central American growers, taking over the banana quota allocated to the Antilles on the European market would merely represent an increase in their already large global exports. In addition, these countries have embarked on a crop diversification program and have already managed to widen the range of manufactured products they can export. On the other hand, for the English- and French-speaking islands, bananas are a staple crop, and a primary source of export income. Agricultural diversification has not advanced significantly and the export of products from other sectors remains minuscule. To this can be added the different productive structures characteristic of the two banana blocs: Latin Americans rely on a powerful agro-processing organization using cheap labor, whereas the small island growers suffer from cost-intensive products and limited profit margins.

Policy-makers in the French Antilles are concerned that any wiping out of the banana production either in their own territories or in the English-speaking islands would immediately result in the loss of jobs for thousands of people. The bulk of the unemployed people in the English-speaking territories would no doubt try to emigrate to the neighboring French islands, which are already faced with heavy immigration from Dominica and Saint Lucia. In addition to the predictable economic disaster that would follow, the specter of social and economic turmoil would soon loom, an unacceptable prospect for both the French government and the local powers.

Apart from NAFTA and related EU issues, the DOM are also involved in the newest regional and most ambitious geographical grouping, the ACS. They, along with the remaining Dutch and British Caribbean territories, are associate members of this grouping. In a move that was debated in Guadeloupe, Martinique, and Guyane, a representative of France signed the ACS charter at the organization's establishment in July 1994. At the first summit meeting of the ACS, held in Trinidad in 1995, France was represented by the president of the Regional Council of Guadeloupe but the remaining territories did not sign the summit communiqué. The first step, therefore, is for the DOM to resolve their status vis-à-vis France with respect to membership in the ACS. A complicating factor is clearly that France's involvement on behalf of the DOM could be construed as the membership of France itself inasmuch as the DOM are integral parts of France.

In any event, willing participants or not, the DOM are integrally involved in the new developments, groupings, and agreements that are being formed in the Caribbean and hemisphere. While not willing to reject their French, therefore European, regional status, the three territories are clearly not willing either to reject their Caribbean, therefore American, roots. To define their position, the DOM will have to reconcile their history and institutional status with the facts of geography.

Bibliography

Eeuwen, Daniel van. 1990. "Caribe francés: temores ante una mayor 'cercanía' europea." *Nueva Sociedad* 110, November/December: 40–49.

Hillcoat, Guillermo and Carlos Quenan. 1991. "L'intégration régionale dans les Caraïbes: Antécédents et perspectives." *Cahiers des Amériques Latines* 12: 139–164.

Hosten-Craig, Jennifer. 1992. *The Effects of a North American Free Trade Agreement on the Commonwealth Caribbean*. Lewiston, N.Y.: E. Mellen.

Lasserre, Guyard and Albert Mableau. 1993. "The French Antilles and their Status as Overseas Departments." Pp. 444–454 in Hilary Beckles and Verene Shepherd, eds., *Caribbean Freedom: Society and Economy from Emancipation to the Present*. Kingston, Jamaica: Ian Randle.

Serbín, Andrés. "América Latina y la 'conexión europea' del Caribe no-hispánico." *Estudios Internacionales* 22 (86), April–June 1989: 248–276.

Zylberberg, Jacques and François Demers, eds. 1992. *L'Amérique et les Amériques*. Sainte-Foy, Quebec: Laval University for Canadian Association of Latin American and Caribbean Studies.

United States Congress. House Committee on Ways and Means. Subcommittee on Trade. 1993. *Caribbean Basin Free Trade Agreements Act*. Washington, D.C.: U.S. Government Printing Office.

5

Regional Trends:
The Role of the "Group of Three"

Andrés Serbín

The G-3 in the Context of Sub-Regional Initiatives

During the course of the fifth meeting of Latin American foreign ministers of the "Group of Eight" countries in 1989, Mexico, Colombia, and Venezuela founded the "Group of Three" (G-3) with the specific aim of promoting economic integration among themselves and stimulating cooperation with Central America and the Caribbean (Serbín 1991b). A series of presidential, ministerial, and technical meetings ensued, culminating in the signing of a free trade agreement on June 6, 1994, in Cartagena de Indias, Colombia.

The foundation and consolidation of the G-3 forms part of a more general revitalization and development of sub-regional integration schemes in Latin America and the Caribbean since the late 1980s. These sub-regional initiatives include the reactivation of the Andean Group and Caribbean Community (CARICOM) and the creation of the Southern Cone Common Market (MERCOSUR). (For details, see Comisión Económico para América Latina [CEPAL] 1991a, 1992b; Sistema Económico Latinoamericano [SELA] 1991; Bouzas and Lustig 1992; Beckerman 1992). This increasing integration responds to the incidence of both exogenous and endogenous factors and to their mutual articulation. Among the exogenous factors are the end of the Cold War, the accelerated globalization and interdependence of the world economy, the growing priority of economic and commercial issues in the global agenda, and the tendency toward the consolidation of three economic blocs: the European Union (EU), the North American Free Trade Area (NAFTA), and the East Asian bloc (Moneta 1992a; Quenan 1991). Endogenous factors include the debt problem and its consequences, in particular the renewed economic crisis that led to the characterization of the 1980s as the "lost decade" in

Latin America and the Caribbean. This sense of crisis culminated in policies of economic adjustment based on attempts to promote an export-led strategy of development as a means of achieving a greater and more competitive integration within the world economy.

At the same time, the regional environment is impacted by the social and political effects of applying economic policies that imply a significant social cost in circumstances in which there is a parallel attempt to renew and consolidate democratic regimes. In this regard, the characteristics of the integration process that is being promoted in the region are quite different from those that inspired the Latin American and Caribbean integration initiatives of the 1960s and 1970s. The integration strategies of the 1990s emphasize trade liberalization, stimulation of non-traditional exports, and a more relevant role for the private sector in the context of an outward-looking process of development (CEPAL 1991, 1992; Rodríguez 1993).

Nevertheless, attempts in the 1990s to stimulate regionalism in Latin America and the Caribbean cannot be interpreted as a mere response to the imperatives of the new conditions imposed by the world economy. In fact, they differ substantially from similar processes taking place in other parts of the world. First, particularly in the case of the G-3, there is a previous history of political concertation and economic cooperation which must be taken into account in order to understand the nature, and gauge the prospects, of the different initiatives (Frohman 1990; Moneta 1992b; Hurrell 1992). Second, these initiatives are not only a reaction to the contradictory tendencies of economic globalization and regionalism but also must be understood within the context of the establishment of the North American Free Trade Agreement/Area (NAFTA) between the United States, Canada, and Mexico. However, the regional initiatives, stemming as they did from a growing concern in the region about its eventual marginalization within the world economy, were underway before the U.S. initiative on NAFTA was significantly advanced (Weintraub 1991).

The creation and evolution of the G-3 is distinctive in being the result of an attempt to graft a new economic dimension onto a previously successful experience of political concertation and regional cooperation, and to do so within the framework of the particular regional problems generated by the new economic and geopolitical realities of the world order.

Political "Concertation" and Sub-Regional Cooperation

The 1970s and 1980s

The roots of the process of previous political concertation among the three G-3 countries can be traced at least as far back as the mid-1970s and must be understood as a response to the general hemispheric context and to the increasing political instability of the Caribbean Basin. By the mid-1970s, the proliferation of military regimes in the continent had left Mexico, Colombia, and Venezuela as the only major Latin American countries firmly committed to the maintenance of civilian rule and, to that extent, relatively isolated. At the same time, the dramatic increase in oil prices on the world market and the favorable market situation of other raw materials enabled these three countries to pursue a more active and autonomous foreign policy as "middle regional powers" (Maira 1983; Grabendorf 1984).

In view of this, their search for allies led to a growing cooperation among the three countries and to their greater involvement in the affairs of the Caribbean Basin, both Central America and the recently independent states of the non-Hispanic Caribbean (Serbín 1991a). In a period in which a concern for third world problems encouraged south-south cooperation, expressed in initiatives such as the creation of the Latin American Economic System (SELA), the increase in diplomatic convergence among the three countries and their growing awareness of common regional interests were clearly reflected in activities such as the incorporation of the three countries as donors into the Caribbean Development Bank (CDB), and initial moves to implement what subsequently become the San José Pact, through which Mexico and Venezuela offered preferential access to their oil to the smaller countries of the Caribbean Basin (Serbín 1991b).

This convergence of political interests increased as a result of the Central American crisis of the late 1970s. The three countries supported the Nassau Initiative that would later culminate in the Caribbean Basin Initiative (CBI) launched by President Reagan in 1983. That same year, Mexico, Colombia, and Venezuela, together with Panama (which at the time had developed closer relations with these countries, particularly in view of their support for the process of the signing of the Torrijos-Carter Treaty of 1977), launched the Contadora Group, which played a crucial role in the Central American crisis by both limiting the possibilities of a direct U.S. intervention and contributing decisively to the regional pacification process through Esquipulas II in 1986 (Díaz Callejas 1985; Cepeda and Pardo 1985; Rojas and Solís 1988). From the 1970s on, therefore, the three countries, despite the different principles and priorities traditionally sustained in their respective foreign policies, succeeded in gradually consolidating an experience of joint diplomatic initiatives and political concertation that was of fundamental importance for the stability and geopolitical evolution of Central America and the Caribbean Basin as a whole (Serbín 1991a). The Contadora experience was also associated with a general process of "re-learning," as Frohman (1990) points out, a process of political concertation in Latin America that led first to the creation of the Support Group to Contadora, then the Group of Eight, and finally the Rio Group. It must also be underlined that this process, despite its ups and downs, went together with the re-affirmation and defense of democratic values and the traditional Latin American foreign policy principles of non-intervention, self-determination, and the peaceful resolution of regional conflicts (Frohman 1990).

Furthermore, the Contadora Group represented an important showcase of the potential for cooperation in the Caribbean Basin of the "middle regional powers" of the area (Grabendorf 1984). This experience was the result of a profound concern, on the part of each of the respective governments, about the stability of the region and the regional effects of the East-West antagonism. For Mexico, the intervention of extra-regional actors and the dimensions of the crisis served to underline possible threats to its own national security and political stability, particularly in the Central American area (Bagley 1990; Jauberth 1992). The same potential problems were perceived by Colombia (Drekonja 1983; Pardo and Tokatlian 1988), and Venezuela (Josko 1992), related to their domestic situations and their regional priorities. For Venezuela, the Central American crisis and the confrontation between the United States and Cuba also signified a real threat to the stability of the insular Caribbean, regarded as of vital strategic importance to Venezuela (Serbín 1993a).

Thus cooperation between the G-3 and the Caribbean Basin countries became a key instrument designed to guarantee an effective contribution to the political stability of the region, and was not simply a question of increasing the possibilities of political leverage. This cooperation was also fostered by a common approach to the roots of the regional crisis, an approach that emphasized its social and domestic political dimensions rather than the eminently geo-strategic focus that inspired U.S. policy.

The 1990s

The above profile helps to explain the contemporary importance attributed by the G-3 to cooperation with Central America and the Caribbean. This focus was clear from the very outset: At the inaugural meeting of the group, a high-level commission was appointed exclusively to deal with this (Grupo de los Tres 1991).

At the same time, however, the emphasis placed on this also reflected, in 1989, the perceptions of a new geopolitical situation that required a greater involvement of the three countries in regional affairs.

The end of the Cold War led to an increasing geopolitical vacuum in the Caribbean Basin as a consequence of a gradual retreat and disengagement of the extra-regional actors. The security agenda of the major powers and particularly of the United States, beyond the inertial effects of the confrontation with Cuba, was no longer dominated by the aim of containing Cuban-Soviet influence. The new security priorities of the United States in the region emphasized issues such as control of drug-trafficking, migration flows to the North, and environmental threats, problems which are not necessarily accorded the same importance by the regional actors and which are not perceived as of a similar impact as the Cold War confrontation in the region.

In view of this geopolitical vacuum and given the traditional economic and political vulnerability of the Caribbean Basin states, the middle powers of the region have increased their interest in the issues of regional security and stability. Illustrative of this are the positions assumed by Mexico, Colombia, and Venezuela with regard to the domestic crisis in Cuba. The potential threats to regional stability of an abrupt political change in Cuba have led the members of the G-3 to promote a policy designed to facilitate the re-incorporation of Cuba into the Latin American and Caribbean community, as was made clear when they invited Fidel Castro to a major meeting of presidents in Cozumel in 1991. Additionally, former Venezuelan President Carlos Andrés Pérez and former Colombian President Gaviria attempted unsuccessfully to develop a personal diplomacy with Fidel Castro aimed at mediating the diplomatic impasse in relations between Cuba and the United States. However, these attempts were frustrated by the domestic political situation in Venezuela, and, in the United States, the passing of the Torricelli Amendment and the pressure placed by Cuban exiles on the Clinton administration. More recently, the re-establishment of diplomatic relations between Colombia and Cuba, and their increasing trade ties, suggest a continuation of the effort in support of Cuba, despite some differences over Cuban government links with guerrilla groups in Colombia.

G-3 interest in the Caribbean is also evident in some of the steps taken toward trade liberalization and closer regional economic ties. Thus the three joined CARICOM as observers in 1990. In the same year, Mexico and the Central American countries signed a free trade accord, and a similar initiative was undertaken by Venezuela in June 1991. Further, a non-reciprocal free trade agreement has been in force between Venezuela and the CARICOM states since January 1993, and Venezuela applied for full membership in CARICOM in 1991. Colombia has pressed to join Venezuela in these cooperative gestures toward Central America and the English-speaking Caribbean. In 1993, a free trade agreement was signed between the G-3 and Central American states, and the signatories pledged to advance toward the creation of a sub-regional free trade zone. In October 1993, a summit meeting took place between the CARICOM and Surinamese heads of state and the G-3 presidents. In July 1994 the accord creating an Association of Caribbean States (ACS) was signed.

At the same time, inevitably, the negotiations that have led to these agreements have dealt with many difficult problems and the process is continuing amid important obstacles. Illustrative of these obstacles has been the reluctance of Costa Rica to sign a non-reciprocal trade agreement with Colombia and Venezuela of the type accepted by the other Central American countries; and the difficulties that have been encountered in trying to effect a free trade agreement between Mexico, on the one hand, and Colombia and Venezuela, on the other (*El Diario de Caracas*, February 12, 1993: 27–29; Economía Hoy, February 11, 1993: 22–26, February 12, 1993:18–19). Nevertheless, these difficulties have not prevented significant advances toward trade liberalization in the region during the last few years. In particular, the initiative to create the ACS with the inclusion of the "Three" points toward a consolidation of this process and serves to underscore the particular dynamics of regionalism in the Caribbean Basin.

The Group of Three and the Caribbean: An Assessment

Despite the apparent success of G-3 initiatives in the region and the optimism provoked by the exercise of greater influence in regional affairs, the rather exaggerated expectations of some observers that the G-3 could be transformed into a genuine free trade area or into the nucleus of a profound process of regional integration point to the need to analyze more carefully the difficulties and obstacles that have not yet been overcome.

The major obstacle in the way of a transition toward an effective economic integration among the members of the G-3 lies in the asymmetry of their economies and, especially, in the different pace at which the three countries have attempted to reform their economies and adjust them to the demands and pressures of the international economic system. For example, differences were apparent in the preparatory stage of the G-3 meeting in 1993 with Central American leaders, as well as in the course of the deliberations at that meeting. Colombia and Venezuela underlined the need to take into account the aforementioned general asymmetries, particularly those related to specific economic sectors such as the automotive industry and petrochemicals, in implementing the free trade agreement and the corresponding schedule of tariff reductions. They suggested, as a solution to the problems posed by the larger size of the Mexican economy, an arrangement similar to that achieved by Mexico in its negotiations with the United States and Canada within the NAFTA (*El Diario de Caracas*, February 11, 1993: 26; *El Universal*, February 12, 1993: 2–1; *Economía Hoy*, February 11, 1993: 23). On the other hand, Mexico expressed concern about Venezuelan (and to a lesser degree Colombian) government support for the mining, steel, cement, aluminum, and petro-chemical sectors through subsidies in energy and water (*El Financiero*, March 25, 1993: 3A). Also, Mexico has been particularly concerned about the inclusion in the negotiations of issues such as services and intellectual property ownership rights.

At the same time, the relative rapidity with which Venezuela and Colombia have advanced in their bilateral agreements on economic inte-gration (Romero 1993) contrasts with the fact that Mexico conceives eco-nomic links among the three countries as defined basically in terms of a free trade agreement without, in the short run, a more far-reaching inte-gration. Thus further advancement in trade liberalization is conditioned by these differing expectations, as also by the different pace with which the respective adjustment programs are being implemented, and evident difficulties in the way of harmonizing macro-economic policies. With re-gard to the last, it is important to underline that there are differences not only in the design of the respective development strategies and the con-sequent foreign policy priorities, but also in the rates at which they are being implemented and the effect on deregulation and tariff policies, in-dustrial reconversion and diversification programs, and technological development strategies that assume particular characteristics in each of the cases.

Furthermore, G-3 economic asymmetries are reinforced by significant differences in the attempts to reform and modernize the respective po-litical systems and the political and social impact of such reform. In Mexico the government succeeded until 1993 in maintaining an atmos-phere of political stability, despite the social costs implicit in the adjust-ment program and integration into NAFTA. It also succeeded in mobi-lizing an important spectrum of interest groups in support of the reform and modernization measures, especially in the case of the private sec-tor. However, the Chiapas crisis, the murder of presidential candidate Donaldo Colosio at the beginning of 1994, and continuing political problems, not to mention the economic crisis of 1994 that necessitated a financial bailout by the United States, all have threatened to jeopardize the liberalization process. Meanwhile in Colombia, the violence associ-ated with the drug cartels and guerrilla operations, and governmental instability as a result of allegations of corruption, have hindered at-tempts to implement various policies; and, in Venezuela, the policies pursued by former President Carlos Andrés Peréz were stymied by popular resistance and discontent within the armed forces, the im-peachment of the president in April 1993 (Serbín, Stambouli, McCoy, and Smith 1993), and more nationalistic policies pursued by President Caldera.

Even in the case of the bilateral negotiations between Colombia and Venezuela which, apart from their relevance for the G-3, have also been identified as a key element in the reactivation of the Andean Pact, discussions were affected by border problems, continually brought to the public attention by nationalist and military sectors in the two countries (Muller Rojas 1992), and tension arising from the competition between Venezuelan Miguel Burelli Rivas and former Colombian President Gaviria for the post of Secretary-General Organization of American States (OAS). (Gaviria emerged the winner.)

In the long run, the prospects for deeper cooperation among the G-3 are conditional above all on the general hemispheric environment and the relationship of these countries with the United States and NAFTA. For the great majority of Latin American and Caribbean countries, economic relations with the United States—their main market and trade partner, main creditor, and main source of technology and capital—is decisive when it comes to defining the general parameters of their foreign policy and, even more so, in the case of any sub-regional project. As a result the NAFTA has become a basic point of reference and a model for negotiating any similar free trade agreement.

Despite early endogenous attempts to advance the sub-regional integration process in Latin America and the Caribbean, no sub-regional initiative can be discussed without taking into account the potential (or actual) interest of its participants in an eventual incorporation into the North American scheme on relatively favorable terms. The addition of environmental and labor conditions to the NAFTA accord with Mexico, the adhesion clauses that could widen membership beyond the hemispheric context, and the rapidity of the implementation of new free trade agreements with Latin American partners, are all aspects of the same process, and as such are closely followed by the Caribbean Basin countries.

NAFTA affects the G-3 members in different ways. Mexico sees the G-3 primarily as a political counterweight to its North American bloc association and, especially, to the United States. For Colombia and Venezuela, the association with Mexico raises hopes (not necessarily well-founded) of simultaneously expanding their economic space and improving their bargaining position vis-à-vis NAFTA (Serbín 1993b).

With respect to G-3 relations with the Caribbean Basin, although their geo-strategic foci differ, there is a convergent concern about the consolidation of democracy in the Caribbean Basin. Mexico's regional strategic and economic concerns are mainly oriented toward Central America, a particularly sensitive area for Mexican economic and geopolitical interests in the framework of the pacification process in the region. On the other hand, for Venezuela, the insular Caribbean is perceived as a crucial strategic area, whose stability can be eventually undermined by changes in Cuba and by destabilization processes in the non-Hispanic Caribbean countries. The insular Caribbean is also an increasingly important market for Venezuelan non-traditional exports. Finally, Colombia's main regional concerns center on the economic potentialities of the Caribbean Basin market and the destabilizing links of drug traffickers and guerrillas.

G-3 concerns and interests are matched by a growing disposition of the Central American and insular Caribbean countries to diversify and deepen their economic and political links with the G-3, in order to counter marginalization resulting from the formation of NAFTA and their decreasing strategic relevance for extra-regional actors.

Conclusion

Despite the distinctive priorities and perceptions of Mexico, Venezuela, and Colombia, it can be concluded that the formation of the G-3 has significantly contributed to increasing the influence of its members in the Caribbean Basin and, in the face of the geopolitical vacuum generated by the gradual disengagement of external actors, the group has succeeded in transforming the three regional middle powers into crucial actors in regional affairs. The G-3, together with CARICOM and the Central American states,[1] are active protagonists in the search for the progressive articulation of a regional economic and political bloc that will supersede the barriers of political, linguistic, and cultural differences, varying levels of vulnerability, and asymmetrical variations in Caribbean Basin economies. The effort is being undertaken despite the domestic difficulties being experienced by the majority of the countries of the region as a result of the implementation of economic adjustment policies.

On the other hand, G-3 members differ as to the importance they assign to the group. They also have different foreign policy priorities on the sub-regional level and varying expectations about their respective economic and political performances. As a result, notwithstanding the successful evolution of the process of political concertation and sub-regional cooperation helped in certain degree by the efforts of the G-3, there remain significant questions about the group's further evolution as a free trade agreement and as an economic and geopolitical focus for the process of regionalism in the Caribbean Basin. In particular, the jury is out with respect to the role that the group and each of its members can perform in the consolidation of the ACS, the region's main response to the changing international environment.

Note

1. The relationship among these three groups of actors is somewhat uneasy. As described in previous chapters, Central American and CARICOM states have conflicted over the issue of the European banana market. Again, despite the collaborative activity elaborated here, there is a growing competition between the G-3 and CARICOM for leadership in the region, which will probably become increasingly evident as a result of the creation of the ACS. Additionally, the traditional rift between the English-speaking Caribbean and the Dominican Republic has led the latter to establish closer links with Central America.

Bibliography

Bagley, Bruce. 1990. "Los intereses de seguridad de México y de Estados Unidos en Centroamerica." Pp. 315–339 in Sergio Aguayo and Bruce Bagley, eds., *En busca de la seguridad perdida*. Mexico: Siglo XXI.

Beckerman, M., ed. 1992. *Mercosur: Oportunidad y desafío*. Buenos Aires: Legasa.

Bouzas, R. and Nora Lustig, eds. 1992. *Liberalización comercial e integración regional: De NAFTA a MERCOSUR*. Buenos Aires: Facultad Latinoamericana de Ciencias Sociales (FLACSO)/Grupo Editor Latinoamericano.

Comisión Económica para América Latina (CEPAL). 1991. "La integración económica en los años 90: Perspectivas y opciones." Doc. LC/R 1024, August 24.

———. 1992. "Convergencia de los esquemas de integración." Doc. LC/R 1192, October 2.

Cepeda, Fernando and Rodrigo Pardo. 1985. *Contadora: Desafío a la diplomacia regional*. Bogotá: Oveja Negra.

Díaz Callejas, Apolinar. 1985. *Contadora:Desafío al imperio*. Bogotá: Oveja Negra.

Economía Hoy (Caracas). February 11–February 13, 1993.

El Diario de Caracas. February 12–February 13, 1993.

El Financiero (Mexico). March 25, 1993.

El Universal (Caracas). February 12, 1993.

Drekonja, Gerhard. 1983. *Retos de la política exterior colombiana*. Bogotá: Fondo Editorial Cerec.

Frohman, Alicia. 1990. *Puentes sobre la turbulencia. La concertación política latinoamericana en los ochenta*. Santiago: Facultad Latinoamericana de Ciencias Sociales (FLACSO).

Grabendorf, Wolf. 1984. "Las potencias regionales en la crisis centroamericana: Una comparación de las políticas de México, Venezuela, Cuba, y Colombia." Pp. 267–296 in Heraldo Muñoz and Joseph Tulchin, eds., *Entre la autonomía y la subordinación*. Buenos Aires: Grupo Editor Latinoamericano.

Grupo de los Tres. 1991. "Coordinar las acciones de cooperación e integración." *Comercio Exterior* (Mexico) 41(1), January: 125–126.

Hurrell, Andrew. 1992. "Latin America in the New World Order: A Regional Bloc for Latin America?" *International Affairs* (London) 68(1), January: 121–139.

Jauberth, Rodrigo. 1992. *The Difficult Triangle: Mexico, Central America, and the United States*. Boulder, CO: Westview/Policy Alternatives for the Caribbean and Central America (PACCA).

Josko, Eva. 1992. "Cambio y continuidad en la política exterior de Venezuela: Una revisión." Pp. 41–76 in Carlos Romero, ed., *Reforma y política exterior en Venezuela*. Caracas: Nueva Sociedad.

Maira, Luís. 1983. "Caribbean State Systems and Middle-Status Powers: The Cases of Mexico, Venezuela and Cuba." Pp. 177–204 in Paget Henry and Carl Stone, eds., *The Newer Caribbean: Decolonization, Democracy and Development*. Philadelphia: Institute for the Study of Human Issues.

Moneta, Carlos. 1992a. "El sistema internacional en la década del noventa." Pp. 19–40 in Carlos Romero, ed., *Reforma y política exterior de Venezuela*. Caracas: Nueva Sociedad.

———. 1992b. "Los espacios de intercambio económico regional." *Capítulos del Sistema Económico Latinoamericano (SELA)* 31, January-March: 10–23.

Muller Rojas, Alberto. 1992. "Venezuela y la seguridad en el Caribe." Paper presented to the workshop "La nueva agenda de seguridad en el Caribe." Caracas: Instituto Venezolano de Estudios Sociales y Políticos (INVESP), July.

Pardo, Rodrigo and Juan Tokatlian. 1988. *Política exterior colombiana*. Bogotá: Tercer Mundo/Uniandes.

Quenan, Carlos. 1991 "Impacto de los procesos internacionales en la realidad latinoamericana: América Latina y la economía de los grandes bloques." *Presidential Commission on State Reform (COPRE) Report*, Caracas, June.

Rodríguez, Miguel. 1993. "Apertura económica e integración en América Latina: La experiencia venezolana." Paper presented to the workshop "La democracia bajo presión: Política y mercado en Venezuela." Caracas: Instituto Venezolano de Estudios Sociales y Políticos (INVESP)/North-South Center, November.

Rojas Aravena, F. and Luís Guillermo Solís. 1988. *Subditos o aliados?* San José: Porvenir/Facultad Latinoamericana de Ciencias Sociales (FLACSO).

Romero, Carlos. 1993. "Venezuela y la dimensión económica del Grupo de los Tres." *Excelencia* (Caracas), March: 6.

Serbín, Andrés. 1991a. "El Caribe: Mitos, realidades y desafíos para el año 2000." Pp. 13–33 in Andrés Serbín and Anthony Bryan, eds., *El Caribe hacia el año 2000*. Caracas: Nueva Sociedad/Instituto Venezolano de Estudios Sociales y Políticos (INVESP.

———. 1991b. "The CARICOM States and the Group of Three: A New Partnership Between Latin America and the Non-Hispanic Caribbean?" *Journal of Interamerican Studies and World Affairs* 33(2), Summer: 53–80.

———. ed. 1992. *El Grupo de los Tres: Políticas de integración*. Bogotá: Fescol.

———. 1993a. "Venezuela y el Caribe: Un reto persistente?" Paper presented to the workshop "El Grupo de los Tres y la cooperación con la cuenca del Caribe." Bogotá, Colombia: Ministry of Foreign Affairs and Fescol, January.

Serbín, Andrés. 1993b. "Venezuela, el gran viraje y las opciones regionales." Paper presented to the 34th International Studies Association (ISA) Conference, Acapulco, March.

Serbín, Andrés, A. Stambouli, J. McCoy, and Bill Smith, eds. 1993. *Venezuela: La democracia bajo presión*. Caracas: Instituto Venezolano de Estudios Sociales y Politicos (INVESP)/North-South Center/Nueva Sociedad.

Sistema Económico Latinoamericano (SELA). 1991. "Apertura comercial e integración regional en América Latina: Diagnóstico y escenarios alternativos." *ED/17*, July.

————. 1992. *La Nueva etapa de la integración regional*. Mexico: SELA/Fondo de Cultura Económica.

Weintraub, Sidney. 1991. "The New United States Economic Initiative Toward Latin America." *Journal of Interamerican Studies and World Affairs* 33(1), Spring: 1–18.

6

Regional Trends: Cuba-Caribbean Community Relations

Damián Fernández and Olga Nazarío

Readjustment in Cuba's Foreign Relations[1]

The stage on which Cuba must conduct its foreign affairs in the post–Cold War world presents significant contextual changes. In addition to the loss of its socialist allies and assistance, Cuba confronts the discrediting of Marxist-Leninist models of government, the end of bipolarity, the internationalization of human rights, the decline of the "third world" movement, the globalization of the economy, and the worldwide trend towards privatization and integration. Cuba is not immune to the repercussions stemming from these changes. The main foreign policy issue facing the island's government is how to redefine its international relations within a new setting, without abandoning a minimal ideological and practical commitment to socialism.

The readjustment of Cuba's international relations has had several dimensions: (1) recognition and re-establishment of economic relations to the extent possible with the newly independent states of the former Soviet Union; (2) partial re-insertion in the global economy through attraction of foreign direct investment, tourism, and export promotion of traditional and non-traditional items; (3) a search for new trade partners; and (4) a turn to the Caribbean and Latin America for economic and political links. These objectives are accompanied by a worldwide effort to weaken the U.S. embargo on Cuba.

The downsizing of Cuban foreign policy after the mid 1980s has led to a rediscovery of the Caribbean. Cuba turned away from distant shores (that is, Africa and Eastern Europe) and back to its own environs. The turn to the Caribbean has been dictated by necessity, born out of limitations imposed by the lack of resources enjoyed in the past. As such, the region encapsulates the constraints as well as the opportunities available to Havana in the years to come.

Seeking CARICOM

Cuba's overtures toward the Caribbean are highlighted by its interest in joining the Caribbean Community (CARICOM). CARICOM is especially attractive to Cuba on political and economic grounds. Unlike other sub-regional groups, CARICOM is willing to accept Cuba without preconditions regarding its political status. Most integration groupings in Latin America (including The Group of Three and the Rio Group) demand that the Cuban government move toward democratization and respect for human rights before its admission can be considered. Instead, CARICOM has opened opportunities for Cuba to gradually join various Caribbean organizations.

Cuba's relations with the English-speaking Caribbean were established when the latter became independent. Despite U.S. pressures to keep Cuba isolated, the four major English-speaking Caribbean nations—Jamaica, Trinidad and Tobago, Guyana, and Barbados—established diplomatic relations with Cuba in December 1972. Cuban officials appreciated this "far-sighted and principled" stand, which also defied the sanctions imposed by the Organization of American States (OAS) on Cuba (CANA, December 7, 1972). Still, Cuba pursued its relations with the Caribbean mostly along ideological lines. Close relations were established with Suriname, Guyana, Jamaica during Michael Manley's first administration, and Grenada under Maurice Bishop. These relations were characterized by close alliances with third world organizations, Cuba's provision of fellowships for Caribbean students, and technical assistance, including dispatch of teachers, doctors, and construction workers. Cuba did not make a serious effort to develop trade relations with the Caribbean countries: in fact, trade with them was insignificant when compared to Cuba's trade with its socialist partners. Moreover, many Caribbean countries felt threatened by Cuba's military might. In the end, Jamaica broke relations with Cuba in 1981 and the 1983 crisis in Grenada left Cuba's relations with the region in disarray.

Cuba's new rapprochement with the Caribbean began in 1988 and coincided with its increased emphasis on tourism. Cuba requested membership in the Caribbean Tourism Association (CTO) in 1989 and shortly thereafter former foreign minister Isidoro Malmierca met with CARICOM representatives in Guyana to discuss Cuba's relations with the region. The collapse of the Soviet Union and the international perception of Cuba's isolation accelerated the pace of Cuba's renewed attention to the

Caribbean. According to the then vice foreign minister Ramón Sánchez Parodi, "Cuba has two options: to be isolated or to integrate" (*Financial Times*, October 17, 1991: 7).

To integrate, Cuba had to make clear its position in the region. Geopolitical concerns were no longer an issue. In fact, Caribbean leaders had asked the United States to review its policy toward Cuba in light of the changes taking place around the world. The big, remaining hurdle was Cuba's attitude toward Grenada. Since the 1983 overthrow of Maurice Bishop, Cuba had refused to recognize the island's government. Havana also had a legal claim pending for compensation for the construction material and two airplanes left behind by Cuban internationalists following the U.S. military occupation. Cuba also attempted to bloc Grenada's participation in the Non-Aligned Movement and other international organizations. As a result, the Grenadian government objected to Cuba's admission to the CTO until Cuba formally and publicly recognized its government.

The issue was finally resolved on March 3, 1992, when the government of Grenada indicated that Cuba had complied in writing with its demands for the normalization of relations. At that moment, Cuba signaled a new diplomatic approach to the Caribbean and, in essence, a new general foreign policy. Confronted with dire economic needs, Cuba toned down its ideological rhetoric as well as its past perceived arrogance toward less powerful states, and put foreign policy in the service of domestic economic needs.

The rapprochement has been fast and, seemingly, rewarding for both Cuba and the Caribbean. In the early 1990s, several meetings were held between Cuban and CARICOM representatives to explore prospects for closer relations. In June 1992, Cuba was finally admitted as a full member of the CTO.[2] This opened the door for Cuba's closer cooperation with CARICOM. Just a week later, CARICOM leaders meeting in Port-of-Spain, Trinidad, agreed on creating a joint CARICOM-Cuba commission, intended eventually to lead to observer status for Cuba in CARICOM. After ironing out some differences and eliminating a clause calling for democracy in Cuba, the joint commission was formalized in December 1993. The agreement on cooperation, termed historic by Cuban officials, includes collaboration in areas such as biotechnology, disaster prevention, tourism, culture, and fishing.

In late November 1993, Roberto Robaina became the first Cuban foreign minister to embark on an official visit to seven Caribbean states. The foreign minister's visit served to underline the dynamism CARICOM-Cuban relations had achieved by that time: Apart from the establishment of the joint commission, there were indications that Cuba would belong to the then-newly proposed Association of Caribbean States (ACS), and bilateral cooperation agreements had been signed with several countries. The new chapter in Cuban-Caribbean relations was evidenced by CARICOM's stance at the United Nations on the issue of the U.S. embargo of Cuba. During the 1992 vote, only Jamaica sided with Cuba in calling on all states to abstain from formulating and applying extra-territorial laws and regulations that affect the sovereignty of other states. In 1993, however, the Bahamas, Barbados, Dominica, Guyana, Jamaica, St. Kitts and Nevis, Saint Lucia, St. Vincent and the Grenadines, and Trinidad and Tobago all voted for the resolution. No CARICOM country voted against it. Only Antigua abstained and Grenada did not vote. Foreign Minister Robaina, visiting the region only six days after the vote, enthusiastically thanked each host country and the Caribbean in general for supporting Cuba. CARICOM, just as it had done in the 1970s, had expressed its independent stand on Cuba. Despite the limited nature of CARICOM's trade links and collaboration with Cuba, Cuban officials welcomed CARICOM's embrace as a major moral and political victory.

Cooperation and Competition

Caribbean entrepreneurs have been key players pushing for a rapprochement with Havana. They are the ones who stand to gain or lose the most in any future scenario. Therefore, they have opted to seek greater access to the island's economy and to cement cooperation, particularly in the tourist sector, rather than risk competition in the future.

Cuba's vast potential for the development of a solid tourist industry could be a threat to the rest of the Caribbean in the long term. The region is aware that Cuba's sheer size, historical attractions, and political uniqueness may present serious competition for the other islands. In fact, Caribbean leaders have for some time been expressing concern about Cuba's potential for tourism. Thus, for example, as early as 1991, when Soviet troops withdrew from Cuba, Dominica Labor Party leader Michael Douglas opined that once Cuba "re-looked [sic] at its geopolitical position," it would become a "well-resourced player coming into the field to tackle us in tourism" (CANA, September 13, 1991). On the other hand, experts on Caribbean tourism, while acknowledging Cuba's potential capabilities, argue that it would take many years to develop, giving the Caribbean time to readjust to the new competition (see, for example, Information Access Company, January 16, 1992: C13). In any event, the Caribbean hopes to cooperate rather than conflict with Cuba on this issue—hence Cuba's admission to the CTO as well as, in 1994, to the Caribbean Hotel Association (CHA).

In the shorter term, Cuba does not seem to pose a threat to Caribbean tourism. Abandoned for many years, Cuba's tourist industry is at present no match for the rest of the Caribbean. The industry would first need to overcome problems related to the lack of administrative and marketing skills and other structural deficiencies. In fact, Cuba's participation in the regional tourist organizations provides a means for Cuba to benefit from existing Caribbean expertise (*Radio Rebelde*, April 6, 1993). Cuba has also used liberalization of the tourist sector through invitations to foreign investment, as a means of compensating for these weaknesses.

The Cuban government, in the interest of reassuring its new friends in the Caribbean, has developed the so-called "multi-destination tourism," a concept based on the sharing of tourists among the destinations. Flights have been established between other Caribbean countries and several Cuban cities, with the idea of bringing mass tourism to the region and then moving these tourists around. The Cuban government is also providing incentives for investment in tourism by Caribbean entrepreneurs. During the first Caribbean Businessmen's Conference held in Havana in April 1993 and attended by more than fifty Caribbean businessmen, Foreign Trade Minister Ricardo Cabrisas highlighted the government's desire to give priority to investments from neighboring countries (CANA, December 30, 1992). Cuba's encouragement to Caribbean investors coincided with statements by Jamaica's former prime minister Edward Seaga, who had broken relations with Cuba during his tenure, urging Jamaican businessmen to enter the Cuban market before it became too competitive. Today, Jamaican enterprises figure prominently in Cuban tourism. Other potential investors from St. Martin, Martinique, and elsewhere are exploring possibilities in Cuba, despite some concern about reprisals from the United States. Cuban-American representatives in the U.S. Congress and other supporters of the Cuban Democracy Act have adamantly criticized the Caribbean for moving closer to Cuba.

Trade between Cuba and the Caribbean remains minimal in the mid 1990s. Cuban imports from Trinidad and Tobago, an exporter of petroleum and petroleum by-products, increased from about $5 million in 1987 to $41.6 million in 1990, dropping back to $13.2 million in 1992. Trade with Guyana, the only other Caribbean country with which Cuba has some significant exchange, has ranged from $2 million to $6 million dollars in exports between 1986 to 1992, and stabilized around close to $2 million in imports per year over the same period (International Monetary Fund 1993).

Political differences remain between the Caribbean and Cuba. Most of the countries that voted against the embargo also voted, just a few days later and also at the U.N. General Assembly, to condemn Cuba's violations of human rights. The Caribbean Institute for Human Rights has urged CARICOM leaders to include Cuba, along with Haiti, in their efforts on behalf of the establishment of democratic societies (for example, see CANA, December 30, 1992). Countries establishing relations with Cuba, as St. Vincent and the Grenadines did in 1992, acknowledged their political differences with Cuba despite a desire to have a "civil relationship" with the island. And CARICOM, despite its embrace of Cuba, has not granted participation to its leadership at heads of state summits.

While in the past some Caribbean leaders did not seem ready to sit with Fidel Castro as an equal and risk unnecessary confrontation with the United States, Cuba became a member of the Association of Caribbean States (ACS) in 1994. In August 1995, Fidel Castro joined other heads of states at the association's first summit in Trinidad and Tobago. Castro's attendance is illustrative of the Caribbean's importance to Cuba in the 1990s. It also showcased the regime's willingness once again to sign declarations in support of human rights and democracy in international fora while sustaining a repressive regime at home.

Closer integration with the Caribbean may challenge Cuba to take sides when conflict arises between CARICOM and Latin America. Although not frequent, serious discrepancies have occurred between the two regions. Such was the case when each region supported opposing combatants during the Argentina-British war over the Falkland/Malvinas Islands in 1982. Since 1993, CARICOM states have engaged in a bitter competition with Latin American banana exporters over quotas assigned by the European Economic Community. Although taking note of the banana war, the Cuban government media has not taken sides on the issue.

Conclusion: Competition or Collaboration?

Although the context and the tactics of Cuban foreign policy have changed, the main goal of Cuban foreign policy has not. The priority has been, and will continue to be, to safeguard the regime in power. The international and the national, the political and the economic, are inextricably intertwined. Nevertheless, one can discern a political agenda as well as an economic one.

The new look of Cuba's international relations features economic pragmatism. The intensified search for trading partners has been the driving force behind the diplomatic offensive since the end of the Soviet aid and trade regime in 1991. The strategy is to attract foreign investment and tourism, locate markets, promote new exports, and deepen economic cooperation with old and new friends. To do so, political relations must be smooth and expanded with as many countries as possible.

The Caribbean has become Cuba's primary target of diplomatic opportunity. By 1995, the approach was firmly entrenched and yielding positive results. Cuba's incorporation into CARICOM through the joint commission and its membership in the ACS provide the first opportunities for the socialist regime to enter a formal regional integration scheme. On the one hand, these arrangements may facilitate Cuba's participation in other schemes such as the Group of Three which has special links with CARICOM and also the ACS. On the other hand, Cuba's role within the ACS or any other integration scheme may depend on how such a role impacts on CARICOM-U.S. relations. The hostile U.S. policy toward Cuba in the middle to late 1990s will present obstacles for any integration organizations that include Cuba, an element CARICOM must take into consideration in developing further relations with Cuba.

For Caribbean nations, Cuba's re-incorporation into the region poses serious questions of competition as well as opportunities for collaboration. The Caribbean is concerned that political changes in Cuba would attract substantial tourism, trade, investments, and financial aid from the United States, which could be detrimental to the rest of the Caribbean. The CARICOM strategy of incorporating Cuba seems to take into consideration those concerns. The central irony is that normalization of Cuban-U.S. relations may not be in the interest of other Caribbean nations.

Cuba and its neighbors face difficult challenges in terms of integration, development, relations with the United States, and issues of national security (defined in non-traditional terms). These inter-connected issues are impacted by how Cuba re-articulates its own domestic political system and its relations with other Caribbean islands and the United States. For the time being, it is in the interest of both Cuba and the rest of the Caribbean to pursue collaboration rather than competition. It is not certain, however, that in the medium to long run competition will not overtake collaboration.

Notes

1. The views expressed here do not necessarily reflect the positions of the Office of Cuban Broadcasting, the Voice of America, the U.S. Information Agency, or the U.S. government.

2. Only Puerto Rico and the U.S. Virgin Islands voted against Cuba's admission to the twenty nine-member organization. The Bahamas, British Virgin Islands, Martinique, and St. Eustatius abstained.

Bibliography

Caribbean News Agency (CANA). News Releases. December 7, 1972; September 13, 1991; December 7/December 30, 1992.

Erisman, H. Michael and John M. Kirk, eds. 1991. *Cuban Foreign Policy Confronts a New International Order.* Boulder, CO: Lynne Rienner.

Falk, Pamela S. 1986. *Cuban Foreign Policy: Caribbean Tempest.* Lexington, MA: Lexington Books.

Fernández, Damián, 1994. "Continuity and Change: Cuba's International Relations in the 1990s." Pp. 41–66 in Jorge F. Pérez, ed., *Cuba at a Crossroads: Politics and Economics After the Fourth Party Congress.* Gainesville: University Presses of Florida

Financial Times. October 17, 1991.

Information Access Company. January 16, 1992.

International Monetary Fund (IMF). 1993. *Direction of Trade Statistics Yearbook.* Washington D.C.: IMF.

Preeg, Ernest H. 1993. *Cuba and the New Caribbean Economic Order.* Washington D.C.: Center for Strategic and International Studies.

Radio Rebelde (Havana). News. April 6, 1993.

7

Regional Trends: Cooperation and Integration— In Search of Viability

Roderick Rainford

Introduction

Previous chapters have discussed the emergence and significance for the Caribbean area, especially the core Caribbean Community (CARICOM) area, of the North American Free Trade Area (NAFTA), the Group of Three (G-3), the Association of Caribbean States (ACS), and the cooperative strategies of Cuba. This chapter provides an evaluation of the significance and viability of all these collaborative trends affecting the Caribbean in the mid to late 1990s.

Declaratory Integration

In looking at the broad picture of integration in the Caribbean region, the analyst needs to be conscious of certain qualifying considerations. The first is that one must guard against overstating the extent to which integration initiatives in Latin America and the Caribbean are firmly anchored. The case of the G-3 is indicative. Indeed, the tendency of those who are not so familiar with the G-3 may be to dismiss it as simply another instalment in the proliferation of groupings—from G-77 to G-7— that confuses and bewilders the unseasoned sojourner in regional and international affairs. But, as Andrés Serbín argues (Chapter 5), the emergence of the G-3 can be seen as an integral part of the continuum of action and reaction in the unfolding of forces (however let loose) in the international system, forces that impact on the national interest of the countries that comprise the G-3. On one level, the argument goes, the G-3 signifies an attempt to graft economic integration on a pre-existing pattern of political concertation in response to problems and challenges stemming from the emergence of a new world order. On another (complementary) level, the G-3 countries, against the background of being, until recently, the only major Latin American countries under civilian rule—and moreover, countries equipped through their oil resources with the means to conduct an independent foreign policy—have felt drawn to exert influence collectively in the Caribbean and Central America, in the wake of great power disengagement from Cold War confrontation in the region.

While these arguments are plausible, the G-3 initiative and others should be analyzed with a certain caution. The mere pronouncement of an integration initiative does not amount to the fact of integration, as there has been a tendency to believe in the past, especially during Latin America's first round of flirtation with integration in the 1960s and 1970s when the air was permeated with heady euphoria about regionalism. This was the height of the era of what one might describe as "declaratory integration," but the tendency toward declarations of this type continues in the region today. It is perhaps on account of their declaratory nature that, in sharp contrast to the concentration of integration initiatives in Europe, there has been such an impressive proliferation of integration initiatives in Latin America and the Caribbean. Initiatives in the 1990s include the economic program of the G-3, the aspirations for free trade between Mexico and Central America, and the free trade arrangement between Venezuela and Central America.

The intention is not, however, to belittle "declaratory integration." An exercise in declaratory integration may often be the required starting point in the progressive consolidation of a regional grouping. The problem arises when declaratory integration is articulated outside of a context of technical, administrative, or political feasibility, and/or when it is articulated without actual or serious prospect of concrete follow-through.

In this respect, empirical experience shows the recent record to be mixed. In the Latin American Integration Association (ALADI), Andean Common Market (ANCOM), Central American Integration System (SICA), Southern Cone Common Market (MERCOSUR), and Caribbean Cmmunity (CARICOM), the reality has been that large doses of declaratory integration have been accompanied by *increments* of consolidation within the respective groupings, though obviously these increments have taken place with varying intensity. It may even be the case that it is the fervor of declaratory activity that has helped in some measure to propel the consolidation, such as it is, that has taken place. This scenario has most certainly obtained in cases where other critical predisposing conditions for integration are present.

In the case of CARICOM, one such critical predisposing condition has been the sense of affinity and mutual belonging—indeed the "sense of community"—that has characterized the peoples of the member states of the grouping. Although there has always been evidence of centrifugal forces at work in CARICOM, these have usually been contained by the centripetal influence of the "sense of community" that animates most CARICOM peoples, even though the strength of this sentiment is not uniform throughout the grouping. In a sense, therefore, CARICOM might be somewhat unique in that the story of CARICOM has been that of an ongoing effort to invest the movement with form and content congruent with the strong sense of kinship felt by the people. In other words, CARICOM integration happens to be effectively rooted, even if tenuously, in the shared culture of its peoples. It is a moot point whether other integration groupings in Latin America are similarly rooted, though this is not necessarily an argument against the merits of their integration efforts. Rather, this is a basic perspective that might usefully be kept in mind as the analyst ponders the prospect of meaningful integration in economic and other spheres within the ACS and within the G-3, and between the G-3 as an entity (if indeed it is an entity), or parts of it, and other countries and groupings within the region.

Impulse vs. Strategizing

The variety of integration initiatives in the 1990s brings up another consideration worthy of comment. Apart from the issue of whether or not these integration initiatives are predominantly declaratory in nature, the question arises: Are these initiatives a mushrooming set of mutually conflicting ad hoc initiatives, or are they unfolding in harmony with some central guiding principle, some grand strategy, some overarching design? How much stems from orchestration of long-term goals, and how much is simply impulse—sometimes literally on-the-spot impulse—as leaders seek to make an impact as they move from one important speech-making event to another?

This is an issue that invites reflection and analysis by scholars of public policy. Carefully focused review might very well point to some amount of blending of impulse, on the one hand, and reaction to underlying long-term trends, on the other. In other words, it may be that some of these initiatives are essentially *reactive* rather than proactive responses to the unfolding of global forces that have gathered self-sustaining momentum and that appear irreversible.

If there is at all an underlying strategy, it is something imposed by the press of circumstances rather than something put together out of conscious collective long-term strategic planning by the Latin American region as a whole. The unfolding circumstances that impose an underlying design are today precisely the global advance of trade liberalization evidenced by the most recent round of negotiations under the General Agreement on Tariffs and Trade (GATT) as well as the establishment of regional mega-blocs. Thus it is not at all surprising that preoccupation with the probable impact of, and/or prospects of accessing, the North American Free Trade Area (NAFTA) is a common thread running through all the proliferating integration initiatives in the Latin American region. The phenomenon is entirely in keeping with the thesis advanced by Worrell (1994) that on the basis of all important indicators, most areas of Latin America and the Caribbean are inexorably being drawn into a process of natural de facto integration into North America.

Can there be any underlying consistency in this Janus-like attention to two directions at the same time? The answer is yes, but only if at least two key conditions are met. One is that the element of impulse in sub-regional integration initiatives must be strictly subordinated to a consciously-constructed framework of long-term strategic goals. The other, which in a sense is an integral part of the first, is that in today's world integration initiatives must be broadly outward looking, that is, manifestations of "open" integration.

CARICOM, ACS, Cuba

Consideration of all the important seminal documents and decisions of CARICOM—from the "Georgetown Accord" of 1973 through the so-called "Wise Men's Report" of 1981, to the epochal "West Indian Commission Report" of 1992—and the process of collective CARICOM trade liberalization in train in the 1990s, would seem to suggest that the CARICOM integration grouping is moving in the direction of consistency between collective preoccupation with NAFTA, on the one hand, and maintenance of the internal integrity of the integration process, on the other. The impetus that has come from within CARICOM, through the work of the West Indian Commission (WIC), to widen integration in the Caribbean Basin by the establishment of an Association of Caribbean States (ACS), even as the deepening of CARICOM itself proceeds, promises to combine with other influences being brought to the ACS imitative by the wider region, to ensure consistency between the general issue of access to NAFTA and the issue of maintaining sub-regional integration. For, hopefully, the ACS, which includes the G-3 countries, is being pursued with more purpose than impulse, and the elements making for open regionalism at the level of the ACS seem to be firmly in place. A few years' experience of the working of the content and form of this latest integration initiative will tell how far this consistency is achieved.

At the same time, there will always be the question of the play of national interest in the attraction of the G-3 members and other countries to the ACS. In the long run, does the rationale for Mexican and Venezuelan interest in the ACS complement their respective rationales for entering into free trade arrangements with Central America? For Mexico, which is already a part of NAFTA, is the purpose of its interest in free trade with Central America and in involvement with the ACS to provide some counterweight, however modest, to its unfolding trade and economic relations with North America? For Venezuela and Colombia, is the purpose of their interest to shape their negotiating positions for entry into NAFTA? Moreover, the ACS could also turn out to be of importance in consideration of the probable modalities for the re-incorporation of Cuba into the economic and political life of the region.

The WIC, in laying the groundwork for the establishment of the ACS, succeeded in establishing the principle that membership would be open to all independent states and non-independent territories in and bordering the Caribbean Basin, including Cuba. Since the commission was a CARICOM exercise, this position on Cuba is in accord with the English-speaking Caribbean's policy on Cuba in the past. It was the relatively new states of Barbados, Guyana, Jamaica, and Trinidad and Tobago that in 1972 defied the hemispheric diplomatic embargo on Cuba and established formal diplomatic relations with that country. Cuba went on to maintain strong friendly relations with several CARICOM countries (notably Grenada, Guyana, and Jamaica) and "correct" relations with others. Cuba's contact with CARICOM survived its strained relations with Jamaica in the 1980s, and with the Eastern Caribbean countries in the wake of the crisis in Grenada in 1983. Relations with Cuba came to the point where, by the end of the 1980s and early 1990s, technical missions at the CARICOM level were being mounted, relations between Cuba and Grenada were normalized through the good offices of the WIC, and a joint Cuba-CARICOM commission was established.

Cuba's overlapping contacts with CARICOM and with the Sistema Económico Latinoamericano (SELA) and the Economic Commission for Latin America and the Caribbean/Caribbean Development and Cooperation Committee (ECLAC-CDCC), both of which include CARICOM countries, were of major importance during the times of the country's closest embrace of the socialist bloc through membership in the Committee for Mutual Economic Assistance (COMECON). These contacts became even more important in the wake of the cutting of Cuba's lifeline to the former Soviet Union and to Eastern Europe.

An interesting issue is that of the probable mix of collaboration and competition that will characterize the process of Cuba's re-incorporation into the region. The resolution of this tension depends on how urgent is

Cuba's need to use a pattern of mushrooming economic and political relations with Latin America and the Caribbean as a means of making its
way back into the hemisphere with its national dignity intact. Clearly
Cuba is focusing on this strategy, with the Caribbean being an important
trumpcard in the game plan, though of course the leadership is seeking
to mount a multi-pronged approach as well. Accordingly, at this stage of
the process, both for strategic and economic reasons, it is not surprising
that Cuba places greater stress on collaboration than on competition for
the time being, even to the extent of foregoing temporarily the kind of
competitive interplay that is normal in regular interstate relations. Developments in tourism cooperation, both at the intergovernmental and
commercial level, are indicative of this orientation. As re-incorporation
advances, however, whether with the *ancien régime* intact or with new interests in control of state power, the region will undoubtedly see a height-
ening of Cuba's competitive stances toward its neighbors.

But the search for a viable path for Cuba back into regional affairs is not
a one-way street. Caribbean eyes are also looking beyond the current deterioration of the Cuban economy to the eventual potential of the Cuban
market in its own right, and the prospect of Cuba becoming a competing
regional pole of attraction with respect to international capital and finance. Although the English-speaking Caribbean has always sought,
largely, to base its relations with Cuba on principles, pragmatism now
seems to underpin much of CARICOM's interest in future developments
in the Cuban market. There is a growing sense that a political resolution
will come sooner rather than later in Cuba, bringing with it a significant
upturn that will benefit those who will have positioned themselves adequately in time. Not to be well positioned in anticipation of this development will mean being crowded out of the pickings. It is very likely that
some such consideration lies behind the readiness of Caribbean political
leaders, formerly hostile to Cuba, to endorse commercial contacts with
that nation, and even to espouse the idea of the incorporation of Cuba
into an enlarged Caribbean common market.

Finally, on the critical issue of the presumed interest of the Cuban authorities in preservation of the social gains of the revolution in any restructuring of the system that they may feel constrained to undertake, it
appears that Cuba's social gains are becoming increasingly unsustainable
on the basis of national resources alone. External official and private inflows are sorely needed. At the same time, it is probably true to say that
if Cuba moves in the direction of internationally-supported reform, the
conventions that shape the flow of external concessionary and commercial financing would tend to constrain Cuba, inexorably, to enter the Bretton Woods institutions which have now reached near-universal membership. Cuba would be constrained to replicate the kind of relations that are

being forged between these institutions and the economies in transition of Eastern Europe and the former Soviet Union.

Curiously, it is within this framework that Cuba might have an interesting option for an approach to the safeguarding of social gains. For Cuba would be entering into these relations at a moment when the concept of the "social safety net" is fully in vogue in the Bretton Woods institutions, which have gained hard-won practical experience in applying the concept concretely to the special circumstances of the economies in transition. The Cubans will undoubtedly want to engage in some hard-nosed assessment of whether this is their best option for defending social gains, and much would depend on whether they would be prepared to work in a quiet pragmatic way toward this objective, or whether they would want to do so in a mode in which they are seen to be on the ramparts defending an embattled socialism. Although Cuba has embarked on certain internal and external readjustments, it may yet be that temptation toward the latter course might prove to be irresistible.

Note

The views expressed here are those of the author and do not necessarily reflect those of the International Monetary Fund.

Bibliography

Demas, Williams G. 1976. *The Political Economy of the English-speaking Caribbean.* Bridgetown, Barbados: Cedar Press.

Gonzales, Anthony. 1986. *Issues and Problems in Caribbean Economic Integration.* Miami, Florida: Latin American and Caribbean Center, Florida International University.

McIntyre, Arnold M. 1995. *Trade and Economic Development in Small Open Economies: The Case of the Caribbean Countries.* Westport, Conn.: Praeger.

Preeg, Ernest H. 1993. *Cuba and the New Caribbean Economic Order.* Washington D.C.: Center for Strategic and International Studies.

Serbín, Andrés. 1991. "The CARICOM States and the Group of Three: A New Partnership Between Latin America and the Non-Hispanic Caribbean." *Journal of Interamerican Studies and World Affairs* 33(2), Summer: 53–80.

United Nations. Economic Commission for Latin America and the Caribbean (ECLAC). 1994. *Open Regionalism in Latin America and the Caribbean.* Santiago, Chile: ECLAC.

West Indian Commission. 1992. *Time for Action.* Barbados: WIC.

Worrell, Delisle. 1994. *Economic Integration with Unequal Partners: The Caribbean and North America.* Working Paper No. 205, Latin American Program, Woodrow Wilson Center for Scholars, Washington D.C.

PART TWO

The Caribbean Public Policy Agenda: Challenges in Culture, Education, and Training

Education is and will continue to be a critical factor in national and regional efforts to sustain and enhance productivity and economic growth. This incontrovertible fact of life now, and for the foreseeable future, should not prevent us from focusing on the broader role which education must play as we seek to establish social solidarity in our region. This can only be built upon a strong sense of common identity and on the increased social understanding and sense of community which can flow from such cultural identification.

—The Future of Education in the Caribbean:
Report of the CARICOM Advisory Task Force on Education
(Guyana: Caribbean Community Secretariat 1993: 3)

8

Caribbean Culture: Paradoxes of the 1990s

Rex Nettleford

Evolution of Caribbean Culture

Caribbean culture, in so far as it is conceded to exist, is at once the cause, occasion, and result of evolved and evolving paradoxes. The psychic inheritance of dynamic response to disparate elements interacting to find ideal, form, and purpose within set geographical boundaries over time could not have produced otherwise. The 1990s have witnessed no less of this, precisely because the decade serves to encapsulate contradictions in human development over the past half a millennium.

Derek Walcott, poet and Nobel laureate, had long described the cultural dialectic of his region's historical experience and contemporary reality in the following way: "But the tribe in bondage learned to fortify itself by cunning assimilation of the religion of the Old World. What seemed to be surrender was redemption. What seemed the loss of tradition was its renewal. What seemed the death of faith was its rebirth" (Walcott 1974: 7). Caribbean existential reality is here portrayed as a creature of paradox. Surface appearances may well be masks for their opposites. What one sees is not likely to be what one gets.

Edward Kamau Brathwaite, the poet-historian, summed up the contradictions in his seminal essay "Contradictory Omens," a profound statement on cultural diversity and integration in the Caribbean (Brathwaite 1974). Fragmentation is visible, the unity is "submarine." My own conclusions on the anguished urgency of Caribbean cultural identity find focus in the agony of choice encountered in the process of "becoming" in a world of diverse elements caught in dynamic interaction and in quest of inner logic and consistency (Nettleford 1978). Turbulence and chaos are ready handmaidens to creativity and renewal.

The entire Caribbean, and indeed all of the modern Americas of which the Caribbean, like the United States, is only one part, are the creatures of the awesome process of cross-fertilization following on the encounters between the old civilizations of Europe, Africa, and Asia on foreign soil and they, in turn, with the old Amerindian civilizations developed on American soil long before Christopher Columbus set foot on it. It is a development that has helped to shape the history and modern condition of the world for some half a millennium and one that has resulted in distinctive culture-spheres in the Western hemisphere, each claiming its own inner logic and consistency.

The Caribbean, at the core of which are a number of island nations, themselves in sub-regional groupings, is conscious of the dynamics of its development.[1] For it rests firmly on the agonizing and challenging process actualized in simultaneous acts of negating and affirming, demolishing and constructing, rejecting and reshaping (see Nettleford 1978: 181). Nowhere is this more evident that in the creative arts, themselves a strong index of a people's cultural distinctiveness and identity.

Admittedly, other indices of culture such as linguistic communication, which underpins the oral and indigenous scribal literatures of the region, religion, and kinship patterns, reveal the texture and internal diversity that are the result of cross-fertilization of differing elements. The result is an emerging lifestyle, worldview, and a nascent ontology and epistemology that all speak to Caribbean historical experience and existential reality, in some cases struggling to gain currency and legitimacy worldwide (and even among some of its own people) for being native-born and native-bred. For this is the original meaning of "creole." Whites born in the American colonies were regarded as "creoles" by their metropolitan cousins. And the Jamaican-born slaves were similarly differentiated from their "salt-water Negro" colleagues freshly brought in from West Africa. The term was soon to be hijacked by or attributed to the mulatto (half-caste) who defiantly claimed certified rootedness in the colonies—a status not as easily claimed by the person of African or European descent whose ancestry lay elsewhere, it was felt, other than in the Caribbean or the Americas.

To this day genuine Caribbean expressions are regarded as those that have been "creolized" into indigenous form and purpose distinctively different from the original elements from which those expressions first sprang. With some of those original elements, especially those from a European source, themselves reinforcing their claims on the region, whether through politics, economic control, or cultural penetration, the Caribbean is becoming even more conscious not only of its own unique expressions but also of the dynamism and nature of the process underlying these expressions. These in turn constitute the basis for the claims made for a Caribbean identity.

The Caribbean Cultural Experience

In the English-speaking Caribbean such identity and expressions invariably bring to ready consciousness the resonant sounds of "cheng" and "ping" of the reggae in electronic flight and the steel pan backing calypso singers or accompanying roadmarchers in carnival. These follow on a time when the mambo, merengue, chachacha, and *son* bore surface testimony to the esthetic energy and artistic vigor of the mass of the wider Caribbean population, the real sources and determiners of a Caribbean ethos which is the hallmark of any true "identity."

For it was to their *hounfors,* santería rituals, shango yards and pocomania tables that one turned for those treasures of creativity that followed on the early encounters between civilizations from the old world of western Europe and western Africa on foreign soil.[2] This soil stretches from Nova Scotia along the eastern seaboard of what became the United States, bulging out into the Caribbean sea linked by an archipelago of limestone rocks that foreign tourists are encouraged to call "pearls" and "paradise," and projecting down the South American coast to northern Uruguay. That tract of real estate became distinctive not simply for the institution of slavery and the colonial system that supported, and all but extended, western Europe's sustained experiment in human degradation and labor exploitation. It became distinctive because of the internal process of adaptation, adjustment, change and dynamic creativity dictated by survival needs and sustained by the invincibility of the human spirit. Caribbean civilization is indeed a creature of paradox, a model of contradictions. It will remain so in the 1990s.

Insofar as "survival" meant "identity," and identity in turn became a function of survival, the suffering, severed hordes of humanity demonstrated from very early their deep grasp of the fact that "the material base of Caribbean existence must always be supported and informed by a native cultural vision which has absolute confidence in its human worth," as George Lamming, the Caribbean writer once stated (*Caribbean Contact,* September 1985). It is this bit of knowledge and the commitment to its dynamic application that has guided the efforts at articulation of a Caribbean identity—more aptly, a Caribbean civilization (or the germ of it) now that power has been transferred to those limestone rocks (by negotiation, granted) following on the more epic independence of Haiti and Cuba, gained by force of arms.

Such a history of severance, suffering, and survival is supposed to be a thing of the past, and many Caribbean inhabitants would wish to be well rid of it even by way of historical amnesia. But the 1990s have not promised any such escape since the processes set in place by slavery, colonialism, and the plantation economy continue apace, replete with paradoxes. These are not likely to disappear in light of yet unrealized efforts at integration, as in the case of significant post-federation attempts at greater and more effective functional cooperation between countries in the region.[3] "Integration" efforts are also evident within individual societies where the "white bias" persists in the face of black majorities or where the claims of a Euro-African posture defy a numerically strong Asian (that is, East Indian) presence, as in the case of Trinidad and Guyana (see Dabydeen and Samaroo 1987; LaGuerre 1974; Despres 1964). There is, as well, the clear evidence of designs for intensified cultural penetration via satellite and continuing economic control from outside via the International Monetary Fund (IMF).

Political independence, which has been regarded as a positive and ennobling response to the systemic denial of freedom and self- expression for the mass of the population, is now seen as having failed, not having delivered all that it promised. The nineties will therefore witness the paradoxes evolving from this. The decade has already seen the retention on the Caribbean political landscape of "dependencies" of Britain, the Netherlands, the United States, and France, scattered all over the region. To many of the inhabitants of the U.S. Virgin Islands, the Netherlands Antilles, Montserrat, the British Virgin Islands, the Cayman Islands, the Turks and Caicos Islands, Martinique, Guadeloupe, and French Guiana ("departments" of France), political independence is not an option. For such a status may well mean penury (see, for example, World Bank 1993, esp. pp. 51–72 dealing with human resource development and poverty). They came to this conclusion looking at the economic fate of Jamaica, Guyana, Trinidad and Tobago, and more recently Barbados, which were all vanguards in the fight for self-government, joining the older independent Haiti, Cuba, and Santo Domingo. And none of the last-named three could be considered "economic miracles" of the Caribbean in the twentieth century.

Yet even while such reservations are expressed, these dependencies seek greater cultural bonds with the newly independent countries that are generally felt to have achieved greater cultural certitude as part of their liberation process. It is possible to regard the Caribbean as a "cultural unit" without its having to be a political or economic one. Cultural sovereignty is here no longer seen as integral to political independence. This is indeed an evolving paradox to those Caribbean men and women who recall that the triumph of colonialism had a great deal to do with the control of the minds and esthetic vision of the colonized and that the self-government movement advocated the unlocking of the creative potential (collectively and individually) of the tribe(s) in bondage, as much as it fought for the acquisition of symbols of statehood.

Back in the independent nations of the regions, the notion of identity and the expressions of it must in the post-colonial era take into account such variables as the administration, distribution and location of power, economic viability, and sovereignty with respect to how the region relates to the rest of the world geopolitically, economically, and culturally. The clear and established "Caribbean expressions" that have been the subject of anthropological investigation and touristic curiosity and have served as mild entertainments for an outside world that expects minstrelsy from exotic climes, must now be seriously put into perspective. For in contemporary life, identity goes beyond jump-up and calypso, beyond reggae, and beyond rastafarian exteriorities of dreadlock, red-green-and-gold woollen cap, and the smoking of marijuana as a sacrament.

It goes, in fact, into the interiorities of self-determination, sovereignty (both territorial and cultural), and independence for individuals and nations alike. And it is precisely for this reason that the centuries of popular cultural expression by the mass of the population who were always central to the process of creolization or indigenization must be taken into account. After all, it is that historical experience that now informs existential reality, giving to the Caribbean well- articulated parameters of concern in building nations and shaping societies as part of a still emerging civilization. Contemporary identity in Caribbean terms must therefore take into consideration not only the notions or theories that have been employed to articulate, explain, and comprehend the phenomenon itself, but also the divisive forces of geography, colonization, and the distinctive "culture-spheres" that have resulted from the geopolitics of superpower rivalry over centuries of plantation slavery and mercantilist greed.

The realities of the latter half of the twentieth century, when the notion of the region being an "American Mediterranean" followed on its proven strategic importance during World War II and the ensuing Cold War, forced the region back to its history of resistance and efforts at self-definition, as well as the deep social forces that long gave it ideal, form, and purpose. The Cold War may have ended and ideological affinities supposedly no longer dictate the capacity of this or that country to attain eligibility for technical assistance or trade, but a Cuba presided over by Fidel Castro determined to stay loyal to revolutionary socialism is still treated as a pariah by a triumphant capitalist United States. Even if the European Community is far less paranoid about the ghosts of fellow-Europeans Marx and Lenin, the global economy in its twentieth century dispensation serves to reinforce the unbroken dependency and congenital vulnerability of the two-thirds world of which the Caribbean is unmistakably an integral part. So the old questions of sovereignty and self-determination are bound to persist with paradoxical tenacity down the decade of the nineties and into the twenty-first century. The entitlement of a North American Free Trade Area (NAFTA) with its threats of exclusion to Caribbean countries in matters of trade, investment, and labor exchange, the inauguration of the European Single Economic Market changing the scenario for traditional exports like banana and sugar in once preferential markets, and the vigorous pursuit of the cultural penetration of the minds tenanting the region via satellite communication, maintain the old areas of concern for survival and introduce new ones for a region that has known struggle and resistance for most of the past five hundred years.

Many of the strategies of survival employed over time have been enshrined in the repertoire of cultural values that describe and govern Caribbean social and political life to this day. I refer to such phenomena as: armed conflict in liberation struggle; maronnage (evident in physical flight from loci of oppression, whether plantation, workplace, or country); psychic withdrawal and calculated duplicity in dealing with the dominant ethos); cultural assertion especially through the exercise of the creative imagination in the production of uniquely Caribbean works and expressions of art (music, dance, theater, plastic arts and crafts, language and literature); the appeal to religion giving rise to Caribbean religious expressions with implications for the durability of a Eurocentric political legitimacy; the appeal to ethnicity with assertion of racial pride and dignity without degeneration into racism; the appeal to nationalism drawing on the inheritance of the territorial impulse of mankind; and the related claim to the right to self-determination that informs all efforts for freedom that characterize Caribbean history.

Regional Cultural Divisiveness

But such underlying unities of Caribbean history and existence do not rule out the fact of differences, deeply entrenched and active enough to present the region with contradictions. As I have said elsewhere:

> The common history of domination and the struggle for political freedom, economic viability, cultural identity and, within that framework, the common process of creolization offer a logical basis for ease of communication between the different communities of the insular Caribbean and the mainland Latin American areas. Yet there are divisive forces rooted in the realities of geography . . . which separate community from community. The dominant European colonizing forces have also bequeathed imprints of language, religion and other cultural forms to their different spheres of influence, placing Caracas nearer to Madrid than to Port-of-Spain and Kingston nearer to London than to Havana (Nettleford 1978: 149).

Despite continuing efforts to address these concerns, the tyranny of psychic distance between geographical neighbors persists with all that implies. Change in this regard may indeed come during the nineties but only incrementally. The fact is underscored by the poignant presence of distinctive culture-spheres known severally as Plantation America, Meso-America, and Euro-America (Nettleford 1978: 149).

But that is not the end of the story: The peculiar and unique circumstances of the encounters at different points of history of migratory hordes of humanity coming into the different geographical areas of the Americas resulted in further variations within and across the different culture-spheres, spawning contradictions and stubborn difficulties, not only for the concept and reality of cultural identity but for practical programs in inter-cultural relations, such as those of the Organization of American States (OAS) where Anglophone Caribbean membership is of recent vintage relative to that of Latin America. It is such contradictions—the source of creative tension as much as of debilitating confusion—that are not always fully appreciated by those outside the region who devise "Caribbean Basin Initiatives" or "Enterprise for the Americas Initiatives" for the Caribbean. The Hispanic, mestizo, and Afro-Saxon cultural realities of "the Basin" are just as likely to defeat the objectives of any plan concocted in Washington, however well-meaning.

Still the possibility of the European Community in Brussels "planning" the redefinition of "the Caribbean" for purposes of administering Lomé IV was clearly evident in the shift of focus there from the English-speaking Caribbean to the Dominican Republic. Some would argue that such enforced forging of links between Hispanic and the English-speaking Caribbean may well be the best thing for meaningful Caribbean integration which is long overdue. The paradox is that the persistence of outside direction in a region that sets such great store by its historical claim to independence is as strong in the 1990s as it was a hundred years ago. What is more, the denial of an underlying unity (through historical experience and socio-economic realities) must be borne in mind if one is to understand the ideological alignments that sometimes transcend geopolitical and geo-cultural spheres.

Thus for all the unease that is evident in the relations between the United States and the English-speaking Caribbean in the burden it bears under structural adjustment, that part of the Caribbean shares more of the values, meanings, and belief-systems with the United States than either shares with the Latin section of the Basin. This is so because both the United States (at least the important, ancestrally significant parts of that country) and the English-speaking Caribbean, as ex-colonies of Great Britain, are the common inheritors of Anglo-Saxon notions of freedom, rights at common law, Lockean ideas of political obligation or accountability, and even views about artistic cultural autonomy, with the mediation of state power being kept either to a minimum or qualitatively as passive as possible, and facilitatory at best. These are cultural values cherished by Anglophone Caribbean peoples and should be easily understood by Americans who are no less insistent in their advocacy of a right to these values.

Yet problems of misunderstandings and ignorance persist. Washington gratuitously insists on holding tutorials on democracy for the English-speaking Caribbean that houses the oldest elected legislature, of unbroken history, in all of the Americas. Admittedly, within the Caribbean itself there are questions rooted in the perceived and actual differences of cultural values and identity among the communities themselves. One question that comes to mind turns on whether Euro-America, which takes in large geographical spaces and psychological postures in both North and Latin America, is able to nurture sensibilities that are compatible with the other two dominant culture-spheres. While Euro-America makes claims to ethnic purity (or cultural purity for that matter), Plantation America thrives on miscegenation (even if with some ambivalence) and cultural pluralism (M. G. Smith 1965, 1991). Then again, if Caribbean Latins see themselves as "Europeans overseas," it is reasonable to suggest that their commitment to the Americas in any deep cultural sense is bound to be seriously flawed, especially in terms of a Latin American development path based on the utilization of indigenous resources. For the notion of Caribbean solutions for Caribbean problems is as rooted in cultural impulses as it is political ones.

A sense of cultural unity will help in no small way to achieve closer cooperation between nations of the wider Caribbean as envisaged by the establishment of the Association of Caribbean States (ACS) which carries with it the pedigree of endorsement by the likes of the late Eric Williams, founding father of Trinidad and Tobago, and José Martí, patron-saint of nineteenth century Cuban revolutionism. It should be added that the problems engendered by cultural divisiveness are not mitigated by the fact that many Caribbean countries would regard themselves as having within their borders all the "culture spheres."

What cannot be denied, however, is that Caribbean countries are all part of "the Americas," itself the creature of the past five hundred years of myriad encounters between immigrants and representing age-long contradictions that will not disappear in the 1990s. A commitment to American civilization (of which Caribbean civilization is but a variant) is a cultural value of strategic importance in the living of life in the western hemisphere. It is a value Caribbean peoples are generally intense about since most of what they have created out of the belly of this Caribbean/American experience (whether it be in language/literature, religion, kinship patterns, artistic expressions, or politico-economic organization) is the victim of Eurocentrism. The Euro-American's entrapment in the ancestral heritage of Mediterranean and Northern European philosophies and systems of knowledge merely makes him ripe for the thought-systems of Europe, whether of the Right or the Left. Indeed, the great intellectual struggles of eighteenth and nineteenth century Europe have continued to find new and welcoming arenas in those parts of the New World that are clearly satisfied with merely preserving the cultural legacies of the Old.

Significance of the African Presence

The habit of falling back on the old is of course all-pervasive and infectious. For Afro-Americans in all parts of Plantation America have attempted to replicate Africa, or what is believed to be Africa, in the New World. The true strength of the Plantation America culture-sphere is, paradoxically, what it shares with Meso-America, namely the consciousness of a "creole" (native-born and native-bred) reality in the Americas. While the latter is posited on a mestizo equilibrium of forces between indigenous Amerindian and invading or settler European cultures, the former (that is, Plantation America), though posited on similar notions of a mixed-blood ideal, carries with it an overt dominant "white bias" reinforced in class categories in the cultural apparatus of the sphere. It is the endemic revolt against this phenomenon by a numerical majority forced to operate as a cultural minority that culturally marks off the English-speaking Caribbean and parts of Meso-America from Euro-America, though *mestije* is reported not to be free of racial preferences tilting to the "white bias."

The assertion of the African Presence for centrality in a nascent Caribbean civilization informs the Plantation American cultural sensibility and presents some psychic problems not only for the United States which has still to deal with this question, but also for Latin American communities where that presence is either denied or has long been submerged. For the politics of this cultural phenomenon turns on a possible raising of consciousness among an underclass who may want recognition far beyond that given to them when they are made to surface for folklore displays before foreign dignitaries on official visits to those lands. Many Caribbean people are becoming increasingly weary of being engaged as minstrels or being treated as specimens for anthropological research. They regard neither opportunity for display of their talents as a cultural value worth taking seriously and they devise secret weapons to fight the tendency both within their territories and outside them.

Within the Caribbean Basin, Latin American countries like Costa Rica, Panama, Honduras, Mexico, Colombia, and Venezuela admit to having spreading "Caribbean segments" based on the African presence. There is of course more than the African presence now seeking a centrality of place and purpose in English-speaking Caribbean life. There are large populations of East Indians in Guyana and Trinidad and Tobago, numerically strong enough to question what has been—until recently—their seeming marginalization in a polity officially committed to majoritarian rule. Fancy franchises involving proportional representation were said to have kept the East Indians out of political power for a long time in Guyana; and cries of racism were heard from a largely East Indian opposition in Trinidad unable until now to dislodge a largely Euro-African ethnic aggregation forming the government. The East Indian-derived Hosay festival and the Hindu Divali festival are "national" events in Trinidad and Tobago but it is the strongly Euro-African pre-Lenten carnival that is all-embracing as a truly national expression spreading to the rest of the English-speaking Caribbean and to the Caribbean diaspora in North America and the United Kingdom (Nunley and Bettelheim 1988: Chapters 4 and 6).

The creolization process must now spread to embrace the East Indian variable as it did Europe and Africa for two centuries before the arrival of Indians after emancipation. It is clearly a matter of time but it is also a matter of commitment on the part of the "creole" population in Trinidad and Tobago as well as of the "African" in Guyana to allow the process to take and run its course. On the other hand, East Indians will themselves have to exhibit a similar commitment to their own transformation into "West Indians" through inter-culturation, without resorting to exaggerated claims on "Mother India," just as corresponding claims by Blacks on "Africa" or by Whites on "Europe" have had to be modified or abandoned. The myth of relations must take precedence over the myth of origins. None of this will be possible without the guarantee of a level playing field for all who are involved and crave for the ease of access not only to political and economic power but also to a sense of social place and purpose, and to an equitable share in the cultural certitude of the Caribbean.

The Search for Consensus

It is clear from the above that the issue of identity is yet to find consensus in Plantation-America Caribbean itself. Perceptions of what constitutes the cultural ethos of that part of the region vary. They have ranged from imperialist notions that that part of the Caribbean is still an extension of Europe to neo-Marxist interpretations about cultural consciousness being determined by the material base and rooted in the experience of a Caribbean proletariat, both urban and agro.

The paradox of the Eurocentric orientation of Caribbean colonization and the creole or Afrocentric struggle against it would be regarded by some as the dialectics of Caribbean existence, a cultural value to be trea-sured. To others the bourgeois synthesis of nineteenth century Europe is all but dead, and claims are therefore made on behalf of an urban prole-tariat who are seen as the true creators of a unique "roots culture," espe-cially in Jamaica with its reggae artists and Rastafarian brethren, and in Trinidad with its steelband men and calypso kings traditionally drawn from the lower socio-economic groups.

Between these two points there is the melting-pot theory that claims inter-racial bliss at its most idealistic and concentrates, at its most analyt-ical, on the phenomenon of syncretism or on the more dynamic process of creolization that now carries its own signature. There is, as well, the pluralist view with its emphasis on segmentation and the institutional differentiation between racial/cultural groups, which has invited the counter-theory of stratification. Then there is black nationalism which sees the African heritage as the engine of cultural dynamics, presenting identity problems for the growing East Indian populations of Trinidad and Guyana as well as for the numerically small but affluent and eco-nomically influential Lebanese and Chinese groups all over the region. Black nationalism also creates unease in some Latin American territories where blacks are traditionally marginal to their ethos. None of these no-tions can be regarded as mutually exclusive for there are elements of most of them in the postures taken by this or that protagonist of Caribbean cultural integrity.

The Caribbean migrant carries with him/her all this textured, if con-tradictory, view of self, society, and the world, and presents to many a host society particular problems of understanding, decoding of behav-ior, and identity, since the Caribbean person is likely to operate on sev-eral levels simultaneously or may exhibit tremendous flexibility in adapting to changing situations as circumstances demand. Where un-predictability is of tactical advantage, such a person may very well think of several identities instead of one. This paradox is likely to intensify in the interest of survival, and against the background of a globalization not only of what one eats or wears but of how one thinks of self and of society.

The quest for a Caribbean cultural identity has of course been a vigor-ous and consistent one within the Caribbean for a long time. And the ef-forts of such Caribbean writers as the Cubans Alejo Carpentier and Nico-las Guillén to defy the imperialist view of Caribbean culture have been continued by others who are firmly against the suggestion that we should be but a distorted echo of what occurs elsewhere. Of course Jean Price-Mars of Haiti, George Padmore of Trinidad, Marcus Garvey of Jamaica, Aimé Césaire and Frantz Fanon of Martinique were in the vanguard of a conscious counter-offensive to the dying but still gasping view that things Caribbean (especially if laced with African ingredients) are subordinate to superordinate European expressions of artistic and intellectual achievement.

Indeed, there has been no shortage of commitment to the cause of putting right a misguided perception that has long outstayed its earlier welcome into would-be civilized society. This has been an underlying theme, indeed a central theme, in copious outpourings in the region's literature, music, dance, and plastic arts, all giving to the African presence elemental cogency in the Caribbean cultural reality since, according to some, the African heritage has been the crucible in which a definitive Caribbean has been forged.

For the Hispanic Caribbean the crucible may well be something else— the Iberian heritage, perhaps. But there is historic significance in the fact that the Cuban leadership of the revolutionary era should have declared the Cuban heritage an Afro-Latin one,[4] no doubt because it is *Caribbean*. This makes modern Cuba a horse of a different color from the pre-revolutionary days of overt racial discrimination and the purity-of-blood preoccupations of the mating-game. It is also different if looked at in terms of the orientation of nationalists like José Martí and even of Alejo Carpentier himself, whose literary concerns were more focused on the dialectical relationships between America and Europe.

The Haitian revolution had of course long presented the French Antilles and the rest of the region with an icon appropriate, if awesome, for its political and cultural struggles. But Latin America, despite the acknowledged insights of Simón Bolívar into the region's cultural realities, seemingly took much longer to make the journey away from that vision of the African presence as an offering of raw sensuality and minstrelsy to perception of the presence as an expression of cultural dynamism and elemental power. The Cuban revolution admittedly stands a far second behind the Haitian in this essential detail but it has carried for many in the Caribbean the burden of that wider-ranging aspiration for freedom, self-determination, and economic deliverance through self-help.

This in good measure explains the ease with which anti-imperialist Caribbean leaders Eric Williams of Trinidad and Tobago, Michael Manley of Jamaica, Errol Barrow of Barbados, and Forbes Burnham of Guyana established full diplomatic relations with Cuba despite the disapproval of the Oval Office ((Nettleford 1978: 150; Mills 1989: 151ff). Washington had long sought to banish Castro and his errant supporters from the international community, much as the fledgling United States did to Haiti in the early nineteenth century after a combination of slaves and their free colored descendants dared to liberate themselves and set up an independent state.

The Uniqueness of Caribbean Cultural Values

An understanding of the shared human thirst for freedom in terms of its cultural significance is critical. For the impulses that drive the Caribbean people (like people anywhere) to freedom within nation-states, to the right to choose their own friends and political systems, and to independent paths to development are the same impulses that drive them to the creation of their own music, their own languages and literature, their own gods and religious belief-systems, their own kinship patterns, modes of socialization, and self-perceptions. All plans made for them from outside must take this fact into account, whatever may be the dictates of military and strategic interests or the statistical logic of tabulated growth rates and gross national products. The Caribbean people, faced as they are with the post-colonial imperative of shaping civil society and building nations, expect to be taken seriously in terms of their proven capacities to act creatively in coordinated social interaction over centuries in the Americas. They feel passionately that their history and experience are worthy of theory and explanation and expect others to understand and appreciate this fact. They are unique, paradoxically because they are like everybody else. The Caribbean has been engaged in freedom struggles and its inhabitants have been at the job of creating their own languages, and designing their own appropriate lifestyles for as long as and, in some cases, longer than most parts of what became the United States. Recognition of this and the according of the status due such achievement is a prized wish of all Caribbean people—Black, White, Mestizo, Indian (indigenous and transplanted), Chinese, and Lebanese.

The great value placed on racial dignity and racial pride by Caribbean people of African ancestry should not be seen as an epidermal indulgence. It merely reflects the determination and resolve by a set of people who understand that their survival depends on the final disappearance from human consciousness of: (a) that view of the world that denigrates things African or African-derived and regards as superior all things European; and (b) that sensibility that violates their sense of person, place and purpose, wherever Western values prevail, rooted in the Greco-Christian heritage and reinforced by the fantastic achievements in science and technology. None of this necessarily leads to racism, despite the high profile of black nationalism and black power in recent American social history. The Caribbean Black is too sophisticated to be racist but not that stupid not to be race-conscious. On that delicate balancing of sensibilities one lives and has one's being. Such a paradox is not evolving. It is fully evolved and will inform Caribbean reality into the twenty-first century as long as racism and its related iniquities continue to rear their ugly heads.

The Caribbean person who is aware of his/her condition sets great store by the escape from colonial dependency. The search for greener pastures by migration to lands which can provide jobs, educational opportunities, and a better material life does not necessarily rob the Caribbean migrant of the thirst for independence. So the Hispanics will invoke an impassioned Hispanicism (language, customs etc.) to ward off the impositions of Anglo-Saxon U.S. hegemony, as the waves of cultural assertion in a place like Los Angeles indicate, or the Latinism of the OAS in the heartland of Anglo-Saxon United States confirms. Yet, both the Caribbean Latin Americans and their Afro-West Indian counterparts treasure the products of their years of symbiotic interaction with the Caribbean environment they leave behind and regard themselves as uniquely "Caribbean." The Anglophone Caribbean person will indulge Anglo-Saxon postures when in New York, if only to lord it over a U.S. Black counterpart. But this is frequently a tactical tool from the armory of weapons utilized to escape the firing line of institutionalized racism against Blacks, if not to combat the growing satellization of the region by the Eurocentric United States. The Anglophone Caribbean person also knows that although the sun has set on the British Empire which once colonized and conditioned people of his ilk, it has not set on the English language, what with the extensive global power of the Anglophone United States. Language here becomes an important instrument of survival in hostile climes.

However, the cultural value of self-definition, through the exercise of one's creative imagination, remains the political imperative of territorial integrity and ideological independence. The calypso and the reggae are not merely artistic vehicles for social comment and social protest: they become the actual weapons of war against dependency and a threatening denigration within Caribbean society itself. Carpentier, Guillén, and Alicia Alonso exercised their creativity *within* the Cuban revolution; the Caribbeanism of Louise Bennett, George Lamming, Derek Walcott, Vic Reid, Kamau Brathwaite, et al. represent the voice of liberation itself. To understand the Caribbean, one must understand these people.

Social Bases of New Cultural Assertiveness

That remains a paradox of politics in the nineties, especially for outsiders in their designs on the region for most-favored trade and investment. In fact, long before perestroika, glasnost, the disintegration of the Soviet empire and, with it, the decline of communist Stalinist ideology, a certain paradox began to evolve within several countries of the region. There was a clear shift of authority and ethical authenticity from the bureaucratic and formally legitimated centers to a broader social base. One began to recognize deeper dimensions of change and cultural expression in the region. As a U.S. intellectual once observed, one began to discern more clearly a world that could no longer be defined by artists, novelists, and social scientists, much less by politicians and publicists who construe the forces of history from private, academic, or "managerial" positions. The region was coming to be defined less by its traditional administrative regimes—Spanish, English, French, or Dutch—and more by the quality of the popular cultures and the messages they transmit to the official realm.[5]

For there is increasing belief within the Caribbean of the capacity of the mass of people in the region to take decisions in their own interest. The people who inhabit it are in many ways insisting on the right to do this. Many who give leadership to the mass of the populations in the region are very aware of the disintegration of a number of the old certitudes that propped up western civilization, what with the impact of science and technology and the clear indications that the new mass society worldwide is not without distinctive forms and expressions of its own. They do not (or they no longer) conceive of a "mainstream culture" outside of what they themselves have to offer to human civilization. They see themselves as part-determiners of that mainstream and not as outsiders to be let in. It is a far cry from the days when they dutifully accepted their sibling status and held on to the apron-strings of mother countries. The new posture is disruptive, admittedly, for it questions in fundamental ways the old relationships that bred the ghastly truth that places like the Caribbean have achieved nothing because they have created nothing. The region has long been disproving this, of course, not only in its political but also in its cultural action.

In sum, the paradox of evolving paradoxes of Caribbean culture is not at all dissimilar to what is already revealing itself in the increasingly globalized twenty-first century which, in any case, has already dawned in the nineties. More and more the "tribes" on Planet Earth, in the face of a threatened homogenization, perceive themselves to be in global bondage. They will therefore want to fall back on reserves of energy generated out of the specificity of their own experience and encapsulated in manifestations of the languages they have created, the gods they have grown to worship, the kinship patterns they have devised for their own survival, the structures of thought and the artistic products emerging from their intellect and collective imagination. What is now seen as "surrender" may well be the "redemption" of humankind, and what seems the "death of faith" may well be its "rebirth," as the Caribbean has long known in its protracted struggle for self and cultural certitude over the past half a millennium.

Notes

1. The "Caribbean" is used here in its broadest geo-cultural sense. It includes the English, Spanish, French, Dutch, and U.S. territories, both independent and dependent, and the circum-Caribbean states of northern South America and Central America. Both Northeast Brazil where Africa met Europe under slavery and which has remained underdeveloped with a high misery index, and New Orleans which has produced music and lifestyles out of centuries of interaction between Africans and Europeans are sometimes regarded as culturally "Caribbean."

2. For information on voodoo, see Courlander 1960, and Yarborough 1959; on santería, Bascom 1950; on shango, Simpson 1965; on candomble, Verger 1980; on pocomania, see Seaga 1969; and on rastafarianism, see Smith et al. 1960 and *Caribbean Quarterly* 1980 (entire edition).

3. Apart from the well-known institutional linkages—Caribbean Community (CARICOM), the regional University of the West Indies (which pre-dates the West Indies Federation), and the Caribbean Development Bank established in 1969—Caribbean collaboration has been encouraged and flourishes in the field of sports (especially cricket), the arts (for example, the Caribbean Festival of Arts or Carifesta), the spread of carnival and calypso throughout the region and of reggae from Jamaica to the Eastern Caribbean, and the media (Caribbean Broadcasting Union, a Caribbean News Agency [CANA], and others).

4. Fidel Castro declared Cuba's "Afro-Latinity" in a marathon speech he delivered to a mass rally in Sam Sharpe Square, Montego Bay, on October 16, 1977 during a state visit to Jamaica.

5. The scholar is Richard Morse in an unpublished paper and discussions when he was head of the Latin American and Caribbean Center, Woodrow Wilson Program, Smithsonian Institution, Washington D.C.

Bibliography

Bascom, William. 1950. "A Focus on Cuban Santería." *South Western Journal of Anthropology* 6 (1): 64–68.

Brathwaite, Edward. 1974. *Contradictory Omens: Cultural Diversity and Integration in the Caribbean*. Mona, Jamaica: Savacou Publications, Monograph 1.

Caribbean Contact. September 1985.

Caribbean Quarterly. 1980. Special issue: "Rastafari." 26(4).

Courlander, Harold. 1960. *The Drum and the Hoe: Life and Lore of the Haitian People*. Berkeley: University of California Press.

Dabydeen, David and Brinsley Samaroo, eds. 1987. *India in the Caribbean*. Warwick, U.K.: University of Warwick.

Despres, Leo. 1964. *Cultural Pluralism and Nationalist Politics in Guyana*. Chicago: Rand McNally.

LaGuerre, John, ed. 1974. *Calcutta to Caroni: The East Indians of Trinidad*. St. Augustine, Trinidad: University of the West Indies, Extra Mural Studies Unit.

Mills, Don. 1989. "Jamaica's International Relations in Independence." Pp. 151–166 in Rex Nettleford, ed., *Jamaica in Independence: Essays on the Early Years*. Kingston: Heinemann Caribbean.

Nettleford, Rex. 1978. *Caribbean Cultural Identity: The Case of Jamaica: an Essay in Cultural Dynamics*. Kingston, Jamaica: Institute of Jamaica and Los Angeles, CA: University of California.

Nunley, John and Judith Bettelheim. 1988. *Caribbean Festival Arts: Each and Every Bit of Difference*. Seattle: University of Washington Press.

Seaga, Edward. 1969. "Revival Cults in Jamaica." *Jamaica Journal* 3 (2), June: 3–13.

Simpson, George Eaton. 1965. *Cults in Trinidad*. Puerto Rico: Institute of Caribbean Studies, University of Puerto Rico, Caribbean Monograph Series 2.

Smith, Michael G. 1965. *The Plural Society in the British West Indies*. Berkeley, CA: University of California Press.

————. 1991. *Pluralism, Politics and Ideology in the Creole Caribbean*. New York: Research Institute for the Study of Man.

Smith, M. G., F. R. Augier and Rex Nettleford. 1960. *The Ras Tafari Movement in Kingston*. Jamaica: Mona, Jamaica: University College of the West Indies, Institute for Social and Economic Research.

Verger, Pierre. 1980. *Iconografía dos Deuses Africanos no Candomble de Bahía*. Raizes, Bahía: Cultural Foundation of Bahía.

Walcott, Derek. 1974. "The Muse of History: An Essay." Pp. 1–27 in Orde Coombs, ed., *Is Massa Day Dead? Black Moods in the Caribbean*. Garden City, N.Y.: New Anchor Press.

World Bank. 1993. Caribbean Region: *Current Economic Situation, Regional Issues, and Capital Flows 1992*. Papers prepared for the Caribbean Group for Cooperation in Economic Development (CGCED). Washington D.C.: World Bank.

Yarborough, Lavinia Williams. 1959. *Haiti-Dance*. Frankfurt: Frankfurt am Main.

9

Caribbean Culture in the 1990s: Toward a Carefully Conceived Policy

Fred Constant

Salient Features of Caribbean Cultural Experience

From whatever perspective one examines it, the question of cultural identity seems, particularly in countries deeply divided along racial or color lines, to be perpetually challenging, for it overlaps issues such as national unity and cultural pluralism, nation-building and the integrity of the state, social cohesion, and ethnic politics. In most post-colonial societies such those of the Caribbean, the search for cultural sovereignty gains high priority alongside political independence and economic sufficiency in the awesome process of decolonization and, beyond, in the arduous struggle against external post-colonial domination. It is the triple threat of economics, politics, and culture that determines the ideological thrust of many who advocate change and that delineates the programmatic stages of growth and development in the region at large.

In thinking about the policy needs of the region in culture, it is useful to go back to some of the points delineated in Chapter 8. There Nettleford synthesized his apprehensions and expectations with respect to the development of Caribbean identity. In the course of the analysis, many interrelated processes that determine the salient features of the Caribbean cultural experience emerged, the following among them:

- Insofar as "survival" for the Caribbean meant "identity" and identity, in turn, became a function of survival, the cultural identity of Caribbean peoples is rooted in contradictory processes set in place by slavery, colonialism, and the plantation economy over the past five hundred years;
- Political independence has not brought about cultural sovereignty; the metropolitan colonial country remains the model of intellectual

excellence. Despite the post-colonial assertion of African or Indian presence, there is a continuing intellectual dependence of the region on Europe and the United States;

- The search for Caribbean solutions to Caribbean problems is as rooted in cultural impulses as it is in political ones;
- In the nation-building process, this search means that creolization must now spread to embrace the East Indian community, as it did Europe and Africa.

These are but some of the crucial points made by Nettleford that are relevant to the consideration of public policy needs in the area of culture. In this chapter, some additional comments on the cultural situation in the region are made from two main standpoints. First, the question is asked: How can we account for the persistence, with paradoxical tenacity, of the disparity between the central place of culture in the political discourse of Caribbean leaders and the weakness or failure of the cultural policies implemented in most countries? Second, suggestions are made with respect to the requirements of a carefully thought-out and integrated national cultural policy, one that can offer the possibility of transcending social and ethno-national divisions.

Cultural Politicization and Underdevelopment

Although it generated controversies across the Caribbean, the 500th anniversary of the so-called "discovery of the New World," celebrated in 1992, was also that of an international reconnaissance of Caribbean artistic creativity. Derek Walcott, a poet born in Saint Lucia, became Nobel laureate in literature while Dulce Maria Loynaz, a Cuban poetess, won the famous Cervantes prize. Rigoberta Menchu, an energetic Guatemalan advocate of the Amerindian cause, received the Nobel Peace prize, and Patrick Chamoiseau, Martinican novelist, became Goncourt laureate. Given the dynamism of Caribbean cultural expression, these awards may appear to be rather unsurprising. Yet, there remains the paradox of the underdevelopment of Caribbean cultural policies, despite the post-colonial assertion of the centrality of culture in the independence process. Except for Jamaica, and to some extent Cuba, no Caribbean country has succeeded in giving significant impetus to the development of a sophisticated national cultural policy. Culture is one area in which post-colonial governments have failed miserably, while paradoxically it is this area that has generated wide local public action, particularly in some non-sovereign Caribbean territories (Constant 1993). On the one hand, culture has been linked primarily to tourism development, a linkage that has had, and still has, important consequences for the Caribbean today.

On the other hand, culture is an area where all too often politics prevail over policies, particularly in plural societies.

For while most countries have sought to incorporate a cultural development policy in their overall national development strategy, too often the policy option has been that of "cultural tourism" as a justification for any activity in this domain, and certainly as a priority before cultural integration. As contributor to the foundation of national development, cultural actions should indeed form linkages with education and tourism, but a careful balance in orientation should be maintained, and this is generally not the case in the region. As a result, education and tourism remain the greatest priorities within the development process, with the largest designated budgets. Culture, which is generally assigned the smallest budget, is dependent on the other policies (usually tourism) for its orientation. Thus despite a rhetorical adherence to the cultural dimension of national development, public cultural actions are frequently seen as mere appendages to tourism.

Here lies another paradox: Despite the rhetorical commitment to culture, no Caribbean country, Belize excepted, has, until recently, had functioning legislation for the protection of its cultural heritage. In most cases, the nation's vulnerability to possible cultural destruction has been aggravated precisely because there was no protective legislation in place for architectural or archaeological remains (Cummins 1989). In addition, a lack of professional curatorial and technical staff has been identified as a major deficiency: There is a need for professional training at all levels. Despite the role of museums, monuments, and sites in fostering national and regional identity, Caribbean museum establishment and development has been left primarily to private non-profit organizations, resulting in a benign indifference on the part of governments. Cannizzo's (1987) exploration of the Barbados Museum's redefining of local culture may be used, to a greater or lesser extent, as illustrative of the pitfalls of museum development in the other English-speaking islands. Cannizzo pointed out that Caribbean museums, while often being active agents in shaping identity, have until recently expropriated culture, using it on behalf of the ruling classes to achieve "self-definition by majority exclusion." Thus even though for most Caribbean governments culture remains a great priority in principle, there has clearly been very little done to foster its development and to put it at the disposal of the public at large.

Jamaica, more than any other country, seems to have benefited from sympathetic governmental interest at important periods in its development, for example under the administration of Michael Manley between 1976 and 1981. This interest nevertheless served unwittingly to politicize the cultural development process, as evidenced at the time by the fact that ambitious plans for the development of a new home for the National

Gallery became the target of bitter attack by the opposition. Similar politicization has occurred in Trinidad with respect to proposals for an Indian Cultural Center and a national theater.

The anti-colonial stances and strident nationalisms of the sixties and seventies on the part of the new Caribbean states gave, on rhetorically admirable terms, added impetus to questions of cultural policy. But by the 1990s, even given the constraints of the internal and external environment, little concrete had been achieved. It is true that financial and other assistance has been given to local artists and cultural associations, but this has not been done in any systematic or coherent way. For the most part, the assistance given has been politically opportunistic.

Infrastructural development also remains weak. Ironically, non-sovereign territories such as Martinique, Puerto Rico, and Curaçao have a better record in this regard than do their independent neighbors. In these territories, there is a higher technical level among the cultural staff. It is not only a matter of the availability of public funds; nor is it a matter of greater governmental cultural expertise. Rather, culture has developed in these non-autonomous islands because of governmental incentives and favorable official orientations based on the fact that this area has been, and still is, the only one where the hegemony of the metropole could be challenged (see Constant 1993). Cultural nationalism has been possible without political emancipation. In the case of the independent Caribbean countries, the reverse is true: Political sovereignty has not led, in most cases, to carefully planned and integrated cultural policies.

Trinidad and Tobago illustrates the type of neglect culture has suffered in many parts of the region. By the 1980s, after thirty years of Eric Williams's post-colonial leadership, culture remained highly undeveloped (Ryan 1988). Since Dr. Williams was a scholar and historian, it was very surprising that he failed to formulate and implement a national cultural policy that could appeal to a wide cross-section of the Trinidadian community as part of the nation-building process. Instead, given that domestic political parties were mainly derived from racial bases, cultural policies usually became enmeshed in political considerations. Instead of promoting a genuine policy of multiculturalism, Williams typically encouraged sub-national divisions based on ethnic politics.

Though the official policy in Trinidad was the eventual absorption of sub-cultural groupings around national values, African culture received far more emphasis and support from the state than Indian culture, viewed as the culture of opposition. Indian culture was also regarded as outside the mainstream of the dominant Afro-Caribbean culture. By not displaying the cultural heritage of a sizable segment of the population, Eric Williams failed to affirm the responsibility of the state to encourage the cultural expression of the nation's peoples as part of the concept

"Unity in Diversity" (LaGuerre 1993), and the effects of this failure are still being felt today. As to Afro-Trinidadian culture, even though more supported, it was not institutionalized. For thirty years, the pan (steelband) movement, Trinidad's most important cultural contribution, remained without a national physical home. Very little by way of public resources was channeled into research into the dynamics of pan music. This has changed somewhat today, with wider popular acceptance and interest in the development of pan, to the extent that the steel pan has been declared the national instrument of Trinidad and Tobago (although not without some complaint on the part of segments of the East Indian community). There is little doubt, however, that the steelband movement still remains under-funded and resource-poor.

The situation is not very different in other cultural areas. Despite the plethora of talent and activity in the performing arts, there is still no permanent home in Trinidad for the performing arts, no national gallery for the visual arts, no proper national archive system, and rehabilitation of the national museum has been undertaken without much government support. In other words, the foundation for cultural development that should have been laid early on by the post-colonial government, was not. Eric Williams, who strongly favored education policies and must have understood intellectually the relationship between culture and national development and education, left no monuments to the cultural genius of the people of Trinidad and Tobago. As Selwyn Ryan wrote in 1988, "the man of culture revealed himself to be a philistine" (p. 157).

Challenges and Opportunities

How is this bias against cultural development, certainly not unique to Trinidad and Tobago, to be resolved and the imbalance in priorities corrected? The role of cultural resources in the overall insular development process has not yet been fully recognized or defined by Caribbean nations. Cultural development can promote a sense of pride, self-esteem, and national identity that will help the people of developing countries to face the future with hope and confidence. This achievement takes not only time but also commitment on the part of each community in every country concerned.

In this regard, the state has a critical role to play by preserving the cultural heritage of each component of the population and encouraging the creolization process to embrace all of said components. While we may disagree with such an interventionist policy on the part of governments, inasmuch as popular sentiments might be manipulated, the state has a duty to guarantee to every citizen equal access to public resources in culture as in all other areas under its responsibility. Without a cultural policy that can appeal to a wide cross-section of the national community, commitment to the state by all segments of the community will be fragile and feelings of alienation will develop.

In order to overcome the weakness of most Caribbean cultural policies, political change must take place. Given the people's fascinating creative energies, it is difficult to understand why the intellectually-focused "doctor politics" of the Caribbean leaders did not lead to more serious attention being paid to culture. Few regions in the world have been cross-fertilized by such disparate elements from Asia, Africa, and Europe "interacting to find ideal, form, and purpose within set geographical boundaries over time," to put it in Rex Nettleford's words (see Chapter 8). The refrain of Caribbean cultural richness resounds everywhere in the various islands. Yet while this refrain may be accepted in principle, there has clearly been very little done to put it into practice. It is time to act by formulating well thought-out and integrated cultural policies. Between "official" culture and the abdication of the state in favor of the market, there is room for reasoned intervention by public authorities. Indeed, the state may assist without dictating, encourage without imposing. This may avoid the rise of conformity of taste, more subterranean in process, but also more harmful. Although it is far from being perfect, the experience of Jamaica is of some interest. This country has long developed a cultural policy, formally dating back to 1959 (upgraded in 1963) but harking back to 1938. Once again, Rex Nettleford has commented on Jamaica's policy: "For all the policy declarations in the 1980s about deregulation and privatization, and despite the untamable individualism of the Jamaican, the role of the state as strategic funder and patron of artistic culture has been a positive and facilitative one" (1989: 291).

Although Jamaican politics has not been totally divorced from cultural development, in most cases artistic culture has transcended the perfidy of political tribalism and the acrimony of ideological conflict. In this perspective, the role of the state is critical. Here is a selective list of the tasks required. First, the state must protect the national cultural heritage by the drafting of appropriate legislation. Second, it has to encourage education in the arts at school, and the training of cultural agents such as art teachers, creative arts practitioners, and the civil servants concerned. Third, it must provide cultural production with appropriate financial and technical assistance without, in any case, imposing what the beneficiaries should paint, sculpt, dance, act, or sing. Fourth, the state must provide cultural infrastructures such as a national library, national gallery, museum, and cultural center, built in different parts of the country in order to facilitate wide access to cultural activities.

Such a serious cultural policy that can appeal to everyone in a country helps not only to shape and consolidate insular national identities, but also to counterbalance external cultural penetration such as the massive influence of the U.S. mass media. While this influence is not new to the region, it has grown with the increasing technical sophistication of these media manifested in satellite broadcasting, home video viewing, cable television, and other electronic devices. The cost of this new technology has put it beyond the reach of most small producers, including local governments who are increasingly forced to rely on relay transmissions, with the result that by the 1980s 85 percent of all programming was originating outside the area (Brown 1983). This massive cultural penetration by foreign mass media is a real danger to the cultural integrity of the Caribbean, notwithstanding the so-called globalization process. Political leaders seem too often unconcerned about this threat to their cultural identity.

Caribbean migration, in particular the circulatory type that is becoming the norm in most areas, is, to some extent, another challenge to the protection of the Caribbean's unique indigenous forms of popular culture. Although some scholars (for instance, Flores 1981) have argued that migration is contributing paradoxically to the cultural revitalization of the Caribbean heritage, it should be noted that migration results also in de-culturation and a loss of cultural identity (Safa 1987). The intense academic debate in Puerto Rico on the validity of a "separate" Nuyorican culture is illustrative of the problem: Is Nuyorican culture not related to the island or is it a new cultural expression with its roots in the island? Caribbean governments are not sufficiently aware of the impact of migration on the cultural identity and even on the socio-economic structure of the sending society. Despite growing evidence about the role of circulatory-type migration in the massive influence of U.S. culture in the Caribbean, the official view is focused on the large-scale remittances in U.S. dollars that are supposed to help bolster the faltering economies.

Undoubtedly, the search for national identity in the Caribbean is not easy, given the region's exposure to North American and European models. Yet it is clear that the Caribbean must look at its own indigenous creative energies instead of reinforcing metropolitan standards. In this search, a national cultural policy that appeals to each component of the population can play a critical role in encouraging the development of indigenous forms of popular culture.

In summation, an effective cultural policy must pay more attention to the historical roots of cultural identity in the Caribbean, with particular emphasis on the Indo-Caribbean contribution which has been, longer than the Afro-Caribbean contribution, devalued in most areas of the region and especially in the plural societies. It must take into consideration the technical requirements without which a cultural policy will inevitably fail. It must also look carefully at the changes which migration and the

mass media are bringing about in the Caribbean's contemporary reclamation of self. Indeed, it must explore the possibilities offered by the
search for a transcendent regionalism that subordinates ethnic and national origin to an overarching West Indian identity. "We must save ourselves together, or together we will disappear," warned José Martí over a
century ago. His warning still has resonance for contemporary Caribbean
policy-makers who look to the twenty-first century.

Bibliography

Brown, Aggrey. 1983. "Mass Communication, Cultural Policy and Identity in the
    Commonwealth Caribbean." Paper presented at Conference on Popular Cul-
    ture, National Identity, and Migration in the Caribbean, University of Florida,
    June.
Cannizzo, Jeanne. 1987. "How Sweet It Is: Cultural Politics in Barbados." *Muse*
    4(4): 22–26.
Constant, Fred. 1993. "Comparing Public Cultural Action in the Caribbean: Poli-
    tics or Policies?" Paper presented at the 18th Caribbean Studies Association
    Conference, Kingston, Jamaica, May.
Cummins, Alissandra. 1989. "Culture, Museums and National Identity in the
    Caribbean." Unpublished Report.
Flores, Juan Attinasi, and John Pedro Pedrazo. 1981. "La Carreta Made A U-Turn:
    Puerto Rican Language and Culture in the United States." *Daedalus* 110 (2):
    73–97.
LaGuerre, John. 1993. "Dilemmas of a Cultural Policy in Trinidad and Tobago."
    Unpublished Paper.
Nettleford, Rex. 1989. "Cultural Action in Independence." Pp. 247–271 in Rex
    Nettleford, ed., *Jamaica in Independence: Essays on the Early Years*. Kingston:
    Heinemann Publishers:
Ryan, Selwyn. 1988. "Dr. Eric Williams, the People's National Movement and the
    Independence Experience: A Retrospective." Pp. 139–161 in Selwyn Ryan, ed.,
    The Independence Experience (1962–1987). St Augustine, Trinidad: Institute for
    Social and Economic Research (ISER), University of the West Indies.
Safa, Helen. 1987. "Popular Culture, National Identity, and Race in the
    Caribbean." *New West Indian Guide* 61 (3/4): 115–126.

10

Caribbean Culture: Ethnic Identity Issues— The Case of Suriname

Rosemarijn van Hoefte

Cultural Decolonization

Although political independence for the Caribbean states has not led to economic emancipation, a level of cultural decolonization has been attained even in those teritories that remain political dependencies. In the first place, Caribbean culture, born out of resistance to colonial domination and characterized by assimilation, dynamism, and cross-fertilization, has been reluctantly accepted and has to some extent replaced the metropolitan culture. Second, the international influence of Caribbean culture by far exceeds what one can realistically expect from a small region with a relatively small population. This influence reaches from the august Nobel Prize committee to the discotheques of Paris where zouk music holds sway, and to the stands in Dutch soccer stadiums, where fans have sported an orange cap with dreadlocks in honor of Ruud Gullit, Dutch star of Surinamese descent. In short, Caribbean culture in its many forms has spread throughout the world and yet is threatened by Americanization, Europeanization, and globalization. Caribbean culture always has been used and will have to be used as a weapon against dependency and disparagement.

In this chapter, another dimension is added to the arguments set forth in the last two chapters. The focus is on the specific issue of ethnic identity, in this case the integration of the East Indian inhabitants of the Caribbean and of Suriname in particular. In Chapters 8 and 9, Nettleford and Constant agreed that the creolization process should today include the East Indian element in the Caribbean as well as Afro-Caribbean and other elements. Nettleford, in particular, has called on Afro-Caribbeans to

allow this process to take place and on East Indians to become "'West Indians" through inter-culturation without resorting to exaggerated claims
on "Mother India." Reality is such, however, that integration is a long
way off in countries such as Suriname. To explain why this is the case we
need to go back in history to understand the present paradoxes in Surinamese culture. Creolization definitely did take place; yet it resulted in
fragmentation rather than unification.

History and Identity

The great majority of the Asians arrived in the West Indies as indentured
laborers, contracted to replace the emancipated slaves on the plantations
(Hoefte 1987). Even though contract laborers were supposed to be temporary migrants, it soon became clear that the majority would settle as
permanent residents. Between 1873 and 1917, 34,000 East Indians arrived
in Suriname.[1] Even though official figures have not been published since
1971, the East Indian population group is the largest group in Suriname
in the 1990s and the group is also economically dominant.

The majority of the Asian immigrants did not want to conform to the
existing western, Christian values of Surinamese society and tried to preserve as much of their cultural heritage as possible, though generally shy-
ing away from confrontation. The newcomers emphasized their own cultural identity to establish a place in an alien world; yet the Asian cultures
did not survive the transfer to Suriname unscathed. The process of adaptation to the new environment can be clearly discerned in, for example,
language and religion. The fact that immigrants originated from different
districts often led to amalgamation of several cultures and languages into
one "East Indian" culture or language. Religion played an important role
in attempts to preserve as much as possible of the Asian cultural heritage.
In addition, the Asians increasingly became politically aware, and this
was primarily expressed in the growing organization of immigrants and
an increasing East Indian nationalism. The relations between religion,
culture, politics, and nationalism have been exceedingly significant
throughout the twentieth century.

Most East Indians originated from northern India, yet there did not
exist a clear majority from any particular district. As a consequence several cultural traditions merged into a single "East Indian" one, which
served to strengthen ethnic identity. Thus several cultural expressions
that exist among East Indians in Suriname do not exist as such in India itself. Perhaps the clearest example of this process is the development of
the Sarnami language. The East Indian migrants spoke a number of different, but closely related, languages. Very quickly, both in India and
aboard ship, the migrants communicated in a new language based on the

amalgamation of languages and dialects spoken in Central Northern India. Sarnami is a grammatical mixture of several Indian languages and not identical to any Indian language. Moreover, Sarnami's further development in Suriname has led to the creation of new unique grammatical forms that cannot be found in any Indian language. In addition, the lingua franca of the East Indians includes adopted Sranan Tongo (Suriname Creole) words (Damsteegt 1988).

Eighty percent of immigrant East Indians were Hindus. The organizing principle of both Hinduism and the social structure in India was the caste system (de Klerk 1953; van der Veer and Vertovec 1991), but most observers agree that the caste system did not survive in Suriname, at least not in its original form. Castes lost their corporative character and gave up their individuality to form a new kind of national Indian caste which was closed to other population groups. However, it cannot be denied that culturally some notion of caste still persisted. For example, the *Brahmin's* priesthood still has an important caste connotation. His is the highest status, and, as in India, this is not necessarily based on material comfort. The *Brahmins* or *pandits* in Suriname maintained and even strengthened their position. The *pandits* were instrumental in preserving and promoting traditional religious and cultural knowledge. Just as respect for the Brahmins continues to exist in Suriname, so does the contempt for the *camars* or outcastes. Thus, while the authentic caste system no longer exists, some of its informing ideas still retain significance, although not as exhaustively and systematically as in India. The absence of caste, however, did not affect the vitality of Hinduism.

The beliefs and rites of Hinduism vary by geographical location, time, and social group. In the Caribbean, different caste beliefs and practices fused into a single unitary religion. Central are cults and rites of passage. Two separate religious traditions may be discerned. A clear majority of the Hindus supports the oldest one, the Sanathan Dharm. This movement preserves the religious heritage as it has developed through the centuries. The second movement, Arya Samaj, was founded in Bombay in 1875 and reached Suriname by way of British Guiana. Its religious and social reformism was coupled with nationalism, for it stressed the significance of the Indian heritage and ethnicity. As it also repudiated Christianity and Christian education, the movement initiated the first cultural renaissance for the Indians. The new life of the migrants explains the success of the progressive Arya Samaj movement.

Failure of Dutch Policy

Different policies demonstrate that the administration in Paramaribo did not have a clear concept of whether to treat the Asian immigrants as temporary or permanent residents. As a result the strategies vacillated between attempts to fully integrate the newcomers and the implementation of different rules and laws for the Asian population. Unlike the case in the Netherlands East Indies where the Dutch attempted to preserve the native customs, traditions, languages, and juridical systems, assimilation was the predominant feature in colonial rule in Suriname. One language, one law, and one culture, all made in Holland, prevailed in the west. However, an extensive, well thought-out plan for the integration of the new population groups never existed. Not surprisingly, soon cracks began to appear in the assimilation policy.

Education policy provides a good example of the wavering governmental goals. The introduction of compulsory education, in Dutch, in 1876 was an important aspect of assimilation attempts. The education of Asian children in Suriname was closely linked to the evolution of the concept and functions of indentured immigration. At first the government believed that the colony had the moral obligation to provide some form of primary education to the children of East Indian immigrants. In 1890 the first "coolie school" was opened. An East Indian teacher instructed the pupils in at least two languages, Hindi and Urdu. After all, the idea was that the children would remain in Suriname for only five years and knowledge of the Dutch language would be useless in case of repatriation to India. Within a decade, however, a conflict between defenders and opponents of this education was brewing. Opponents argued that separate education of the Asian children would not enhance their assimilation into society and would prevent their christianization. In 1907 the government abolished the "coolie schools" in favor of integrating Asian children into Suriname society.

Another attempt at assimilation was the law of 1927 that made all Indians born in Suriname Dutch subjects. But the definitive break in Dutch assimilation policy were the so-called marriage laws. Most immigrants did not contract a civil marriage and their religious unions did not have any legal validity. In 1913 the Suriname Immigrants Association requested the legal recognition of marriages solemnized by acknowledged Indian priests. Only in 1937 did the governor of Suriname propose to legalize the marriages concluded according to the Muslim or Hindu religion. This draft bill ran into strong, creole, white collar opposition in the Surinamese parliament whose members feared the dissolution of society into different cultural and ethnic communities. The creoles felt that it was a deliberate attempt to "divide and rule" the ethnic groups. Although this aspect might have played a role in charting the new course, a pragmatic adjustment to existing circumstances seems to have been the major motivation (see Ramsoedh 1990 for a good description of developments in the 1930s). Despite this opposition, the Asiatic marriage decrees came into effect in 1941. The government legally recognized marriages performed before Asian priests. This constituted a definitive break in the assimilation policy of the colonial regime.

The immigrants themselves also undermined assimilation policy by organizing along ethnic lines. During the first decades of indentured immigration, little organized political action took place among the Asians. In the early twentieth century the majority of the migrants directed their energy toward looking after the immediate interests of their ethnic group. Clearly, the most important goals were the promotion of communal interests and the forging of an East Indian ethnic identity. Political impulses often originated from outside Suriname and the leaders of the first hour were not immigrants themselves but officials or politicians. The preferred strategy called for cooperation and not confrontation with the colonial authorities. A lack of radicalism and a rather curious attachment to Holland, and the Queen in particular, characterized the dozens of unions founded during the first decades of the twentieth century. Only in the period of change after World War II did the Asian groups gain real power in the Surinamese political arena.

Cultural Divisiveness

In the first years after World War II, urbanization and better educational opportunities were divisive forces in the East Indian community. The urban elite increasingly adopted western ideas. This elite preferred the Dutch language over Sarnami and added the Netherlands to India as a source of cultural inspiration. Furthermore, economic and social mobility led to a split between religious culture and secular culture, the latter including clothing, music, movies, cuisine, and name giving.

However, political developments led to a restrengthening of East Indian culture (see Meel 1990 for a fine analysis of these developments). First, after the watershed caused by World War II, mass political parties were organized in Suriname, founded not on ideology but on ethnicity. Especially in the East Indian case, politics and religion were inextricably intertwined. Often national interests were considered subservient to parochial ethnic interests. Political leaders were also prominent in the Sanatan Dharm and Arya Samaj movements and this made religion an important instrument of political mobilization. Second, Suriname's autonomy, granted in 1954, did not create a strong Surinamese nationalism but rather emphasized the difficult relations between the different population groups. Colonialism was on the decline as was the political and cultural significance of the European elite. Several creole intellectuals argued that cultural decolonization should pave the way for political and economic independence and thus advocated a cultural nationalism based on the existing Afro-Surinamese culture. All population groups were to conform to this creole cultural heritage which was regarded as the sole "true" Surinamese culture. Of great importance was the attempt to make Sranan Tongo, Suriname's linga franca, the national language. Throughout the colonial era a good command of Dutch was an essential prerequisite to obtain white collar jobs and thus social acceptance. As a result Sranan Tongo and other expressions of Afro-Surinamese, and Asian-Surinamese for that matter, culture were despised and seen as a clear mark of low social status. This did not mean, however, that the creole heritage was erased; officially many creoles adhered to Dutch values, yet at home they continued to speak Sranan and covertly tried to preserve their cultural, African legacy. Not surprisingly, this situation resulted in double standards and a growing lack of self-confidence. The cultural nationalists regarded Sranan Tongo as the exclusive Surinamese language and started to publish literature and hold discussions in Sranan.

This creole cultural, and later political and economic, nationalism led to a reverse reaction among the Asians. They equated nationalism with a Surinamese version of negritude. The East Indian population advocated pluralism: "unity in diversity." The East Indians (re)evaluated their own secular and religious cultural heritage. For example, Hindu and Moslem schools and first names became popular again. An essential point was that the Asians did not share the anti-Dutch feelings of the creole nationalists. Rather they preferred a continued Dutch presence that would enable the Asian populations to complete their emancipation and to become equal to the creole segment. They also wanted Dutch, instead of Sranan, to remain the official language of Suriname. This pro-Dutch sentiment loomed large during the discussions about Suriname's political independence. According to opinion polls in 1975, 99.9 percent of the East Indian population was opposed to independence.[2]

The triumph of of Sranan Tongo and political independence did not create one people and one nation. East Indians continued to search for their roots and to strengthen their cultural heritage. In the 1970s Sarnami poetry and prose were published for the first time. These cultural developments may be regarded as progressive, new, and enriching Surinamese culture, yet at the same time as conservative because they strengthened ethnic identity and as a consequence served as divisive elements in Surinamese society.

A final paradox in Surinamese culture is the influence of migration. Amsterdam has always been closer to Paramaribo than, say, Port-of-Spain or Caracas, but in the 1990s the pull of the former metropole seems to have become stronger rather than weaker. The tens of thousands of Surinamese migrants leaving Suriname following the enormous political and economic problems of the 1970s, 1980s, and 1990s, included many intellectuals. The intellectual climate in the Netherlands is more appealing, with a good infrastructure in the form of freedom of expression, publishing houses, bookstores, libraries, a healthy mass media, and other advantages. The negative side is that the market dictates that authors write in the Dutch language, and this generates feelings of disorientation and estrangement, feelings that so long have influenced culture in Suriname and the Caribbean.

This ambivalence will continue to characterize Surinamese and Caribbean culture in the 1990s and beyond. Surinamese poets Dobru (Robin Ravales) and Shrinivasi (M. Lutchman), the first person to write a poem in Sarnami, have illuminated the identity issue in two well-known poems. In one, Dobru (1982) speaks of "one Suriname/so many kinds of hair/so many colors of skin/so many languages/one people"; in the other Shrinivasi laments: "I would like to bind you/to one people/prevent it from remaining a fairy tale/for in speech we are Surinamers/but in deed still Negro, Hindustani, Javanese or Chinese" (1974). These poems highlight not only the cultural contradictions that still exist between creoles and East Indians in Suriname today but more generally the tension between one Caribbean identity and the geographical, historical, social, and ethnic fragmentation so characteristic of the region.

Notes

1. Also 33,000 Javanese migrated to Suriname in the period 1890–1939. This Javanese presence is unique in the Caribbean. At present approximately 15 percent of the population of Suriname is of Javanese descent. For the history and culture of the Javanese in Suriname, see Malefijt (1963) and Hoefte (1990.)

2. According to these figures, 80 percent of the Javanese and 50 percent of the creoles were opposed to independence. See Dew 1978: 182.

Bibliography

Damsteegt, Theo. 1988. "Sarnami: A Living Language." Pp. 95–120 in Richard K. Barz and Jeff Siegel, eds., *Language Transplanted: The Development of Overseas Hindi.* Weisbaden: Otto Harrassowitz.

de Klerk, C.J.M. 1953. *De Immigratie der Hindostanen in Suriname.* Amsterdam: Urbi et Orbi.

Dew, Edward. 1978. *The Difficult Flowering of Surinam: Ethnicity and Politics in a Plural Society.* The Hague: Martinus Nijhoff.

Dobru, R. 1982. *Boodschappen uit de zon.* Amsterdam: Meulenhoff.

Hoefte, Rosemarijn. 1987. *Plantation Labor After the Abolition of Slavery.* Ph.D. Dissertation, University of Florida.

———. 1990. "De Beeldvorming Omtrent de Javanese Cultuur in Suriname." *Oso* 9(2): 7–18.

Malefijt, Annemarie de Waal. 1963. *The Javanese of Surinam: Segment of a Plural Society.* Assen: Van Gorcum.

Meel, Peter. 1990. "A Reluctant Embrace: Suriname's Idle Quest for Independence." Pp. 259–289 in Gary Brana-Shute, ed., *Resistance and Rebellion in Suriname: Old and New.* Williamsburg, VA: College of William and Mary.

Ramsoedh, Hans. 1990. *Suriname 1933–1944: Koloniale Politiek en Beleid onder Gouverneur Kielstra.* Delft: Eburon.

Shrinivasi. 1974. *Oog in oog (frente a frente).* Paramaribo: El Dorado.

Van der Veer, Peter and Steven Vertovec. 1991. "Brahmanism Abroad: On Caribbean Hinduism as an Ethnic Religion." *Ethnology* 30: 149–166.

11

Toward a New Caribbean Manager: Caribbean Management Education and Training

Dennis J. Gayle and Bhoendradatt Tewarie

The Caribbean Business Environment

The prototypical managerial functions of planning, organizing, directing, controlling, recruitment, and representation must articulate with a specific organizational environment, whether within the public or the private sector. For it is in the framework of this business environment that managers formulate, evaluate, and implement strategies that systematically organize available resources into the means of achieving selected objectives and fulfilling an agreed-upon mission.

The business environment in the English-speaking Caribbean is characterized by small, developing, mostly democratic states with very limited domestic resource bases and markets. Consequently, the world market prices of both imports and exports may be regarded as given. This suggests that the availability of goods and services within the Caribbean will vary directly with the extent of privatization, deregulation, and market liberalization. At the same time, diseconomies of scale as well as scope may imply increased unit production and infrastructural and investment costs. Very small size may impose special constraints on the respective roles of government and private enterprise, while the optimal role of government may vary with national resource endowment (Brewster 1993: 60).

During the 1960s and 1970s, post-independence Caribbean politicians tended toward populism and public sector expansion. By contrast, in the 1990s, the implementation of privatization, deregulation, and market liberalization assumed the aura of received wisdom, particularly in Jamaica but also in the Bahamas, Trinidad and Tobago, Guyana, and Dominica, consequent on the widespread stagnation of regional economic growth experienced in the 1980s and, in several cases, the imperatives of structural adjustment agreements with the International Monetary Fund (IMF). Domestic initiatives have been complemented by regional (Caribbean Community [CARICOM]) moves to liberalize trade. In July 1989 CARICOM heads of government agreed to a Single Market and Economy. A new common external tariff was introduced in October 1992 and the new rules of origin became effective May 1, 1993.

A single market economy would make it possible to address the development of the region's three key economic sectors—agriculture, manufacturing, and tourism—on a "symbiotic" basis, as recommended by the West Indian Commission (WIC 1992: 182). Such an integrated approach could be a tremendous stimulus to production, export expansion, and increased foreign exchange earnings in the region. However, if CARICOM is to continue to play an effective role as a regional bloc within the hemisphere, the strategic vision and management skills of the region's public and private sector leaders must be engaged.

It is not clear, however, that the Caribbean needs fewer public and more private sector managers. Indeed, the concepts of the public and private sectors are not mutually exclusive, static, or unidimensional. In this chapter we argue that the Caribbean needs a new type of manager, capable of functioning effectively in *either* sector and able to provide the strategic vision necessary to be competitive in the new international business environment. First we consider the concept of privatization and explore the respective roles of the public and private sector. Subsequently, we discuss the relative scarcity of entrepreneurs in the region and the need for management education. We conclude with an expanded specification of the new Caribbean manager.

Defining Private and Public Sector Roles

In considering the nature of the new Caribbean manager, it is essential to examine the concept of privatization itself. As a process, privatization denotes reducing the roles of government while increasing those of the private sector in activities or asset ownership. In practice privatization may include "load shedding" or divestiture; the replacement of budgeted public activity by private market mechanisms such as consumer cooperatives; co-production or variously structured public/private sector partnerships; state management contracts such as monopoly franchises for the private supply of public services; user charges; lease-purchase arrangements; the creation of ownership transfer companies; and even tax reduction intended to stimulate private-sector investment. Accordingly, privatization includes a spectrum of categories, from "pure government department" to "pure private entrepreneur," with a range of hybrid organizations in between (Dunsire 1990: 54).

Since 1984 when the British government divested $4.9 billion in British Telecom shares, worldwide privatization proceeds have totaled an estimated $250 billion. In 1991 alone, governments raised some $50 billion by selling public enterprises to private investors. There is abundant evidence that privatization produces a net increase in wealth as a result of expanded investment, managerial innovation, improved price structures, and the shedding of surplus workers. However, freedom from state management may be followed by economic losses, as in the case of Mexicana Airways, and privatization may produce losses for employees as well as customers, as exemplified by British Airways. In some sales, such as Mexico's Telmex, foreigners demonstrably benefit more than all domestic groups combined. Even so, Mexico was able to attract $15 billion in foreign investment during 1990–1992 as a result of privatization (The Economist 1992: 73–74).

On the other hand, it is simplistic to posit an uncomplicated dichotomy between the public and private sectors. First, some aspects of government may grow while others remain static or even decline. Second, private-sector productivity growth depends significantly on public capital investment in basic infrastructure such as airports, highways, and waterworks. Third, the private sector is highly differentiated along several dimensions including the informal-for-profit and non-profit sectors, private professional associations, and the private household economy. Indeed, the public and private sectors both overlap the social sector comprising health, education, and social service providers who work on either a salaried or *pro bono* basis. Fourth, the principal-agent problem persists in both the private and the public sectors. Management does not necessarily act in the best interest of either widely diffused shareholders or taxpayers, so that effective performance monitoring remains problematic (Gayle and Goodrich 1990: 1–23).

By increasing the relative role of the private sector in activities and asset ownership, privatization expands the scope of the market, a process by which buyers and sellers of a good interact to determine its price and quantity. The market economy consists of a network of transactions where relative prices determine what shall be produced, how, and for whom. At the core of the process is the efficiency norm: Managers and owners are given a stake in reducing costs so as to widen profit margins. However, market institutions are also premised upon a set of beliefs that rewards are commensurate to effort and skill, that most human wants can be satisfied through market mechanisms, and that private gain produces social value (Samuelson and Nordhaus 1985: 21, 41, 43). Yet goods and services, as well as the income that produces them, are only intermediate goods, whereas satisfaction or happiness and human development are final goods (Lane 1991). Utility or satisfaction is a reactive, not a predictive concept. Markets emphasize consumer rather than worker welfare. But the greatest subjective well-being is most often experienced during work, not consumption (Jahoda 1989: 309–314). Interpersonal relations, external to the market, remain one of the most significant sources of happiness and satisfaction.

It remains essential to deal with the sources and consequences of market failure, such as imperfectly distributed information, negative externalities, inadequately safeguarded merit and public goods, involuntary unemployment, real demand deficiencies, and the presence of natural monopolies. As Stephen Smith (1991: 151) observes, after reviewing the record of Newly Industrializing Country dynamic growth, sectoral promotion rather than comprehensive market liberalization is crucial, and government-private sector collaboration is necessary to development success. In partial consequence of this realization, some consensus may be developing that the Caribbean requires not necessarily less government, but a better public sector.

In 1992 one influential Caribbean report concluded that apart from the functions of law and order, defense, security, and foreign affairs, government should position itself to more effectively undertake a wide range of functions. These include facilitating, regulating, and monitoring private enterprise; playing a catalytic role in improving education and training, and stimulating research and development; encouraging the growth of small business as well as the development and diffusion of entrepreneurial skills; providing a social safety net for disadvantaged citizens; promoting exports and negotiating market access; and participating in international policy networks intended to deal with transnational issues such as environmental degradation and communicable diseases (Nettleford, Brown, and collaborators 1992: 6–7).

New Entrepreneurs, New Skills

The West Indian Commission (WIC) took the view that the diffusion of entrepreneurial skills was the single most formidable development challenge facing the Caribbean. According to the report, "Surveys done of the projected private sector demand for graduates over the period 1991–1996 indicate demand levels in the range of 4,800 to 7,200 per annum over the period. Net current output is about one-half to one-third of projected private sector needs. When this is added to the requirements of the public sector, it is clear that the Region faces very major shortfalls in high-level managerial personnel"(WIC 1992: 238–239).

What is therefore required is the creation of a cadre of new entrepreneurs, especially those who can build small businesses. In turn, such businesses will create linkages and offer support services that can foster industrial expansion across the region, thus filling up the cracks in a fragmented and disjointed Caribbean regional economy. Currently the massive restructuring effort that is taking place throughout the region has led to the collapse of several businesses into receivership and efforts to "rightsize" those that have survived. Since 1988 for instance, over 250 businesses have gone into receivership in Trinidad and Tobago, according to Ministry of Labor statistics. Again, during a 1993 CARICOM private sector conference in Guyana, the President of the Jamaica Manufacturing Association noted that the sector had become a mere shadow of its former self in terms of the number and diversity of operations.

All this has produced leaner, flatter, and more competitive organizations but it has also led, in this region as elsewhere in the world, to the retrenchment of workers on a significant scale. Anecdotal evidence suggests that many of these retrenched workers have been fairly well-educated people at middle and higher levels of management with a substantial stock of experience gained in industry. An entire entrepreneurial sector can be created through this group which can readily be supported by training in needed skills, including the creation and successful management of small business.

Drucker (1992) has noted that today's small businesses can rapidly become internationally competitive because the growth and sophistication of information technologies have opened up global communication pathways. Indeed Caribbean entrepreneurs need to take into account the fact that this is the age of the "knowledge worker" or, put another way, intellectual capital. Huge organizations, driven by mass production and marketing and controlled by powerful managerial elites, no longer possess an assumed competitive edge. Instead, business is driven and supported by information technology which is generated by and accessible to the managerial mind within small new enterprises created by a new generation of entrepreneurs.

Adaptability to the environment is also important. Because the Caribbean countries are engaged in economic restructuring and market liberalization at the same time, there is an urgent need for organizations that are more effective in responding to a changing environment, with leadership that can motivate people in the direction of a clearly defined strategic vision. The times also demand a capacity to develop skills and strategies that allow for adaptation and survival. This implies a need for managers who are at home in a world of mergers and acquisitions, joint ventures, and international alliances. It also means that managers must learn to speak the languages and to develop an appreciation of the cultures of others with whom they conduct business.

Like private firms, state-owned enterprises are also engaged in restructuring efforts because most Caribbean governments have refused to subsidize loss-making agencies. Many public sector managers have had formal training in relevant fields. The task, however, is for such managers to offer leadership that can transform the culture of their organizations. A key task in transforming the culture of state enterprises is to develop an entrepreneurial spirit among workers, despite a tradition in which public employees have normally seen state sector jobs as sinecures. In this sense, the requirements for public sector managers are little different from those of private-sector managers.

Finally, in keeping with the new international business environment, the Caribbean needs to transform the curricula of management education to ensure that the demands of the market place are met as well as the requirements of a concerted effort to achieve sustainable development. Expansion of management programs at all levels should aim to upgrade existing skills in the workplace, create a crop of new graduates with managerial training, provide some measure of managerial training to all university graduates regardless of discipline, foster advanced managerial and leadership skills, and create the organizational capacity in the region to compete in the global business environment.

The Special Case of the Tourism Sector

The need for innovative managers is particularly pressing in the tourism sector because the Caribbean's most profitable long-term exports to North America and Europe consist of vacation opportunities. Indeed, tourism is the only Caribbean Basin industry that has shown steady growth since 1973. In 1990, visitor receipts provided 25 percent of total Caribbean exports, a larger proportion than in any other region of the world. Alternatively stated, such revenues funded more than 41 percent of total regional imports (Caribbean Tourism Organization 1996: 1–2).

By 1994, the Caribbean had been the largest regional tourism supplier among the developing countries for a decade, with $12 billion in gross earnings. The sector has provided direct employment to 500,000 workers. Between 1970 and 1994, the number of stayover tourists visiting the Caribbean each year expanded by 600 percent to 13.7 million. Annual cruise-ship arrivals increased at an even faster rate, to 2.3 million passengers (Caribbean Tourism Organization 1996: 1–2). Yet critical issues of socio-economic and ecological impact and marketing and management effectiveness remain on the agenda in the 1990s. Despite the centrality of tourism, regional public and private entrepreneurs have yet to capitalize on this pivotal sector.

Within the Caribbean tourist industry, the overriding issue is how best to improve competitiveness while effectively integrating tourism with national and regional development strategies. The tourist-generating markets of Caribbean destinations are often inherent competitors. Other aspects of competitiveness that pose recurrent challenges involve transport and communications systems, domestic food production, quality control and distribution, operating cost control, marketing, and the incidence of taxation.

Both public and private management capabilities are at issue here. For example, within regional governments, ministers dealing with related portfolios such as agriculture and industry are often insufficiently informed about the needs of the tourist sector. Additionally, there is typically a pronounced resistance to rapid change among national tourist bureaucracies and hotel staff. A well-managed project may be programmed for failure because incomplete or inconsistent decision criteria are specified. Furthermore, good advertising may only call attention to a mediocre product (Gayle and Goodrich 1993: 11–16).

These management limitations highlight the need for expanded management education and training programs specifically targeted to the tourism sector. Although there are relevant programs offered by institutions such as the University of the West Indies' Center for Hotel and Tourism Management in the Bahamas, these institutions have unfortunately not yet developed the capacity to meet the needs identified.

Toward a New Caribbean Manager

The term "'new Caribbean manager" is intended to define successful regional entrepreneurs from the viewpoint of managerial process. Such managers understand that technology continues to create a single world market and that capital liberalization has combined with micro-technology to create new potential advantages for small enterprises. They are sensitive to the imperatives of functional specialization and flexibility and thus willing to contract-out supporting functions in the interest of competitiveness, and to re-engineer their companies when required by applying simpler, leaner, and more productive processes. At the same time, the new Caribbean manager is attuned to employee-centered competitive advantage, which emphasizes team-based production, job security, performance-related pay, in-house promotion, managed growth, employee share ownership incentives, and open book management or the supply of full information to all workers.

These managers may be driven by compelling strategic vision, as exemplified by the manner in which the all-inclusive SuperClubs and Sandals hotel chains have expanded across the Caribbean from their initial bases in Jamaica, or by the merger between 1992 and 1994 of the Trinidad-based Neal and Massy Group with the Jamaica-based T. Geddes Grant Group. This strategic vision is capable of considering the world as a potential market, of rapidly reviewing managerial options, applying modern information technology, and selecting appropriate market niches with strong potential for competitive achievement. However, the new Caribbean manager also requires a sense of social responsibility, rooted in an awareness that not all human wants can be satisfied through market mechanisms and that private gain does not inevitably produce social value. In this era, a company or a government is moving toward excellence when its managers and employees are committed to the creation of motivated workers and satisfied customers, or a satisfied electorate, on the basis of a market-oriented strategic plan.

Accordingly, the new Caribbean manager may also be identified by the flexibility to function effectively in either the public or private sector. The rationale is that once the organizational mission is clearly defined, the tools required for goal attainment will be increasingly identical, to the extent that Caribbean political leaders are able to generate a consensus on the need for improved public as well as private sectors. This is by no means intended to suggest diminution of the unique regulatory, extractive, and distributive roles carried out by any functional government driven by inclusive socio-economic and political goals of the kind advocated by the Nettleford report. However, as a result of the changes described, regional "states" and "markets" could eventually develop distinctive but truly complementary roles.

Finally, managers of the kind required may be typified by the creativity to identify new opportunities, even in mature markets, using innovative resource combinations to optimize profit potential. Given the Caribbean's traditional diseconomies of scale, scope, and socio-political volatility, the demand for new Caribbean managers is increasingly intense. The extent to which the Caribbean region can survive and prosper in this era of global liberalization will significantly depend on whether the changes that we project will occur, and whether an effective management education and training capacity can be put in place to support them

Bibliography

Brewster, Havelock R. 1993. "The Report of the West Indian Commission: Time for Action—Critique and Agenda for Further Work." *Caribbean Affairs* 6 (1), January–March: 56–72.

Caribbean Tourism Organization. 1996. *Quarterly Statistical Report.* Spring.

Drucker, Peter. 1992. *Managing the Future: The 1990s and Beyond.* New York: Plume.

Gayle, Dennis J. and Jonathan N. Goodrich, eds. 1990. *Privatization and Deregulation in Global Perspective.* New York: Quorum Books.

———, eds. 1993. *Tourism Marketing and Management in the Caribbean.* London: Routledge.

Jahoda, Marie. 1979. "The Impact of Unemployment in the 1930s and the 1980s." *Bulletin of the British Psychological Society* 32: 309–314.

Lane, Robert E. 1991. *The Market Experience.* Cambridge: Cambridge University Press.

Nettleford, R. M., G. Arthur Brown, and collaborators. 1992. *Report of the Committee of Advisors on Government Structure.* Kingston, Jamaica: Ministry of the Public Service.

Samuelson, Paul A. and William D. Nordhaus. 1985. *Economics.* New York: McGraw Hill.

Smith, Stephen C. 1991. *Industrial Policy in Developing Countries: Reconsidering the Real Sources of Export Led Growth.* Washington D.C.: Economic Policy Institute.

The Economist. 1992. "Escaping the Heavy Hand of the State." June 13: 73–74.

West Indian Commission. 1992. *Time for Action: Report of the West Indian Commission.* Barbados: West Indian Commission.

12

Environmental Education: Training for Coastal Management

LaVerne E. Ragster

Issues in Environmental Management

Proponents of institutional management of activities in coastal areas have had to face the need for compromise with respect to the sharing of the resource base. A large portion of the communities in the wider Caribbean are situated in coastal areas, and there is a high level of diversity and productivity associated with the mangrove forests and lagoons, coral reefs, beaches, estuaries, and seagrass beds found in the coastal zone of the insular and continental Caribbean. Consequently, since the 1960s, increasing portions of development activities and economic policies have been based on the natural resource base of coastal environments. At the same time, poorly-planned inland development activities (such as clearing land for buildings and roads) have indirectly stressed and degraded coastal marine ecosystems. Illustrative of this is the degradation of coral refs and seagrass beds through the increased freshwater and sediment runoff into Caribbean bays.

Increases in resource use from both the public and private sectors have led to higher demands and pressures on defined areas or resources. Groups compete for resources to fill a number of needs: raw materials for building and industry; habitats to support fisheries and hunting; sites for disposal of solid and liquid wastes; sites for recreation and other socio-cultural activities, including spiritual rituals; and sites for socio-economic activities such as tourism.

In response to the need for an agreement to share the resource base, approaches to management necessarily expanded beyond natural science perspectives to focus on interdisciplinary approaches. Additionally, in the region as a whole, public policy measures began to reflect consultations between professional managers and the general public. These consultations were usually associated with "environmental awareness" or "environmental education" efforts. However, the terms "coastal zone management," "integrated management," "resource planning," "regional planning," and "watershed management" often simply described management approaches, more often than not with a "top-down" orientation, that were mainly concerned with the allocation of resources among users.

The continuing evolution of the interdisciplinary approach and "lessons learned" have brought the concept of resource management to an increased level of complexity and a more appropriate name—environmental management. Instead of focusing mainly on the natural resource base, the economic and social contexts within which the resource use is produced become a significant point of convergence for management. Hence, in environmental management the idea of unsustainable development becomes linked to losses of natural resources and environmental degradation which lead to decreased economic returns and a reduction in future outputs. This is elaborated further in the following pages and some suggestions are made with respect to the specific area of training.

Characteristics of Coastal Zone Use

In the coastal areas of the Caribbean, the ecosystems and the resource users are diverse and complex in their organization and behavior. One bay with fringing coral reefs and seagrass beds can have a border of mangrove forests as well as a sandy beach with two salt ponds (habitat for water fowl) behind the berm. The bay may serve nearby communities as the site for making and setting fish traps, collecting sea eggs (urchins), making charcoal, recreational swimming and scuba diving, environmental education field trips for a school, hunting, church services, and meditation. Additionally, due to its esthetic appeal, the bay is seen by the government and developers as a potential site for a hotel complex. The professional managers, planners, political decision-makers, and all the resource users of this area will at some point compete for the use of these resources or impact another group's use of a resource. It is noteworthy that if the human activities were removed from this ecologically complex bay, it would very likely not require any management. The point is that resource problems are more human problems than they are environmental problems. Therefore, the individuals who become part of the institutional approach to the management of the environment face complex, imprecise, dynamic conditions created by human political, social, and economic activities and their impacts on the natural resources in the area.

Development and management of coastal areas require an acknowledgment of the unique conditions inherent in coastal ecosystems. Coastal areas occur, for example, at the interface of land and sea and are therefore strongly influenced by both. These areas are subject to conditions such as salinity gradients and tides which impact and even control many aspects of the coastal zone. The area is also characterized by diverse ecosystems that are often connected to each other physically or through outputs and are sensitive to activities in adjacent areas. The diversity of natural resources in the coastal area provides the basis for multi-use and direct and indirect effects from human activities. Coastal area management with the objective of "wise use" would require integrated approaches to planning and management involving a number of agencies, users, activities, and resources.

Management Training

Given this scenario, the training of professional managers, planners, and decision-makers, especially those involved with development, must provide the skills and appropriate orientation that allow for a sweeping view of the connections between environment and associated economic activities. Additionally, training should foster the development of approaches that utilize many disciplines to produce understanding of the issues and viable solutions. Although this perspective of training for environmental management may be logical, it creates tremendous challenges for traditional, and even evolving, tertiary institutions that offer degree programs in areas related to resource and environmental management.

Two areas that have been noted as especially problematic to the development of effective resource and environmental management programs are the organizational structure of academic areas and the inadequacy of traditional pedagogy. The single-discipline organization and focus of most university programs have not been able to meet the requirements of the multidisciplinary nature of environmental management. Institutions such as the University of the Virgin Islands that have acknowledged this requirement and constructed interdisciplinary programs have often had to assist the new team of faculty to reorient their approach toward subject areas, teaching, and research. Also, the development of environmental management programs and courses has illuminated the need for more problem-solving and team-oriented learning situations and approaches.

Historically, resource management training has adopted mainly a natural sciences perspective that supported the idea that additional information and data on the resource base would eventually solve most management issues or problems. Hence, people were trained in areas such as fisheries management/ biology, coastal management/ecology, and forestry management. Problem-solving was often approached in very narrow contexts and seldom involved the role of social, economic, and political structures and activities in the management process, at least at a conceptual level.

The high levels of frustration experienced by many professional managers, the many management failures, the evidence of continued environmental degradation, and increasing pressures from resource user groups to buy into the process of institutionalized management have helped to bring about changes in the way universities and others view training in environmental management. Basically, the changes come from a growing new attitude that supports a more holistic approach toward designing and implementing environmental management curricula and teaching or facilitating methods. Aspects of this approach include:

- The development, implementation, and recommendation of courses with an integrated approach to management such as *resources and economic development, community-based resource management, resource policy*, and *parks and protected areas management*.
- The promotion of internships and practical experience in degree programs along with field studies involving actual resource management issues that provide problem-solving and critical-thinking opportunities.
- Opportunities to address complex, imprecise issues as part of an interdisciplinary team.
- The use of case studies of local and regional relevance to introduce and develop dispute resolution skills, group dynamics, critical-thinking, and the integration of various kinds of data (for example, traditional practices, economic opportunities and constraints, ecological conditions and limits, political structure, and so on) into analyses.

In this more integrated approach to training and education in environmental management, the orientation of research, information transfer, and management in general becomes more social, political, and economic even though this approach acknowledges the role of the resource base. This means that research in environmental management will also have an expanded scope. It would be most appropriate, for example, to investigate the harvesting of sea eggs (urchins) in the context of the environmental and biological needs of the organism. However, the complete study should determine which socially acceptable and economically viable methods of harvesting would allow for long-term harvesting of the resource. For the future environmental manager, observation and communication skills are as important as knowing the life stages and habitat of a living resource.

A Hands-On Approach

It was noted earlier that university faculty trained in single disciplines who become part of the teams teaching or conducting research in resource management also require some assistance to reorient their teaching and investigative approaches and methods. In this regard, Caribbean universities working together within the consortium of Caribbean Universities for Natural Resource Management (CCUNRM) have agreed that faculty are more likely to use a holistic approach in teaching and to use case studies and field visits as part of the learning experience for students if they have participated in similar experiences (Ragster and Bacon 1990). Learning the dynamic skills of working as part of an interdisciplinary team requires more than reading or lectures. Faculty also have to learn to use uncertainty as part of their program as they assist students to explore and understand the issues of environmental management.

Case studies illustrating the political and economic patterns and activities that often drive the impacts of society on the natural resource base are valuable teaching and learning tools. Many of the skills (for example, observation, communication, and analysis) needed to assess human participation in the process of environmental management require practice and interactions in similar situations. Field studies, internships, development and manipulation of models, and role playing are becoming standard components of training and education programs that attempt to produce effective, competent professionals for the environmental management area.

Environmental management brings variables such as human motivation, responses, and uncertainty (for instance, size of stocks and how the political system will react to management initiative) into the same milieu as species recruitment and habitat status. The development of research programs and more effective methods of facilitating learning of resource and environmental management concepts requires new ways of structuring courses and the learning experiences of students. Needless to say, the way education and training initiatives in environmental management will be ultimately evaluated is by the effectiveness of their outputs, both professional and research results, in assisting society to attain the elusive goals of sustainable development. The environmental management of the coastal areas of the Caribbean has the potential to be one of the more challenging parts of this evaluation. Tertiary institutions in the region need to seriously begin to prepare for this real-life test.

Bibliography

Barker, David and Duncan F. M. McGregor, eds. 1995. *Environment and Development in the Caribbean: Geographical Perspectives.* Kingston, Jamaica: University of the West Indies.

Beanlands, G. 1992. "EIA Procedures in the Framework of Environmental Management." Paper presented at the 13th International Seminar on Environmental Assessment and Management, Aberdeen, Scotland, June 28–July 11.

Buelow, F. H., ed. 1991. *Strategies for Teaching and Learning: Proceedings of the North Central Regional Teaching Symposium.* Madison, Wisconsin: University of Wisconsin.

Eyre, L. A. 1989. "The Caribbean Environment: Trends Towards Degradation and Strategies for their Reversal." *Caribbean Journal of Education* 16, Special Issue "Environment Education: Global Concerns and Caribbean Focus": 13–45.

Girvan, N. P. and D. A. Simmons, eds. 1991. *Caribbean Ecology and Economics.* St. Michael, Barbados: Caribbean Conservation Association.

Ludwig, D. R., and C. Walters. 1993. "Uncertainty, Exploitation, and Conservation: Lessons from History." *Science* 260: 17–36.

Ragster, L., and P. Bacon. 1990. *Human Resources Development: Education and Training in Resource Management in the Caribbean.* U.S.V.I.: Consortium of Caribbean Universities for Natural Resource Management (CCUNRM).

Snedaker, S. C., and C. D. Getter. 1985. *Coastal Resources Management Guidelines.* Prepared for U.S. Department of the Interior National Park Service, and U.S. Agency for International Development.

United Nations Economic Commission for Latin America and the Caribbean (UNECLAC). 1991. *Rapporteur's Report on Roundtable Meeting on Human Resources Development Strategies.* Havana, Cuba: December 2–5.

United Nations Environment Program (UNEP). 1991. *The Countries of Latin America and the Caribbean and the Action Plan for the Environment.* Mexico D.F: UNEP Regional Office for Latin America and the Caribbean.

Valdés-Pizzini, M. 1990. "Managing Resources or People? A Social Science Agenda for Resource Management in Puerto Rico." Paper presented at the 15th Annual Caribbean Studies Association Conference, Trinidad, May 22–26.

13

Training for Health: The Management of HIV/AIDS

Cora L. E. Christian

Dimensions of the AIDS Problem

It is becoming increasingly clear that the most striking characteristic of the problems that imperil the world—war, hunger, environmental destruction, depletion of natural resources, and others—is that they are global in scope and as such require worldwide cooperation for their solution. To solve them, nations will have to recognize themselves as participants in the larger purpose of securing the well-being of humankind.

The management of Acquired Immune Deficiency Syndrome (AIDS) is certainly one of these global issues that require collective effort. The World Health Organization (WHO)'s provisional estimates of adult and pediatric cases of AIDS stood at 6 million as of late 1995. WHO estimated that by the end of 1994 17 million adults worldwide had the human immunodeficiency (HIV) virus, 11 million in Africa alone. The prevalence rate in fifteen countries of South and Central Africa was over 500 per 10,000 inhabitants (WHO 1995). HIV is now the major cause of loss of productivity and life in the average African city—greater than malaria, gastroenteritis, or pneumonia. In one district in Uganda, one in three households has lost parents due to AIDS (Ndungu 1993: 3; STD Bulletin 1992: 3). In the Americas, about 2 million cases of adult HIV infections were reported by early 1995 (WHO 1995). And in the Caribbean region, by 1993 there were over 3,500 cases of AIDS in the English-speaking territories, and 9,401 cases in Puerto Rico. Puerto Rico alone had 75,000 HIV-positive individuals (Salmon 1993: 1–2).

At the Thirteenth Meeting of the Conference of Ministers Responsible for Health of the Caribbean Community (CARICOM), convened in Barbados in 1992, AIDS was given careful consideration. A commitment was made to improve the national capacities to diagnose and treat all sexually-transmitted diseases, but especially AIDS. In this fight against AIDS, the health care provider is in the forefront. Patients have always viewed their physicians, dentists, nurses, and other health care providers as healers and helpers. The prospect of contracting the human immunodeficiency virus, no matter how small the risk, challenges that image and function in the minds of many health care workers. We often read these days about the concerns of medical students and other health care workers regarding the risks of acquiring HIV infection in the course of their work. Clearly the risk is small but it is real. In Rwanda, half of all midwives trained in the last ten years have died of AIDS (*STD Bulletin* 1992: 3). And in the United States there has sometimes been a reluctance on the part of physicians to provide care for HIV-positive patients.

This chapter reports the results of a survey conducted among health care providers in the U.S. Virgin Islands. The survey was conducted to find out how health professionals felt about treating HIV/AIDS patients, given the increasing numbers of infected persons in the U.S. Virgin Islands (full-blown AIDS cases rose from 8 in 1987 to 130 in 1993, and in 1993 there were 725 reported HIV positive cases [Ndungu 1993: 3]). In addition to the survey, the actual care rendered to HIV/AIDS patients was reviewed in order to find out how well health providers assess and document information on the HIV patient. Documentation and assessment are the first steps in the diagnosis and treatment of any illness, and they represent a clear process used to evaluate the quality of the care given to any patient or client. The intent, then, was to learn what training was needed by the health care provider to adequately care for HIV/AIDS patients. The analysis was limited to the U.S. Virgin islands; however, it is felt that the findings reported below are relevant throughout the Caribbean region. It may be noted that as of December 1995 WHO reported that the total number of AIDS cases was a relatively high 1,892 and 1,876 in the Bahamas and Trinidad and Tobago respectively (Table 13.1).

Methodology

A questionnaire on needs assessment, developed by the New York/Virgin Islands AIDS Education and Training Center-Partnership for Excellence in HIV Care, was mailed to all 135 licensed physicians and dentists residing and practicing in the U.S. Virgin Islands. This needs assessment instrument has been piloted throughout New York and New Jersey and focuses on the following: area of specialty, affiliation, admitting privileges, barriers/problems encountered, unmet needs, willingness to care for HIV/AIDS patients, interest in receiving training, and actual training programs desired.[1]

Table 13.1 AIDS Cases Reported for Caribbean Area, 1995[a]

Country	Total	Country	Total
Antigua and Barbuda	41	Haiti	4,967
Anguilla	5	Jamaica	1,314
Bahamas	1,876	Martinique	344
Barbados	586	Montserrat	7
Bermuda	291	Netherlands Antilles	177[b]
Belize	100	Saint Lucia	73
Cayman Islands	18	Saint Vincent	67
Dominica	31	Saint Kitts and Nevis	47
Dominican Republic	2,948	Suriname	209
French Guiana	489	Turks and Caicos Islands	39
Grenada	63	Trinidad and Tobago	1,892
Guadeloupe	623	British Virgin Islands	10
Guyana	698		

[a]Based on reports received through 15 December 1995. Date of last report ranges from March through December.
[b]Includes 20 cases reported in Aruba.
Source: World Health Organization (WHO), *Reported Aids Cases for the Americas* (Geneva: WHO, 1995).

For the patient chart review and audit, the New York/Virgin Islands AIDS Education and Training Center shared with the investigators the quality assurance checklist for HIV-Medical Services. The checklist is divided into a comprehensive data base that details past medical history (including family, social, and sexual history), and data assessing the patient inclusive of physical examination, laboratory, staging of the illness, and plan of care. A third part of the checklist focuses on subsequent visits.

Health Care Providers' Views

Twenty-two percent of the physicians, 17.1 percent of the dentists, and 14.5 percent of the nurses responded to the questionnaire. All specialties resident in the islands were represented, as were providers practicing within hospitals, in clinics, and in private practice. Although the results were based on a small return rate, they provided important though disturbing information. Table 13.2 shows that 10 percent of nurses, one-fourth of the physicians, and one-half of the dentists were not willing to care for HIV/AIDS patients. Despite that, a substantial proportion of the physicians (76 percent) and the nurses (91.1 percent) were interested in

Table 13.2   Willingness to Care for HIV/AIDS Patients

Health Care Provider (Category)	Yes (%)	No (%)	No Response (%)
Physicians	70	26.6	3.3
Dentists	50	50.0	0.0
Nurses	90	10.0	0.0

Table 13.3   Interest in Training in HIV/AIDS Care

Health Care Provider (Category)	Yes (%)	No (%)	No Response (%)
Physicians	76.0	20.0	3.3
Dentists	33.0	66.0	0.0
Nurses	91.1	8.9	0.0

receiving training. Only a small proportion (33.3 percent) of the dentists was interested in training in direct contrast to other health providers (Table 13.3).

When it came to barriers and problems encountered in treating patients, findings were uniform across providers. The most common barriers encountered were access to medication, access to lab services, continuity of care in hospital/clinic, and confidentiality.

In terms of training requested, again similar needs were identified by the providers. HIV medications review and update was the top training need, requested by 50 percent of physicians and dentists, and 60 percent of nurses. However, requested levels of training varied widely from group to group: 66.6 percent of the dentists, 23.2 percent of the nurses, and 13.3 percent of the physicians requested basic information. No dentist, 1 percent of nurses, and 13.3 percent of the physicians requested advanced information on HIV medications review and update.

Patient Management

Eighty percent (104) of the AIDS patients' charts were reviewed. Over 64 percent of the questions had omissions, that is, there was nothing filled out in the data base. Note that questions referring to gender or the pediatric group were not included in the omission rate as they might inadvertently have been answered even where inapplicable. All questions in

Table 13.4   Response to Questions Pertinent to the Care of HIV/AIDS Patients[a]

Yes	4.3%
No	0.5%
Not applicable	3.9%
Omitted	91.3%

[a]Percent questions answered positively/negatively more than 50 percent of the time.

the comprehensive data bases dealing with medical and family/sexual history had an omission rate of 50 percent. There was only one question pertaining to historical information that had greater than 50 percent response and this had to do with the presenting complaint.

The second part of the questionnaire dealt with the initial assessment of the patient. Here omission rates were greater than 50 percent for items such as height and weight, vital signs, genital/pelvic exam, rectal with hemoccult, neurologic exam, mental status, neuro-psychological assessment, and laboratory information. In addition, omission rates were greater than 50 percent for plan of care inclusive of anticipatory guidance, risk education, partner notification, and counseling on nutrition, exercise, and compliance with therapy. Omissions were greater than 50 percent for immunizations and for referrals to appropriate specialists.

Only 4.3 percent (9 out of 205) of all the questions had a "yes" response at a rate greater than 50 percent. Only one question had a "no" response greater than 50 percent of the time, and that was "treatment appropriate to stage: AZT, DDI, DDC." Of the 8 questions that were gender- or age-specific, 5 were filled in greater than 60 percent of the time as not applicable, indicating that these questions need not have been eliminated from the analysis of the omission rate. Therefore, as an overall review of the chart audit, 91.3 percent of the questions had an omission rate greater than 50 percent, indicating that no information was recorded on the chart in reference to those questions (Table 13.4).

Conclusion

The results of the needs assessment can be used to evaluate the general willingness of the health provider population in the U.S. Virgin Islands to care for HIV/AIDS patients/clients, to compare knowledge level by professions, to identify particular HIV/AIDS educational needs, and to determine the barriers and unmet needs of the HIV/AIDS population. Coupled with the chart review/audit, it is clear that there are serious documentation deficits that can affect the management of the HIV/AIDS client. With the high rate of oral manifestations of this illness, the U.S. Virgin Islands may face a serious problem in reference to dental care since 50 percent of the responding dentists will not knowingly care for an HIV-positive patient. Will the unwillingness of the health care provider to treat HIV patients lead to further cover-up, lack of reporting, and perhaps lack of care when needed? Will it bring harm to the health care providers insofar as their belief that none of their patients has HIV/AIDS leads them to not take the necessary precautions against blood-borne exposure?

The educational challenge is not focused only on the clinical management of HIV/AIDS patients but also on the unwillingness of so many professionals to care for this growing body of patients. Is this unwillingness attributable to a lack of knowledge about the transmission of the disease, as it was in two London hospitals where the health care workers actually believed that AIDS could be caught from toilet seats (McKinnon, Gooch, and Cockcroft 1990: 15–18)? Or is the unwillingness attributable to a lack of confidence in the Center for Disease Control's description of the modes of transmission of HIV?

While these questions are interesting, the results given here must be viewed cautiously because the number of respondents was small and no stringent statistical tests were applied. Yet, the data do clearly show that there is a significant number of health care providers who, even after more than ten years of this major epidemic, are unwilling to live up to the responsibilities of their professions. It is clear that the majority of the records have major documentation deficits in areas that are needed for the management of the patient and are absolutely essential in any audit trail of a health care management plan. In addition, these omissions at times result in agencies such as social security agencies not having sufficient information to make educated decisions about benefits for those very needy individuals. It is clear also that there are major barriers to the care of these very ill and complex cases. Further analysis is warranted. Certainly further training is being planned for Virgin Islands health care providers and for the entire region through the New York/Virgin Islands AIDS Education and Training Center.

Even though the analysis above focused on the Virgin Islands, similar biases, prejudices, and misunderstandings obtain throughout the Caribbean. AIDS is a regional issue, one that has to be solved regionally. The first task for decision-makers and opinion-shapers is to get the people who are trained to take care of AIDS patients to take the fear out of their care of the patients. This fear in administering adequate care may hurt everyone in the long run. Albert Camus, Nobel Prize winner, focused his 1947 description of the plague on the health care worker faced with the risk of contracting the deadly plague in the course of caring for the sick. According to Camus, everyone knows that pestilence has a way of recurring in the world; yet somehow we find it hard to believe in ones that crash down on our heads from the blue sky. By the end of *The Plague*, Camus has shown graphically that the thing to do is to know your job, and do it well, for what you do not know will indeed hurt you.

Note

1. Additional details on the methodology used for this study are available directly from the author.

Bibliography

Blanchet, Kevin D. 1988. *AIDS: A Health Care Management Response.* Rockville, MD: Aspen Publishers.

Braithwaite, A., B. S. Mahabir, F.R.K. Zacarias, S. Sadal, and J. P. Narain. 1992. *A Practical Manual on Sexually Transmitted Diseases for the Caribbean.* Port-of-Spain, Trinidad: Caribbean Epidemiology Center.

Camus, Albert. 1948. *The Plague.* New York: Knopf.

Clark, David, ed. *1993. The Sociology of Death: Theory, Culture, and Practice.* Oxford, UK; Cambridge, MA: Blackwell Publishers/The Sociological Review.

McKinnon, Insall S., C. D. Gooch, and A. Cockcroft. 1990. "Knowledge and Attitudes of Health Care Workers About AIDS and HIV Infection Before and After Distribution of an Educational Booklet." *Journal of Occupational Medicine* 40: 15–18.

Miller, David, and John Green, eds. 1986. *The Management of AIDS Patients.* Basingstoke, U.K.: MacMillan.

Ndungu, J. 1993. "HIV Cases Top 725." *The St. Croix Avis*, February 1: 3.

Salmon, B. 1993. "V.I. Aids Fight Hurt by Region." *V.I. Daily News*, March 2: 1–2.

STD (Socially Transmitted Diseases) Bulletin. 1992. 11(5), November/December.

United States Early HIV Infection Guideline Panel. 1994. *Evaluation and Management of Early HIV Infection.* Rockville, MD: U.S. Dept. of Health and Human Services.

Witt, Michael D. 1986. *AIDS and Patient Management: Legal, Ethical, and Social Issues.* Owings Mills, MD: National Health Publications.

World Health Organization (WHO). Global Programme on AIDS. *The Current Global Situation of the HIV/AIDS Pandemic.* News Release, 15 December

———. 1995. "Provisional Working Estimates of Adult HIV Prevalence as of the End of 1994 by Country." *Weekly Epidemiological Record*, 15 December.

PART THREE

The Caribbean Public Policy Agenda: Human Development Issues

The concept of human development has gone beyond its basic premises to emphasize the sustainability of the development process. It not only puts people at the centre of development. It also advocates protecting the life opportunities of future generations as well as present generations and respecting the natural systems on which all life depends.

—United Nations Development Program,
Human Development Report 1995: 12.

14

Drugs and Crime: Policy Perspectives

Ivelaw L. Griffith

The Drug Problem: Many Facets[1]

The Caribbean "drug problem" is really four separate but related problems: drug production, consumption and abuse, trafficking, and money laundering. These problems are region-wide but not uniform. They are problematic for the entire region but are not manifested in the same way in every part of the region. These drug operations are also multidimensional, with ripple effects on almost all aspects of social, economic, and political life. Thus they affect all issue areas. This chapter analyzes the impact of the multifaceted drug problem on the public policy arena. The four problems mentioned will not be examined extensively, given space limitations, which also preclude examination of a wide range of public policy issues. Attention will, instead, be focused on the criminal justice arena.

Patterns of Drug Production and Use

The three main "danger drugs" in the Caribbean are cocaine, heroin, and marijuana, but only marijuana is produced there, and not throughout the region. Moreover, cultivation varies from place to place. Belize, Guyana, Jamaica, St. Vincent and the Grenadines, and Trinidad and Tobago are among the countries with the highest levels of marijuana production, and among them, Belize and Jamaica have the highest levels of production and export. In both countries, marijuana production has at times been the largest cash crop, once producing some $350 million annually in Belize and about $2 billion in Jamaica (MacDonald 1988: 89).

The Bahamas, which figures prominently in drug transshipment, has traditionally been neither a drug-producing nor a drug-refining country.

However, the production alarm was sounded in 1991 following the discovery and destruction of 40,000 cannabis seedlings and 1,000 medium-sized plants and the seizure of 22 kilos of prepared marijuana, all on Andros Island. By the early 1980s Belize was the fourth largest supplier to the United States after Colombia, Mexico, and Jamaica. But production has plummeted since 1985, largely due to countermeasures taken by the Belize government, often under pressure from the United States. Most of the marijuana that is discovered is destroyed immediately by aerial eradication or by hand in areas that are in close proximity to residences or to legitimate crops.

Large-scale cultivation of five to fifty acre plots of *ganja,* as marijuana is popularly called in the Caribbean, was once common in Jamaica. However, because of eradication measures, most cultivation is now done in plots of one acre or less, with yields of about 1,485 pounds per hectacre. The Bureau of International Narcotics Matters (INM) of the U.S. Department of State estimated that only 744 hectares were under cultivation in 1993. Aerial spraying of cannabis in Jamaica is more controversial than in Belize because marijuana is an even larger source of income there. In the late 1980s it is said to have contributed between $1 billion and $2 billion to the island's foreign exchange earnings, more than all other exports combined including bauxite, sugar, and tourism (MacDonald 1988: 90).

The problem of narcotics consumption and abuse in the Caribbean involves mainly marijuana and cocaine, with heroin becoming problematic in some places. As with production, drug use differs from place to place. The greatest concern is in Jamaica, the Bahamas, Barbados, the Dominican Republic, Guyana, Trinidad and Tobago, and parts of the Eastern Caribbean.

Legal proscription notwithstanding, marijuana has had a long history of accepted socio-religious use, dating from the introduction of indentured workers from India following the abolition of slavery. Indeed, the word *ganja* is itself a Hindi word, as is *kali,* a term also frequently used (Rubin and Comitas 1976: 16). Marijuana's socio-religious pattern of use has changed over the years. It is now associated primarily with the Rastas, and hence is found in places where there are large numbers of this group, including Jamaica, Guyana, and Trinidad and Tobago. It is important to note, however, that Rastas are not the only group to use *ganja.*

Cocaine and heroin abuse in the Caribbean results from the spillover of the illicit cocaine trade. This problem is found mainly in the principal transit states, including Bahamas, Jamaica, Belize, the Dominican Republic, and Guyana. In the case of the Bahamas, the INM has noted: "The Bahamas suffers from a serious drug abuse and addiction problem brought about by the ready availability of drugs as they transit the country. Cocaine is the drug of choice for addicts" (U.S. Department of State 1991:

182). Belize continues to suffer from an increase in the availability of cocaine, clearly demonstrated during the September 1991 Belize Games when 44 out of 180 winning athletes tested positive for illegal drug use. Other data also point to the extent of the cocaine problem. In Trinidad and Tobago, for example, hospital admission of cocaine and marijuana addicts rose from 376 in 1983 to 1,041 in 1989 (Sanders 1990b: 20; U.S. Department of State 1992: 142; Frankson 1992: 5, 8).

Apart from trading their own marijuana in the United States, some Caribbean countries are important transshipment centers for South American cocaine, heroin, and marijuana bound for Europe and North America. For more than two decades the Bahamas, Belize, and Jamaica dominated this business, but in the 1990s Barbados, the Dominican Republic, Guyana, Haiti, Trinidad and Tobago, and Eastern Caribbean countries have featured more prominently.[2] For instance, in 1993, 1.5 metric tons of cocaine and 750 kilograms of marijuana were seized in St. Vincent and the Grenadines. Guyana's 1993 cocaine seizures were 463 kilograms, 1,000 percent higher than in 1992, and Trinidad had its biggest ever cocaine seizure in June 1994 with the confiscation of 226.2 kilos of the substance valued at U.S. $18 million (Gilbert 1993: 1; Alonzo 1994: 1; U.S. Department of State 1994: 189, 214).

The geography of the Bahamian archipelago makes it an excellent candidate for cocaine transshipment, given its 700 islands and cays and strategic location in the airline flight path between Colombia and South Florida. One island, Bimini, is a mere fifty miles from the U.S. mainland and, along with some other islands, has been used frequently by drug traffickers (Government of the Bahamas 1984: 9–51). When the Bahamas first became a transshipment center, the drug involved was mainly marijuana with a few consignments of hashish. There is evidence of drug trafficking dating as far back as 1968 when 250 to 300 pounds of marijuana were shipped from Jamaica to Bimini. One of the earliest cocaine seizures, a shipment of pure cocaine with a street value of $2 billion, was made in 1974 at an airport in George Town, Exuma. That same year, the Bahamas police discovered a store of marijuana more than six feet high and more than two miles long off Grand Bahama Island (Government of the Bahamas 1984: 7–8).

The geography and topography of Belize also facilitate drug smuggling in that country. There are large jungle-like areas, sparse settlements, and about 140 isolated airstrips that facilitate stops on flight from South America to North America. Moreover, there is virtually no radar coverage beyond a 30-mile radius of the international airport at Belize City. However, use of maritime routes has been increasing. "Crack" has also been featuring more prominently in the drug trade in Belize. According to the 1994 Department of State report, "for the first time [1993], there was evidence of Belizean export of crack cocaine to the United States" (U.S. Department of State 1994: 136).

Several features of the Dominican Republic also make that country a prime trafficking candidate: proximity to Colombia, the Bahamas, Puerto Rico, and the southern United States; a long, often desolate, border with Haiti; and poorly-equipped police and military authorities. The scope of the problem is reflected in the fact that in 1993, the country's National Anti-Drug Directorate, supported by the navy, seized 1,073 kilograms of cocaine, 305 kilograms of marijuana, 1,444 grams of crack, and other drugs. In a total of 812 anti-drug operations, 5,635 people were arrested.

Money laundering is another aspect of the narcotics phenomenon. The countries known to be involved are Aruba, the Bahamas, Cayman Islands, and Montserrat, and there is also evidence of Puerto Rican involvement. According to the U.S. Department of State, one major cocaine/heroin group in Puerto Rico laundered over $7 million through casinos. Drug money is also said to be "structured" using U.S. postal money orders sent to Colombia (U.S. State Department 1994: 184, 185, 513). Guyana is a money laundering suspect while Antigua and Barbuda, St. Vincent and the Grenadines, and Trinidad and Tobago are considered countries with "the potential to become more important financial centers and havens for exploitation by money launderers," given their bank secrecy, willingness to cooperate, and limited, usually poorly trained enforcement resources (U.S. State Department 1991: 364–365).

Most money laundering allegations, however, have been directed at the British dependencies. A 1989 study by Rodney Gallagher of Coopers and Lybrand revealed some telling reasons for this development. According to Gallagher, over 525 international financial companies have had offices in one of these territories, the Cayman Islands. The Caymans accommodated 46 of the world's 50 largest banks, including Dai Ichi Kangyo and Fuji, Japan's two largest banks; Bank America; Barclays of the United Kingdom; Swiss Bank Corporation; and Royal Bank of Canada. Banking sector assets in 1987 were $250 billion. The Cayman Islands offer attractive business incentives including no income, corporate, or withholding taxes, and bank secrecy guaranteed under the 1976 Preservation of Confidential Relations Act.

Public Policy Implications

These drug operations have multiple ripple effects in several policy areas including health, criminal justice, education, foreign policy, and economic policy. The nature of public policy itself creates linkages among policy areas. Hence, although the focus of this chapter is on criminal justice, a brief reference to the general public policy context is in order.

Policy-making and implementation in relation to drugs in the Caribbean are challenging, partly because of resource limitations and the variety of social and economic costs involved in dealing with drug operations and problems. Among the costs are those related to controlling drug-related crime through education and treatment, those related to protecting private and government property through improved security measures, and costs stemming from enforcing drug laws, and prosecuting and punishing violators of those laws.

Providing public and private health care for drug users, children exposed to drugs before and after birth, and victims of drug-related crime also exact high social and economic costs. Moreover, there is lost labor productivity due to absenteeism and the lower productivity of addicts and those affected by them, or those not participating in the labor force because of imprisonment for drug crimes, drug crime victimization, or drug-related work place or traffic accidents. Further, there is a cost attached to having legitimate industrial production, such as agricultural land, labor, and equipment, diverted to the production and distribution of illegal drugs. In addition, one has to factor into this social and economic matrix the diminished quality of life caused by illegal drug use, such as pain and suffering of families, friends, and crime victims (see discussions in Tonry and Wilson 1990; U.S. Department of Justice 1992).

As regards criminal justice, there is an obvious relationship between the drug phenomenon and crime. The drug operations mentioned above are illegal, and these operations themselves lead to or require other criminal conduct. One study sees two basic categories of drug crimes: "enforcement" crimes, and "business" crimes. The former involves crimes among traffickers and between traffickers and civilians and police, triggered by traffickers' efforts to avoid arrest and prosecution. The latter category encompasses crimes committed as part of business disputes, and acquisitive crimes such as robbery and extortion (Kleiman 1989: 109–117). Another typology posits three types of crime: "consensual" ones, such as drug possession, use, or trafficking; "expressive" ones, such as violence or assault; and "instrumental" or property crimes, examples being theft, forgery, burglary, and robbery (Anglin and Speckart 1988: 197–231; see also Hunt 1990; Chaiken and Chaiken 1990).

Irrespective of which typology is used, there is a wide range of drug-related criminal activity in the Caribbean. Table 14.1 shows a progressive increase in drug offenses reported for most countries between 1985 and 1990, and there is every reason to believe that this has continued through the 1990s. The table also points to increased criminality in the areas of theft and fraud for some countries, and homicide and serious assault for others.

There is no available evidence of region-wide causal linkages between drug activities on the one hand, and fraud, homicide, theft, and assault on the other. However, three observations are apropos. First, these are precisely the crime categories likely to be associated with drug production and trafficking. Second, in a few countries there is clear evidence of linkage. In Jamaica, for instance, where there were 561 reported cases of murder in 1991, the Planning Institute of Jamaica indicated that "there was a 75 per cent increase in the incidents of murder linked directly or indirectly to drug trafficking" (Planning Institute of Jamaica 1992: 21.3–21.4). The third observation is this: The countries with the high and progressive crime reports in the theft, homicide, and serious assault categories are the same ones that have featured prominently over the last decade as centers of drug activity, namely the Bahamas, the Dominican Republic, Jamaica, and Trinidad and Tobago.

Drug-related crime is all the more problematic for some of these countries because it affects tourism, a national economic economic enterprise in most Caribbean countries. The link between drugs and tourism needs substantive assessment, but there is evidence to suggest a negative effect of drugs on tourism due to media reports that scare potential tourists away, and the high incidence of drug-related crime in some places.

Dudley Allen, a former Jamaican Commissioner of Corrections once noted that "it is no longer possible to think of crime as a simple or minor social problem. . . . Mounting crime and violence have been declared leading national problems, and the issue of law and order has assumed high priority in national planning and policy making. Fear of crime is destroying . . . freedom of movement, freedom from harm, and freedom from fear itself (Allen 1980: 29). This statement is still relevant today, in fact even more dramatically so. Allen was speaking mainly in the Jamaican context, but the observation now has region-wide validity because crime has skyrocketed for a variety of reasons that cannot be explored here.

Drug-related criminal activity within some Caribbean countries is complicated and aggravated by the activities of nationals who are convicted and sentenced elsewhere and later deported. Jamaica's National Security and Justice Minister K. D. Knight reported to the country's parliament in July 1993 that "nearly a thousand Jamaicans were deported from other countries last year, with over 700 coming from the United States. Most of them, nearly 600, were deported for drug-related offenses. . . . Intelligence indicates that many of them become more involved in criminal activity here [in Jamaica] . . ." (Government of Jamaica 1993: 11). In Guyana's case, in 1992 67 nationals were deported from the United States and scores from Suriname and Trinidad. And as one government official noted, "those deportees . . . tend to become involved locally in the trafficking network" (Philadelphia 1993a: 16).[3]

Attention to the criminal justice impact of drugs must, however, extend beyond crime itself to law enforcement, adjudication, and punishment.

Financial, personnel, and technical resource limitations place serious constraints on Caribbean countries in all of these areas. Drug offenses are taxing the capacity of the agencies responsible for these areas. Illegal drug operations and the problems they generate have created the need for new and expanded drug units for intelligence and prosecution, and new and additional drug courts. Guyana planned to create a special court to deal with corruption, one of the serious consequences of the drug phenomenon (Naraine 1993: 20). New and revised legislation has also become necessary. Examples of legislation passed are the Dangerous Drugs Act passed in Jamaica in 1987; the Narcotic Drugs and Psychotropic Substances Act approved in Guyana in 1988; the Drug Abuse (Prevention and Control) Act adopted in Barbados in 1990; and Trinidad and Tobago's Dangerous Drug Act that became law in 1991. Antigua and Barbuda passed the Proceeds of Crime Act in April 1993, and a similarly-titled law was approved in St. Lucia four months later. Calls have been made for capital punishment for certain drug offenses, but generally the new laws impose stiff fines and terms of imprisonment and provide for the confiscation of property acquired through drug-trading. The scope and gravity of drug activities prompt many judges to apply provisions of some laws fully, without regard to extenuating circumstances.

The breath of some of these laws and the potential for abuse, given the wide discretion and power they give to law enforcement officials, are cause for some concern. A former Jamaican attorney general had just this in mind in observing:

> In our effort to rid our societies of the scourge of drugs and with some international pressures, we are being invited to reverse burdens of proof and adopt a retroactive confiscatory regime. All this is understandable. The perceived danger is real, the consequences of the mischief which we would excise disastrous. As we contemplate effective measures, the nagging question, though, for all of us remains: Are they just?
>
> I remember too that in Jamaica, the mongoose was imported from India to kill out the snakes. It did a very good job. The snakes were eliminated. The mongoose then turned its attention to the chickens. There is a lesson in this. Effective measures against vermin may be turned to effective use by the ill-intentioned against decent and law abiding citizens (Government of Jamaica 1991: 7).

Resource constraints not only limit the capacity of criminal justice agencies to execute their mandates meaningfully, they also cause considerable frustration among policy-makers as well as the line and staff personnel involved in the counter-narcotics battles. In referring to the counter-narcotics efforts in Guyana, one writer found a wide gap between what the legislation mandates as sanctions and what criminal justice officials accomplish,

Table 14.1 Volume of Crime in the Caribbean[a]

Country	Year	Homicide	Sex Offenses	Serious Assaults	Thefts (All Kinds)	Fraud	Drug Offenses	Total[b]
Bahamas	1985	68	150	210	10,149c	416	1,161	12,154
	1986	69	158	157	11,539	549	1,259	13,731
	1987	75	177	197	12,425	397	1,214	14,485
	1988	111	228	233	12,555	446	94	14,521
	1989	93	201	243	11,618	448	955	13,558
	1990	134	301	295	12,288	441	1,172	14,631
Barbados	1985	16	101	200	4,088	317	259	4,981
	1986	10	134	215	4,401	308	274	5,342
	1987	24	118	234	4,644	321	401	5,742
	1988	NR	NR	NR	NR	NR	NR	—
	1989	18	137	292	6,389	334	510	7,680
	1990	30	150	280	7,057	448	555	8,520
Dominican Republic	1985	588	815	5,791	47,048	286	1,121	55,649
	1986	608	1,323	4,010	38,609	339	1,358	46,247
	1987	780	1,066	15,308	38,890	815	1,329	58,188
	1988	837	321	2,162	30,085	335	1,036	35,376
	1989	NR	NR	NR	NR	NR	NR	—
	1990	NR	NR	NR	NR	NR	NR	—
Grenada	1985	10	32	750	599c	49	181	1,623
	1986	12	54	1,021	823c	58	172	2,140
	1987	NR	NR	NR	NR	NR	NR	—
	1988	NR	NR	NR	NR	NR	NR	—
	1989	10	53	880	855c	51	211	2,000
	1990	NR	NR	NR	NR	NR	NR	—

Country	Year						
Jamaica	1983	483	825	681	22,030	1,544	4,250	29,813
	1986	449	NR	729	23,949	1,584	4,123	30,834
	1987	442	1,007	894	22,055	1,563	4,395	30,356
	1988	414	1,118	812	19,769	1,533	3,533	27,179
	1989	439	1,090	651	19,684	1,393	4,086	27,343
	1990	542	1,006	12,375	16,278	1,297	5,433	37,031
	1991	561	1,091	10,698	16,476	1,661	6,711	37,198
	1992	629	1,108	12,368	14,521	1,721	6,298	36,645
	1993	653	1,121	12,710	15,454	2,039	6,915	38,892
St. Lucia	1985	10	NR	829	1,845c	107	250	3,041
	1986	15	78	806	1,885c	94	253	3,131
	1987	NR	NR	NR	NR	NR	NR	—
	1988	NR	NR	NR	NR	NR	NR	—
	1989	10	90	1,017	2,181c	67	279	3,644
	1990	NR	NR	NR	NR	NR	NR	—
Trinidad and Tobago	1985	121	272	334	25,794	242	3,162	29,925
	1986	101	276	348	28,131	230	2,175	31,201
	1987	118	215	1,032	29,748	377	2,401	34,981
	1988	119	377	2,901	33,689	1,839	2,473	41,398
	1989	128	311	534	31,971	506	2,361	35,811
	1990	104	289	2,031	16,551c	423	2,921	22,319
	1991	106	305	2,275	30,437	645	2,706	36,474
	1992	109	372	2,221	31,764	626	2,317	37,409

NR: Not reported.

a Select category of crimes. Figure are number of cases reported to the police.

b This is a total of the categories presented here, not a total of all crimes reported in the country.

c All categories of theft not reported.

Source: Interpol, *International Crime Statistics* (various years); *Economic and Social Survey 1993* (Kingston, Jamaica, 1994).

noting that "the difference between persons charged and those found guilty suggests either a certain limitation in the court system or inefficiency in the enforcing organization." He adds that "over the period 1989 and 1992, in spite of several seizures of property, not one case of forfeiture has been completed to date" (Philadelphia 1993b: 14). Guyana is not alone in this regard.

Given the tough, often mandatory, imprisonment sanctions in some of the draconian counter-narcotics legislation, successful drug arrests and prosecution create the need for more prison space, something that does not exist. Indeed, most Caribbean prisons are overcrowded. In Jamaica in December 1991 the total inmate population of the adult correctional centers was 3,705, about 33 percent above the official capacity of 2,781 (Planning Institute of Jamaica 1991: 21.7). The justice minister himself acknowledged that overcrowding in the two maximum security correctional institutions was a serious problem and that these prisons contained twice as many inmates as they were designed to hold (Government of Jamaica 1993: 78). In the case of Trinidad and Tobago, one study shows that most of the country's six penal institutions house three and four times the number of people they were intended to hold (Hagley 1993: 147–154).

In sum, while not every country suffers from the same difficulties, the penal situation is critical or near-critical in many places in the Caribbean. Not only are the physical facilities insufficient, they are often in disrepair. Trained personnel are in short supply, medical attention is woefully inadequate, and for most the ability to undertake rehabilitation simply does not exist. Court facilities and resources fare no better. Indeed, a former Jamaican official once made a pointed reference to the many "squalid, dilapidated, and decaying court rooms and dark, dank, and ill-ventilated chambers" in the region (Green 1991: 311).

This chapter suggests that Caribbean countries are facing grave narcotics-related problems with a variety of public policy implications. As the West Indian Commission declared in relation to the English-speaking Caribbean: "Nothing poses greater threats to civil society in CARICOM countries than the drug problem; and nothing exemplifies the powerlessness of regional governments more" (West Indian Commission 1992: 343). Drug problems present serious criminal justice challenges. Although several important initiatives have been introduced in the region, the increasing scope and gravity of the problem suggests that these are certainly not enough.

Notes

1. This work has been supported by grants from the MacArthur Foundation and the North-South Center at the University of Miami.

2. Among the many sources supporting this conclusion, see Morris 1990: 1; *New York Carib News,* October 16, 1990: 4 and February 29, 1990: 4; Sanders 1990a: 79–92; *Sunday Chronicle* (Guyana), January 6, 1991: 6, 7; *Stabroek News* (Guyana), February 15, 1992: 3; July 29, 1992: 7; and U.S. Department of State 1994.

3. "John Philadelphia" was the pseudonym used by Lt. Col. Fabian Liverpool, then the permanent secretary in the Ministry of Home Affairs, Guyana.

Bibliography

Allen, Dudley. 1980. "Urban Crime and Violence in Jamaica." Pp. 29–51 in Rosemary Brana-Shute and Gary Brana-Shute, eds., *Crime and Punishment in the Caribbean.* Gainesville, FL: University of Florida.

Alonzo, Robert. 1994. "Third Antiguan Charged with Trafficking in 'Coke'." *Trinidad Guardian,* June 14: 1.

Anglin, M. Douglas, and George Speckart. 1988. "Narcotics Use and Crime: A Multisample, Multimethod Analysis." *Criminology* 26 (2): 197–231.

Chaiken, Jan M. and Marcia R. Chaiken. 1990. "Drugs and Predatory Crime." Pp. 203–239 in Michael Tonroy and James Q. Wilson, eds., *Drugs and Crime.* Chicago: Chicago University Press.

Frankson, Howard. 1992. "An Upsurge of Crime in Belize." *Caribbean Contact,* July-August: 5, 8.

Gilbert, Frederick. 1993. "Police Discover G$1 Million of Ganja in Berbice." *Stabroek News* (Guyana), May 23: 1.

Government of the Bahamas. 1984. *Report of the Commission of Inquiry into the Illegal Use of the Bahamas for the Transshipment of Dangerous Drugs Destined for the United States.* Nassau, The Bahamas.

Government of Jamaica. Parliament of Jamaica. 1993. *Presentation of the Honorable K. D. Knight, Minister of National Security and Justice, Sectoral [Budget] Debate,* 15 July.

Government of Jamaica. Ministry of Justice. 1991. *Crime and Justice in the Caribbean. Keynote Address by the Honorable R. Carl Rattray, Q.C., Minister of Justice and Attorney General of Jamaica.* Kingston, Jamaica, May 10.

Green, E. George. 1991. "The Role of Government in Strengthening Human Rights Machinery." Pp. 309–316 in Angela D. Byre and Beverly Y. Byfield, eds., *International Human Rights Law in the Commonwealth Caribbean.* Dordrecht, The Netherlands: Martinus Nijhoff.

Hagley, Lystra. 1993. "Crime and Structural Adjustment in Trinidad and Tobago: On the Exercise of Judicial Discretion." *Caribbean Affairs* 6, January/March: 147–154.

Hunt, Dana E. 1990. "Drugs and Consensual Crimes: Drug Dealing and Prostitution." Pp. 159–201 in Michael Tonry and James Q. Wilson, eds., *Drugs and Crime.* Chicago: Chicago University Press.

Kleinman, Mark A. R. 1989. *Marijuana: Costs of Abuse, Costs of Control.* Westport, CT: Greenwood.

MacDonald, Scott B. 1988. *Dancing on a Volcano: The Latin American Drug Trade.* New York: Praeger.

Morris, Roy. 1990. "Bajan Connection Arrested in London Cocaine Catch." *Daily Nation,* May 16: 1.

Narraine, Ryan. 1993. "Plans for Corruption Moving Ahead in Guyana." *Stabroek News*, July 20: 20.

New York Carib News. October 16, February 29, 1990.

Philadelphia, John. 1993a. "Drug Wars: The Threat to Guyana." *Guyana Review*, March: 15–16.

———. 1993b. "Drug Wars: Can Guyana Win?" *Guyana Review*, April: 14–15.

Planning Institute of Jamaica. 1992. *Economic and Social Survey 1991*. Kingston, Jamaica.

Rubin, Vera and Lambros Comitas. 1976. *Ganja in Jamaica*. Garden City, NY: Anchor Books.

Sanders, Ronald. 1990a. "Narcotics, Corruption, and Development: The Problems in the Smaller Islands." *Caribbean Affairs* 3, January/March: 79–92.

———. 1990b. "The Drug Problem: Social and Economic Effects: Policy Options for the Caribbean." *Caribbean Affairs* 3, July/September: 20–28.

Stabroek News. February 15, March 3, April 14, July 29, 1992.

Sunday Chronicle (Guyana), January 6, 1991.

Tonry, Michael and James Q. Wilson, eds. 1990. *Drugs and Crime*. Chicago University Press.

United States Department of Justice. 1992. *Drugs, Crime, and the Justice System*. Washington D.C.: December.

United States Department of State. 1991. *International Narcotics Control Strategy Report*. Washington D.C.: March.

———. 1992. *International Narcotics Control Strategy Report*. Washington D.C.: March.

———. 1994. *International Narcotics Control Strategy Report*. Washington D.C.: April.

West Indian Commission. 1992. *Time for Action: The Report of the West Indian Commission*. Barbados: West Indian Commission.

15

Caribbean Women in Transition to the 21st Century: The Need for Strategies to Develop Their Potential

Rita Giacalone

Introduction[1]

Women are one of the most underestimated human resources in the Caribbean. The lack of proper appreciation of women and their roles in the Caribbean is attributable to cultural, economic, and political reasons that are detrimental to both men and women and to Caribbean society as a whole. In this context, there are no winners on either side as attempts to advance the economic and political well-being of the region often are blocked not only by external forces but also by internal idiosyncracies. This essay examines these external forces and internal idiosyncracies in the context of dealing with women's participation in the economic and political life of the Caribbean and suggesting what could be done to help them develop their human resource potential.

The essay is predicated upon the assumption that women are rational subjects and actors in Caribbean economic and political life and thus have the inherent right to be part of any attempt to solve the problems affecting the region and develop their own capabilities. Unfortunately, we approach the end of the twentieth century with many in the Caribbean region, including some women, not fully understanding, accepting, or embracing that right. The first part of the article will analyze women's participation in Caribbean economic and political processes in order to establish that, although the universe called Caribbean women is not homogeneous but fragmented according to cultural sub-regions, social classes, and even generational groups, its members share many notable similarities in the economic and political fields (Bifani 1987: 55). The second part of the article addresses several issues around which strategies could be developed by the Caribbean state, private sector, and women's organizations in order to maximize to the fullest extent the development and utilization of all human resources in the region as it prepares for the twenty-first century.

Caribbean Women in Economic Life

Official statistics do not provide an adequate and accurate basis to evaluate women's participation in the economic process of the Caribbean because the purposes for which these statistics are collected and the methods utilized for collecting and presenting these statistics exclude important categories of female economic activities.[2] Massiah has shown that if statistics reporting on female economic activities were taken at face value, more than half of the English-speaking Caribbean women would not be included among the economically active population (cited in Senior 1991: 110). Also, Senior provides information on rates by sex from census reports between 1891 and 1980 to show a consistent pattern of reduction in the participation of women in the workforce across this period. The official picture and perspective(s) on this matter are important for, as Senior points out, "statistics compiled by censuses and labor force surveys are a critical tool in the formulation of policies by government and other planners" (p.110).

While a series of recent studies conducted within and outside the Caribbean (including Deere, 1990; McAfee 1991; Acosta-Belén 1986; Coordinadora Regional de Investigaciones Económicos y Sociales [CRIES] 1993) have helped convey a better sense of the economic value of women as economic subjects, consumers, entrepreneurs, and workers, their participation and contribution to the economic life of the region is still hidden by official statistics, except those on unemployment and/or under employment (Forde 1980). If this fact makes it difficult to assess their contribution, it makes it even more difficult to evaluate their capabilities and value as human resources. Non-recognition of the contribution of women to the economy as workers, for example, is unfair in an environment where families may assume different patterns but where, in general terms, a large number of women must support themselves and their dependents, including children, the elderly, and even able-bodied males.[3]

Classic concepts predicated upon the idea of women looking for jobs outside the home only or primarily as a means to supplement family income to cover the cost of goods and services beyond their unpaid domestic activities, have no relevance for the Caribbean except perhaps among certain middle- and upper-strata social and economic groups

(Garabaghi 1983). A considerable proportion of Caribbean women, willingly or not, have to resort to what Barrow (1986) has called economic "survival strategies." It is important to recognize as well that this is not a new trend but the continuation of a long history of female participation in the Caribbean economy, from plantation slaves and Cuban and Puerto Rican tobacco workers to free zone workers and "higglers" (Lobdell 1988; Stubbs 1988, and Harraksingh 1988).

Traditionally, agriculture has been the economic sector where women have made and continue to make significant contributions. Though female participation in labor-intensive tasks has declined due to mechanization efforts in some areas of agricultural production (Senior 1991: 123), women still play a central role in Caribbean agriculture. In one case, that of Cuba after 1959, a deliberate process of incorporation of rural women into agriculture has taken place as part of the agrarian reform. But by 1983, though women made up 26 percent of the membership in Cuban production cooperatives, their participation in agricultural production was not on "equal terms with men" (Deere 1985: 202).

What is the general situation of Caribbean women in agriculture? A survey made in Guyana in the mid-1980s showed that there was a low percentage of land ownership among women working in agriculture (Odie-Ali 1986). Senior (1991: 145) claims, however, that the percentage of approximately 30 percent was considerably higher than that found in similar surveys in St. Vincent and Barbados. The Guyanese survey showed that 26 percent of women in agriculture, mostly of East Indian origin, have not had formal education even at the elementary level. Women were also engaged in selling agricultural products in the nearby markets but they deferred to men in decisions regarding the purchase of land, animals, furniture, and such matters. All these factors—lack of ownership of the land, formal education, and the means to make important economic decisions—were considered obstacles that inhibited women's access to public credit, technical assistance, and other programs aimed at improving agriculture in the Caribbean (Safa 1986). In fact, in the English-speaking Caribbean, farms on which women are the decision-makers tend to be smaller, more isolated, and have less fertile soils than those operated by men. Advancing this argument, Henshall (1987: 345) stressed that "the feminization of agriculture without concurrent institutional support has led to declining productivity . . . an increasing proportion of uncultivated land, and a retreat into subsistence agriculture by women forced to feed their children from the land without extension or credit."

Even in places where women's participation and responsibility for agricultural production and commercialization are fundamental, as in Haiti, it is still concentrated in activities that provide few possibilities of advancement while demanding a lot of hard work. "Trillage," or hand selection of coffee beans, a monotonous, underpaid activity that requires long hours, or "chiripeo," the purchase of small quantities of coffee from peasants to be sold to illegal intermediaries who in return advance women money or goods for peddling, provide good examples of the type of work that some Haitian women must do to survive (Girault 1983). Higglering or petty vending in the English-speaking Caribbean is an extension of women's agricultural activity in the region. Changes are occurring in this area as many who used to sell home-grown agricultural products now increasingly engage in selling smuggled manufactured goods (Stone 1989; Katzin 1971; Deere 1990).

While these types of activities have been culturally-accepted forms of employment for women in the Caribbean, the expansion of the regional economy between 1960 and 1980 created new opportunities for other types of female employment. In Aruba women's participation in employment outside the home increased from 34 percent in 1960 to 45 percent in 1981 (Emerencia 1986). In the English-speaking Caribbean a similar trend is noticeable: A "shift from agriculture to the development of industry and large-scale undertakings, a rapid expansion of the public sector, and the broadening of the educational base" are reasons that, according to (Senior 1991: 123), explain the change to a broader variety of employment for women. But the broadening of the employment spectrum seems to be more apparent than real: Female employment patterns have been altered to a lesser extent than expected, with the result that women are heavily concentrated in a reduced number of occupations. At the lower level, women in domestic service, "*trabajadoras de la aguja*," and petty traders, and at the level of the most educated, office workers, nurses, and teachers—these still account for the highest number of female workers in most of the Caribbean (Barrow 1986). In the case of Cuba, in 1973 the government revoked the Labor Code of 1968 which had established employment for men and women as a way to protect the latter (Segundo Congreso Nacional 1975; Randall 1978). Even with this obstacle removed, between 1980 and 1985 women were under-represented as factory workers and over-represented in services and administrative positions (Comunidad Europea 1984, 1985). While the number of professional women in Puerto Rico increased between 1947 and 1982, most of them went into teaching and social work, making limited inroads in fields like law and accounting (Acevedo 1987: 60).

Even though an increasing number of women are engaging in paid employment outside the home in fields other than those of traditional agriculture and petty trade, they are heavily concentrated in jobs defined as female work. An important qualitative change has taken place, however: From the 1960s to the 1980s, more married women, or women with families, have entered the workforce. For Cuba, this group of women recorded a 33 percent increase during those years, and a similar trend became evident in other islands as well (Emerencia 1986). Female unemployment, understood as those women actively seeking employment at a given moment, also rose in the same period.

A similar pattern is confirmed from the evidence for Jamaica in the 1980s. Most of the disadvantages women faced in the job market derived from gender segregation of jobs. According to Gordon (1986), Jamaican women who entered the workforce with the same qualifications and at the same time as men soon noticed disparities between their salaries and those of men. The disparities were smaller for middle-strata workers, teachers, and other selected types of white-collar workers, and bigger among manual workers. In the informal sector women were not usually owners or employers, and their activities tended to be less remunerative than the ones managed by men. Women who left the agricultural sector tended to go into service-related activities, especially domestic service, whereas their male counterparts had more and better chances of finding jobs that offered opportunities to move up the ladder to supervisory positions. In general, at every social and educational level, women tend to be found in more labor-intensive and monotonous jobs that offer fewer options for social and/or economic mobility.

An interesting question is how the economic crisis of the 1980s affected women's participation in the Caribbean economies. It can be said that with very limited exceptions women were forced to engineer survival strategies outside formal employment as the entire spectrum of traditional female occupations was negatively affected by the crisis. In the case of the Netherlands Antilles, cuts in salaries, layoffs, and diminution of working hours curtailed the economic gains of public and Catholic school teachers, while the closure of the Lago Oil Refinery in 1985 forced most of the Dominican women working the "red light" district of St. Nicholas out of Aruba (Emerencia 1986). Other islands had their share of hardship as shown by Davies and Anderson (1989), and Nettleford (1989).

The crisis also accelerated the pace of female migration from the Caribbean region. Female migration, which began to grow in the 1960s, surpassed that of men in the 1980s (Deere 1990: 74). Saint-Rose (1991:120) noted that in 1982 there were 52 women per hundred French Antilles migrants living in France, whereas twenty years before, Antillean male immigrants in France had outnumbered female immigrants. A 1981 survey of Dominicans in New York revealed that 55.8 percent of them were women between 20 and 45 years of age (Deere 1990: 77).

During the 1980s, female employment expanded considerably in the assembly industries in the free production zones (FPZs) that were established thanks to the Caribbean Basin Initiative and the Twin Plants Program under the auspices of the Puerto Rico Development Program (see

Deere 1990; McAfee 1991). Already in 1985, women constituted 80 percent of workers in these FPZs where younger women were preferred on the grounds that they were "more pliant and manageable" (Senior 1991: 121; Safa 1985). In this regard, there are no marked differences among the cultural sub-regions, with studies for the English-speaking Caribbean, the Dominican Republic, and Haiti confirming the trend (Henry 1988; Girault 1983).

Work requirements tended to be the same in the free trade zones. A survey of three free zones in the Dominican Republic found a set of characteristics that are generally repeated in the rest of the Caribbean region: Salaries were 20 percent below the minimum national wage and a there was a six-month apprenticeship period during which women were paid only 50 percent of the minimum national wage. The lack of adequate facilities and long working hours, along with provisions that discouraged or prohibited any type of workers' organization, became the norm (Cortén and Duarte 1981). For transnational companies operating in the FTZs, as well as for those in the area of tourism, another sector in which women's participation is growing, female work is still considered supplementary to male earnings, an argument that is used to justify lower salaries for women (Forde 1988; Barry, Wood, and Preusch 1984). An added element of concern is that export manufacturers are increasingly sub-contracting work to home-based workers (informal sector) to further reduce labor costs and avoid any move to organize female workers in the plants (Deere 1990: 62).

Anderson (1986) has summarized the situation by noting that while Caribbean women are very actively engaged in paid employment at all levels of the production of goods and services, their earning power continues to be blocked by limited employment opportunities and below-average wages. Anderson concludes that there is little hope that this economic picture will change as long as women accept the predominance of male leadership in trade unions and remain unprepared to re-examine the gender basis upon which Caribbean societies distribute rewards for work.

Political Participation Among Caribbean Women

Another issue to be addressed is that of political participation of women in the region. Political participation among women can be differentiated at three levels: as voters in the electoral process; as members of political parties and trade unions; and as members of social movements or organizations.[4] In the first case, it should be noted that women are constrained by the same socio-political factors affecting men's political participation as voters. In other words, their ability to exert their right to vote is affected by the political culture of a society relative to the presence or absence of democratic traditions (Comisión Económico para América Latina (CEPAL) 1989). But it is at the second level, as members of political parties and trade unions, that gender differences in participation may be found. A 1987 survey undertaken by the Inter-American Commission on Women found that women accounted for between 0 and 13 percent of members in congresses and parliaments of Latin America and the Caribbean, strikingly low in comparison to the number of women voters in the whole population (CEPAL 1989). Even in nations with democratic governments, where women were encouraged to vote, there was more emphasis on stimulating women's "modernization," without encouraging a more active role for them in unions and political parties. Political participation seems to be directly influenced by the social class and background of women, with higher participation found in the middle- and upper-strata groups, which usually correlate with a higher educational level and better living conditions that allow women to mobilize for political participation..

A new trend dating from the 1980s has been the growing participation by women in "alternative forms" of female organization such as cooperatives, community organizations, NGOs, workshops, "ollas populares," and a host of gender-based activities. The growing number of these organizations and activities and the fact that more women than men are actively involved in them suggest that they seem to provide a better place for female action than traditional political organizations that are unable or unwilling to grant women an active and equal role. The analysis by CEPAL (1989), however, did not consider that alternative organizations facilitate the process of political apprenticeship of women in the region.

The Caribbean region is characterized by political environments ranging from newly-democratic Haiti and still-socialist Cuba to Western-style democracies, either presidential like Dominican Republic and Guyana or parliamentary as in Barbados. Leaving aside the case of Haiti where popular political participation by Haitians in general was until recently neither allowed nor encouraged by the system, we will review features of the political participation of women in the region.

Senior (1991: 153) stressed the following in her summary of political participation of women in democracies of the region:

> While women today constitute a substantial number of registered voters, indeed a majority in Barbados, and turn out to vote at elections, while they are active as party workers, especially in "women's arms" or auxiliaries of national parties, and although women do serve if nominated to senates or upper houses of parliament, official boards and commissions (but only a token few are), they are hardly represented at all in the highest reaches of po-

litical power—as elected representatives in national parliaments. They do not generally play a major role in the inner circle of their parties and have never introduced specific women's issues into Caribbean national electoral politics. Although they campaign for the rights of workers and are active in trade union movements, they play a minor role in trade union leadership, 25 percent in the English-speaking Caribbean.

Studies of political participation among Cuban women have shown that by 1984 women made up 21.9 percent of the municipal district leadership, 18.9 percent among the provincial (state) leadership, and 12.8 percent of the national leadership of the Communist Party of Cuba (PCC) (Espín 1986). These proportions seem to justify the assertion that "the higher the hierarchy, the fewer the women . . ." (Rodríguez and Díaz 1986). On the whole, while Cuban women accounted for between 21 and 22 percent of leadership at all levels of elected positions in the different organs of government in 1984 (Espín 1986), female representatives made up around 45 percent in trade union sections, the lowest level of workers' organizations, but only 14.7 percent in the national leadership. Objective factors such as an insufficient number of child care centers, inadequate household appliances that made domestic chores very labor-intensive, and subjective factors such as prejudices against women's participation in public activities and male resistance to being led by women were said to account for this imbalance in female participation in Cuba.

Despite differences between the political systems and political parties of Cuba and the English-speaking Caribbean, and accepting that there is a relatively much larger political participation of females in the former, the most striking observation is the under-representation of women in leadership positions and the importance of gender-related reasons in explaining this phenomenon across the systems. Underlying the stated objective factors is the assumption that women are responsible for household chores and the care of children. Thus most of the obstacles that hinder women's political participation in positions of responsibility seem to be derived from cultural factors, affecting not only men in and out of political parties but also women themselves (lack of self-confidence, fear of speaking in public, concerns about unfair attacks on their images, etc.) (Forde 1980).

These obstacles notwithstanding, individual women like Maria Liberia-Peters of Curaçao, Maria Eugenia Charles of Dominica, Viola Burnham of Guyana, and Portia Simpson of Jamaica have been quite successful in key political positions at the highest level in their countries. The first two became prime ministers running as candidates of a Christian democratic and a conservative party respectively, while the other two achieved positions of power within their own parties, the People's National Congress (PNC) and the People's National Party (PNP), respectively. Of the four, only the third achieved a political position due to family connections with the leader of the party. Of the three remaining examples, Portia Simpson has been credited with being a charismatic populist leader who also is eloquent in public discourse. In spite of this, her party ran very few women as candidates in key elections in 1989, only five against eight by the Jamaica Labor Party (JLP). Moreover, all female candidates ran in districts with higher concentrations of the better-off segments of the Jamaican population, usually urban, and linked to tourism and other service activities where professional women have been able to penetrate the medium and medium-to-upper levels of the system (Stone 1989: 148–149). Senior (1991: 158) has also pointed out that of the two main political parties in Barbados, one had only four women among the 23 members of the executive council and the other had 7 out of 41, "at a time when female-registered voters exceeded male."

It can be said, therefore, that women who have reached the highest political positions in national life or party life are the exception rather than the norm Usually women are segregated in female arms of parties that are reserved for organization and support work as well as "cultural" activities. There is no difference among conservative, liberal, and progressive parties. For instance, at the end of the 1970s, the National Joint Action Committee (NJAC) in Trinidad established an auxiliary support group made up of women, with the explicit restriction that it should not have links with any movement of female liberation (Henderson 1988: 364). Once established, this women's organization, in a pamphlet entitled "The Black Woman: A Handbook," reminded its members that men were the heads of the family and gave detailed instructions regarding the raising of boys and girls in order to facilitate their acquisition of adequate gender roles at home.

Arocho (1987) has documented the situation in Puerto Rico where both "establishment" parties, the Partido Nuevo Progresista (PNP) and the Partido Popular Democrático (PPD), and the radical opposition Partido Independentista Puertorriqueño (PIP) and Partido Socialista Puertorriqueño (PSP), relegated women to selling tickets and organizing political events, handing out leaflets, raising funds, and in fact marginalized them from participating in any meaningful process of learning how to actively participate in political life or the core aspects of party decision-making. Strategies and male behavior within these four disparate parties were the same—men supported men for positions of power in the party, and only nominated women candidates for irrelevant party positions or for districts where the chances of a party victory were nonexistent. It is not surprising then that, in the fifty years between 1932 and 1982, only 26 women were elected to the senate and the House of Representatives (5 percent in 50 years); 34 women became party majors (4 percent of the total number of majors during the same period), and women never obtained more than the 18 percent representation in municipal councils that were ironically established in 1932 when Puerto Rican women voted for the first time (Pico 1985). In the English-speaking Caribbean, between independence and 1984 only 13 women had become members of national parliaments, and of these 2 were wives of prime ministers (Emmanuel 1984, cited in Clarke 1986).

The situation within the regional trade unions has not been different. The Transport and Industrial Worker's Union (TIWU) of Trinidad and Tobago has a women's unit, but members of this unit had been unable until the mid-1980s to get the Central Committee to discuss their demands for equal opportunities in employment and promotion policies, or gain support for the establishment of child care centers for women workers (Henderson 1988). Few changes have since been made, and the record of Caribbean trade unions in organizing women workers is quite poor. In recent times, the Caribbean Congress of Labor has called for an end to discrimination in employment and increased child care opportunities (Deere 1990: 99).

In summary, political parties and trade unions and other formal channels of political participation in the Caribbean do not offer women an adequate medium to express their needs and demands in an organized, acceptable way. These institutions do not offer women the possibility of learning how to improve their potential for more structured and systematic political action and involvement.

What, then, is the situation with respect to women's organizations created by women themselves? Women's organizations have a long history in the Caribbean and cover a wide spectrum that includes the "Gremio de Damas" (Ladies Trade Union) of Puerto Rico (1908), the "Cedros Bees" of Trinidad (1926), the Jamaican Federation of Women (1944), the League of Women Voters (Trinidad, 1952), and Friendly Societies in most of the English-speaking islands in the Eastern Caribbean (Azize 1986; Clarke 1986; Ramkeesoon 1988; French 1986).

It was after the 1960s that most regional women's organizations concerned with affecting the political life of these countries appeared. During the 1980s, as their numbers increased, they began to put pressure on the state and political parties to improve the delivery of services to women and to reduce or eliminate inefficiency and corruption in the public sector and in the political parties.

It is questionable whether all women's organizations provide an adequate environment for political participation among females. In the English-speaking Caribbean, surveys have shown that the leadership of these organizations is controlled by middle-strata women with a relatively high degree of formal education (Clarke 1986), a phenomenon that can also be observed in the women's units of political parties. These women define the strategies, tactics, and objectives, and determine the battles to fight; yet there is no common agreement around objectives in all organizations. A classic example of disagreement over objectives could be seen when female church groups walked out of the Barbados National Organization of Women (NOW) in opposition to attempts to alter the pattern of gender domination which they viewed as an issue that had become "too politicized" (Clarke 1986). In addition, other studies have concluded that several of these organizations, which work at improving the quality of life among women and presenting women as rational political and economic actors, have the effect of reinforcing segregation in the gender-based division of labor. An example can be found in the numerous projects in agriculture, nutrition, and education that concentrate on teaching women how to cook, sew, and take care of children (Clarke 1986:133–134; Yudelman 1987).

A survey of the Eastern (English-speaking) Caribbean showed that there is a higher proportion of women in these organizations than in political parties and trade unions, with the exception of Barbados where there are more women in the trade unions. The highest levels of female participation in women's organizations can be seen in the poorest islands where the motivation to participate stems from the need for programs of social and political action (Clarke 1986: 141). Incentives like training programs and courses that provide women with badly-needed vocational and technical skills seem to be the best way to attract women to these organizations. Antrobus (cited in Clarke 1986) concluded that English-speaking Caribbean women are not motivated to join organizations that have as their central objective the achievement of formal equality for women vis-à-vis men, but they are interested in promoting themselves economically.

Efforts by women's organizations in the Spanish-speaking Caribbean can be characterized as disperse and erratic, and the creation of Women's Offices and Women's Bureaus at the governmental level in most of these nations is mainly window-dressing effort to give the impression that something concrete is being done (Arocho 1987). Even in Cuba, the Federation of Cuban Women has consistently pressured the government to establish more child care centers, reduce discrimination against women in employment, and monitor the implementation of the Family Code that was enacted in 1975 (Baloyra 1983). However, these demands have never been effectively articulated, and they are limited by the fact that it is impossible to create alternative organizations outside of the state to fight for them.

Political participation among Caribbean women ranging from the poor to the affluent and from the poorly educated to the highly educated seems to be limited to voting or supporting political parties, with little expectation of leading or influencing them to take action in women's direct interest and benefit. It has been documented by Deere (1990) and McAfee (1991) that a considerable part of the weight and impact of the economic crisis has fallen upon female heads of household, with the effect of aggravating their already-eroded economic position. The impact of the crisis and the structural adjustment measures taken to adjust economies to the new global economic reality demand more concerted efforts to address the pain that is being visited upon large numbers of women. For these reasons, it is now more necessary than ever for women to assert themselves and exert leadership and influence to change existing conditions. A basic prerequisite to enhance women's economic and political participation is a clear understanding by Caribbean society of the importance of women as human resources.

The foregoing analysis makes clear that the main obstacle Caribbean women face in developing their potential as human resources is no different from that encountered in Panama by the Foundation for the Advancement of Women and the United Nations Food and Agriculture Organization: "Women are a productive force always on the lookout for ways to improve their situation, but they are often excluded from community decisions and the country's political and economic mainstream" (Latin America Press, May 13, 1993: 4). Women's overall negative situation has been compounded by measures taken by governments in response to the economic crisis. As noted by Deere, "It appears that governments have in fact taken advantage of women's ability to draw on traditional networks of support to introduce policies which have been particularly devastating to women and those for whose care they have been traditionally responsible—children and the elderly" (1990: 71). In effect, as women suffer the impact of unemployment or employment at lower wages, cuts in government services in health and education, and increases in the cost of living, "they are working even harder, spending and eating less, and migrating more" (Deere 1990:79). In some Caribbean countries, survival strategies adopted by women put them at high risk of violent death or contracting dangerous diseases. Perhaps the most dramatic case is that of the Dominican Republic which is considered "the world's leading supplier of prostitutes" with more than 50,000 Dominican women working overseas in this profession (Latin America Press, May 13, 1993: 6).

Some Steps to Help Develop
Women's Economic and Political Potential

What are some of the issues around which strategies for the development of Caribbean women's potential could be devised? Our attention turns to three issues that the state, the private sector, and women's organizations can address toward enhancing the quality of women's lives and providing them with tools for their own self-actualization. Regarding the state, an important issue is that of democratizing existing institutions through broader and more direct participation by Caribbean citizens, of which women comprise a considerable segment. In discussing this issue, McAfee (1991) has already highlighted areas where efforts should be concentrated: providing women with access to information that they can utilize to change their role in the economy; and changing policy and attitudes among those public officials with whom women have to deal at every level. This means the building of more and better channels of communication between the state apparatus and women in all sectors, together with an enhanced willingness of the former to understand and accommodate the special needs of the latter. In this sense Antrobus' words to a U.S. Congressional delegation in Jamaica are still relevant: "The ones most in need of training are those that women . . . have to deal with" (cited in McAfee 1991:178). The benefits of enhancing the communication process between the state and women could be multiple, ranging from more access to credit for women in agriculture and more facilities to transport their crops, to decreasing the amount of foreign currency needed by most of the islands to import foodstuffs for their population. Obviously this requires that the state undertake a careful planning process in which women, as well as all other small farmers, are taken into consideration and also trained to take care of new crops.

The Caribbean private sector seems to be less suited than the public sector to the development of a strategy that may enhance women's participation in the economic and political life of the region. This is the sector that has traditionally exploited cheap female labor to its advantage, reaping the benefits of keeping them unorganized and ready to work for abysmally low wages. However, for independent Caribbean entrepreneurs or those working as sub-contractors for transnational companies in manufacturing and tourism, the two areas where female employment has steadily grown, the development of women's capabilities are in the long run, essential to their economic well-being.

In effect, if the Caribbean private sector has serious plans to make itself competitive in the global economy, it cannot postpone the question of training and developing the region's human resources to meet that end. Training and retraining of the workforce has become more important than maintaining a large pool of unskilled and unemployed workers. Given the cuts in public funds mandated by structural adjustment programs in the Caribbean and the divestment and privatization strategies adopted by the state, training is going to fall increasingly upon the shoulders of the private sector, which could discharge it by directly implementing it at the workplace or by shifting guidelines and financial resources to the public educational system. Either way, the private sector must come to terms with the reality that Caribbean women make up a considerable portion of the workforce and have special needs.

Women's organizations in the Caribbean have the task of organizing women to take advantage of any available opportunities, making them understand and accept their role as full-fledged Caribbean citizens with rights but also responsibilities for the overall well-being of the region. In this sense, the challenge to them is to reach out to as many women as possible, in all types of organizations and social sectors, in order to heighten their awareness of their strengths and weaknesses, to enhance the former and overcome the latter. The task of women's organizations does not end with reaching out to women themselves and to social movements where women are active; it includes the establishment of linkages with the state and the private sector in order for them to develop the strategies sketched above. In fact, the responsibility for making both the state and the private sector understand the need for changes rests in the way women's organizations relate to women. Detailed diagnosis of women's conditions should be followed by concrete proposals that take into consideration the well-being of the society as a whole. Even when economic programs applied by the state and private sector are seen as detrimental to women and negative for the well-being of Caribbean people in general, women's organizations should strive to advance more effective alternatives to those programs with efforts to strengthen the lines of communication to the state and the private sector if they are going to exert any policy-relevant influence on their decisions.

In conclusion, if birth and mortality rates in the Caribbean region remain at existing levels, the number of females in the population will increase and so will their economic and political participation. It is imperative that they be prepared to undertake the many responsibilities that will fall on them. Organizing themselves, establishing better channels of communication with the state apparatuses, and training and retraining at the workplace or within the education system are only a few of the strategies needed today in order to ensure the full development of this neglected human resource within Caribbean society.

Notes

1. This article is reprinted by permission from *Century Policy Review: An American, Caribbean, and African Forum* (Largo, MD: International Development Options Research Organization), 2 (1–2), Spring 1994: 219–243. Appropriate editorial changes have been made with the permission of the author.

2. It should be noted that we are not exclusively referring to the debate over whether domestic chores constitute an unpaid economic contribution to the production of a family or household unit (Colón de Zalduondo 1987), but to economic activities undertaken in an informal way or without remuneration, as in the case of family agricultural activities (see Massiah 1986, p. 189).

3. Deere (1990) calculated that in 1985, at least 39 percent of Jamaican households were headed by women, and in Kingston 45 percent of households were headed by women.

4. According to Acosta-Belén (1986: 80), women's organizations are political when they identify with political parties or "perceive their role as political in terms of producing social change."

Bibliography

Acevedo, Luz del Alba. 1986/1987. "Política de industrialización y cambio en el empleo femenino en Puerto Rico, 1947–1982." *Homines* 10 (2), agosto/febrero: 40–69.

Acosta-Belén, Edna. 1986. *The Puerto Rican Woman: Perspectives on Culture, History and Society*. New York: Praeger.

Anderson, Patricia. 1986. "Conclusion: Women in the Caribbean." *Social and Economic Studies* 35 (2), June: 291–324.

Arocho, Sylvia. 1986/1987. "La mujer y el aceso al poder en Puerto Rico" *Homines* 10 (2), agosto/febrero: 401–404.

Azize, Y. 1986/1987. "La mujer obrera en el movimiento sindical." *Homines* 10 (2), agosto/febrero: 432–445.

Baloyra, Enrique A. 1983. "Cuba." Pp. 522–539 in J. W. Hopkins, ed., *Latin America and Caribbean Contemporary Record, 1981–1982*. New York: Holmes and Meier.

Barrow, Christine. 1986. "Finding the Support: Strategies for Survival." *Social and Economic Studies* 35 (2), June: 131–176.

Barry, T., B. Wood, and D. Preusch. 1984. *The Other Side of Paradise*. New York: Grove Press.

Beauvue-Fougeyrollas, Claudie. 1985. *Les Femmes Antillaises*. Paris: L'Harmattan.

Bifani, Patricia. 1987. "Opresión y poder: La mujer del Tercer Mundo." *Nueva Sociedad* 90, julio-agosto: 52–60.

Comisión Económico Para América Latina (CEPAL). 1989. *Notas sobre Economía y Desarrollo*. No. 483–484. Santiago de Chile, octubre/noviembre.

Clarke, Roberta. 1986. "Women's Organizations, Women's Interests." *Social and Economic Studies* 35 (3), September: 107–155.

Colón de Zalduondo, B. 1986/1987. "El valor económico y social del trabajo de la mujer en el hogar." *Homines* 10 (2), agosto/febrero): 32–38.

Comunidad Europea. 1984/1985. *Anuario Estadístico de Cuba*. La Habana, Cuba.

Coordinadora Regional de Investigaciones Económicos y Sociales (CRIES). 1993. *Nota # 4*. Santo Domingo, Repúbllica Dominicana, enero.

Cortén, André and Isis Duarte. 1981. "Proceso de proletarización de mujeres: Las trabajadoras de industrias de ensamblaje en la República Dominicana." *Revista de Ciencas Sociales* 23 (3/4), julio/diciembre: 529–567.

Davies, O. and P. Anderson. 1989. "The Impact of the Recession and Structural Adjustment Policies on Poor Urban Women in Jamaica." Paper presented at the Annual Meeting of the Caribbean Studies Association, Barbados, May.

Deere, Carmen Diana. 1985. "Rural Women and Agrarian Reform in Peru, Chile, and Cuba." Pp. 189–207 in J. Nash and H. Safa, eds., *Women and Change in Latin America*. South Hadley, MA.: Bergin and Garvey.

Deere, Carmen Diana, coordinator. 1990. *In the Shadows of the Sun: Caribbean Development Alternatives and U.S. Policy*. Boulder, Colorado: Westview Press/Policy Alternatives for the Caribbean and Central America (PACCA).

Emerencia, L. A. 1986. "Hende muhe den e proceso laboral na Aruba." Pp. 45–61 in Grupo Aruba. *Sembra awe pa cosecha manan*. Aruba: Groningen.

Espín, Vilma. 1986. "La batalla por el pleno ejercicio de la igualdad de la mujer: Acción de los comunistas." *Cuba Socialista* 20. La Habana, Cuba, marzo/abril: 50–58.

Forde, Norma. 1980. *The Status of Women in Barbados*. Occasional Paper 15. Cave Hill, Barbados: Institute for Social and Economic Research.

————. 1988. "Exploitation by EPZs." *Caribbean Contact*, December: 1–2.

French, Joan. 1986. "Colonial Policy Towards Women after the 1938 Uprising: The Case of Jamaica." Paper presented at the Annual Meeting of the Caribbean Studies Association. Caracas, Venezuela, May.

Garabaghi, Ninou. 1983. "Un nuevo enfoque sobre la problemática de la participación de la mujer en la vida económica." *Revista Internacional de Ciencias Sociales* 35(4): 705–727.

Giacalone, Rita. 1991. "La mujer en los procesos políticos y socioeconómicos del Caribe." Pp. 201–22 in A. Serbín, ed., *El Caribe hacia el 2000*. Caracas: Editorial Nueva Sociedad.

Girault, Christian A. 1983. *El comercio del café en Haiti*. Bordeaux, France: University of Bordeaux.

Gordon, Derek. 1986. "The Sexual Division of Labor and Intergenerational Mobility in Jamaica." Paper presented at Annual Meeting of the Caribbean Studies Association. Caracas, Venezuela, May.

Harraksingh, K. 1988. "Sugar, Labor and Livelihood in Trinidad 1940–1970." *Social and Economic Studies* 37(1/2), March/June: 271–291.

Henderson, Thelma. 1988. "The Contemporary Women's Movement in Trinidad and Tobago." Pp. 363–372 in P. Mohammed and C. Sheppard, eds., *Gender in Caribbean Development*. Mona, Jamaica: University of the West Indies.

Henry, Ralph. 1988. "Jobs, Gender and Development Strategy in the Commonwealth Caribbean." Pp. 183–205 in P. Mohammed and C. Sheppard, eds., *Gender in Caribbean Development*. Mona, Jamaica: University of the West Indies.

Henshall, Momsen J. 1987. "The Feminization of Agriculture in the Caribbean." Pp. 331–347 in J. Henshall Momsen and J. G. Townsend, eds., *Geography of Gender in the Third World*. Albany, New York: State University of New York/Hutchinson.

II Congreso Nacional de la Federación de Mujeres Cubanas. 1975. *Memoria*. La Habana: Orbe.

Katzin, Margaret F. 1971. "The Business of Higglerism in Jamaica." Pp. 340–381 in M. Horowitz, ed., *Peoples and Culture of the Caribbean*. Garden City, New York: The Natural History Press.

Lobdell, R. 1988. "Women in the Jamaican Labor Force, 1881–1921." *Social and Economic Studies* 37 (1/2), March/June: 203–240.

Massiah, Joyceline. 1986. "Work in the Lives of Caribbean Women." *Social and Economic Studies* 35 (2), June: 177–239.

McAfee, Kathy. 1991. *Storm Signals: Structural Adjustment and Development Alternatives in the Caribbean.* Boston, MA.: South End Press.

Nettleford, Rex. 1989. "Caribbean Crisis and Challenges to Year 2000." *Caribbean Quarterly* 35 (2), March: 2–10.

Odie-Ali, Stella. 1986. "Women in Agriculture: The Case of Guyana." *Social and Economic Studies* 35 (2), June: 241–289.

Pico, Isabel. 1986/1987. "Women and Puerto Rican Politics Before Enfranchisement." *Homines* 10(2), agosto/febrero): 405–420.

Ramkeesoon, G. 1988. "Early Women's Organizations in Trinidad: 1920s to 1950s." Pp. 353–356 in P. Mohammed and C. Sheppard, eds., *Gender in Caribbean Development.* Mona, Jamaica: University of the West Indies.

Randall, M. 1978. *No se puede hacer la revolución sin nosotras.* La Habana, Cuba: Casa de las Américas.

Rodríguez, L. and E. Díaz. 1986. "Participación de la mujer cubana." Avance de Investigación.

Safa, Helen. 1985. "Female Employment in the Puerto Rican Working Class." Pp. 84–97 in J. Nash and H. Safa, eds.,*Women and Change in Latin America.* South Hadley, MA.: Bergin and Garvey.

———. 1986. "Economic Autonomy and Sexual Equality in Caribbean Society." *Social and Economic Studies* 35 (3), September: 1–21.

Saint-Rose, Pierre Leval. 1991. "Le retour des migrants aux Antilles et en Guyane Francaise." Pp. 117–143 in M. L. Martin and A. Yacou, eds., *Études Caribéenes. Société et Politique.* Toulouse, France: Presses de l'Institut d'Études Politiques.

Senior, Olive. 1991. *Working Miracles: Women's Lives in the English-speaking Caribbean.* Cave Hill, Barbados: Institute for Social and Economic Research.

Stone, Carl. 1989. *Politics vs Economics: The 1989 Elections in Jamaica.* Kingston, Jamaica: Heinemann.

Stubbs, Jean. 1988. "Gender Constructs of Labour in Pre-revolutionary Cuban Tobacco." *Social and Economic Studies* 37 (1/2), March/June: 241–269.

Yudelman, S. 1987. "The Integration of Women in Development Projects." *World Development* 15, Fall: 179–187.

16

Caribbean Labor at Issue: Labor Migrations and ILO Standards

Mario Trajtenberg

The Role of Labor Migrations

Labor migrations play a fundamental part in the life and the economy of Caribbean nations. These countries were created by migratory flows, some of them highly involuntary. For the past four decades they have been an unending source of migration to wealthier countries, first the United Kingdom, and now mainly the United States, Canada and, in the special case of Suriname, the Netherlands.

This chapter discusses the status of existing international labor legislation affecting migrants from the region to the developed countries. It is strongly felt that both migrants themselves and the sending governments need to be knowledgeable about this legislation and how it might be used to their advantage.

Some History

If one leaves aside the transport of enslaved Africans, migratory movements *into* the Caribbean can be dated back mainly to the nineteenth century. After emancipation, the authorities of some of the larger territories such as Jamaica, Trinidad, and Guyana induced workers from the smaller islands and from Portugal and Madeira to come to work on the plantations. The largest inflow—one that to this day has shaped the make-up of the population, especially in Guyana and in Trinidad—was that of indentured laborers from India, about half a million of whom made their way across the ocean and, except for exceptional cases, stayed in their new country. The collapse of world sugar prices in the 1880s slowed down this process and started a new pattern that was to become dominant in this century: migration *outwards* from the Caribbean territories.

New opportunities were created with the abolition of slavery in Cuba, the construction of railways and the Panama Canal, and the growth of the banana plantations in Central America. World War II brought new job openings on U.S. military bases and in the United States itself to make up for the war-induced shortage of industrial and agricultural labor.

For more than a decade after the war, the United Kingdom acted as a powerful magnet and allowed for almost unrestricted immigration of Caribbean citizens to Britain where they manned the reconstruction effort and, later, some public utilities such as transport. During this time, Barbados and Grenada also received many agricultural workers from St. Vincent, Saint Lucia, and Grenada, and these tended to remain in the host countries. Policies have since become more restrictive in the U.K., where immigrants have had to contend with scarcity of jobs, inflows from other parts of the Commonwealth, and racism. In the United States, the national quota system was abolished in 1965, thus increasing substantially the numbers of immigrants from the Caribbean, but later legislation reduced the choice to immigrants having specific skills and professional qualifications. Canada remains a very large job market for expatriate islanders.

It is now obvious that even if the job opportunities are not as plentiful, many immigrants are there to stay. One is therefore entitled to consider Caribbean labor migration in the same breath as its counterparts in other parts of the world and to analyze its problems and advantages with the same yardstick, even if neither the receiving nor the sending countries seem particularly sensitive to the need for enshrining protection in ratified international instruments.

Ambiguous Advantages

There has been some misunderstanding of the effect that migrations, in their current form, have on the economies of the sending and receiving countries. The effects on development are highly topical for the International Labor Organization (ILO) in that the agency is involved in the collective effort of the United Nations system to promote balanced economic growth on a plank of adequately-trained human resources.

The argument for promoting free circulation of workers toward the wealthy markets of the north is that when they return to their countries, they will have acquired skills and work habits that will prove beneficial to the various economic sectors. This line of reasoning has been widely promoted in Europe as a justification for sending the migrants back when they are no longer needed.

Highly-trained professionals, however, do not return quickly. For countries like Jamaica and Suriname, the social cost, in terms of brain and skills drain, of a migration movement that had some political motivation has been enormous precisely because the migrant nurses, doctors, and managers do not feel encouraged to return. On the contrary, they become more and more aware of how well they fit into the economic fabric of wealthy countries that have spent little or nothing on their training.

In the case of workers that may have upgraded their skills while abroad, the usefulness of their new training to their countries of origin remains open to doubt when one considers the vastly different environments in which they will have to operate after their return—if they find a job, and if such employment is in the sector in which their newly-acquired skills can be of any use. Many islanders came back from England with manufacturing skills that could not be put to use because there was very little investment in that particular sector. Moreover, returnees sometimes felt constrained by possible resentments they might stimulate in colleagues who had not migrated.

Many migrants do bring back savings that can serve as a starting-point for the creation of small enterprises, provided that they receive technical and managerial assistance as well as appropriate lines of credit. The drawback, assuming that economies should develop according to their own modalities and independent of pressure from the north, is that migrant enterprise has contributed to continued economic and cultural dependence on developed countries.[1]

The International Labor Perspective

The ILO is an international agency whose business it is to set world labor standards and see to it that they are applied. The standards are, of course, drawn up with a full knowledge of existing circumstances and also with the added advantage of empowerment by the social partners: The legal standards set by the ILO and the technical cooperation it delivers to facilitate their application originate not only in action by the International Labor Office and approval of the member governments, but in the active participation of workers' and employers' associations in the work of the ILO. This may not seem to be so important if one considers that migrants seldom belong to unions or, if they do, take little part in union activity. The reality is also that many immigrants are illegal and that many employers know this. On the other hand, we are dealing with an instrument that can help to correct reality and to avoid social injustice.

An ILO Convention is a treaty drawn up by the International Labor Office and, after some elaborate consultation with the governments and with representatives of the workers and the employers, adopted by the International Labor Conference in Geneva. These treaties are binding only on the countries that have ratified them. There is further machinery, which has proved effective in the course of seventy-five years, to ensure that governments actually take all measures needed to give effect to the provisions of the conventions they have ratified. A different kind of ILO standards are in the form of recommendations which set flexible guidelines for national policy and practice. Usually recommendations supplement the provisions contained in conventions and spell them out in greater detail.

Although the constitution of the ILO dates back to 1919, the year of the agency's creation, twenty years were to elapse before the first convention dealing with migration for employment was adopted, and ten more years before the convention attained the form in which it is known today, that of Convention No. 97 on Migration for Employment (revised). This Convention has the basic purpose of regulating the conditions under which migrations for employment take place, and of ensuring some equality of treatment for migrant workers. The general protection envisaged is the following:

- the establishment of free services to assist prospective migrants;
- the adoption of steps against misleading propaganda relating to emigration and immigration;
- measures to facilitate the departure, travel, and reception of migrants for employment;
- the establishment of appropriate medical services before departure and after arrival;
- the permission accorded to migrant workers to transfer their earnings and savings.

Another set of provisions in Convention No. 97 deals with equality of treatment. The provisions involve, for ratifying states, the obligation to apply to immigrants residing lawfully within their territory, without discrimination in respect of nationality, race, religion, or sex, treatment no less favorable than that which they apply to their own nationals in respect of the following:

- employment conditions, vocational training, membership of trade unions and enjoyment of the benefits of collective bargaining, and housing;
- social security;
- employment taxes, dues, or contributions payable in respect of the person employed; and
- legal proceedings with regard to such treatment.

Recommendation No. 86, adopted at the same session of the International Labor Conference that adopted Convention No. 97, and also revised in

1949, includes a number of supplementary measures covering information and assistance for migrants, recruitment and selection, and equal treatment with respect to access to employment. It also includes provisions aimed at protecting migrant workers against expulsion on account of their lack of means or the state of the employment market.

Convention No. 97 has been ratified so far by eight Caribbean states that are members of the ILO: Barbados, Belize, Dominica, Grenada, Guyana, Jamaica, Saint Lucia, and Trinidad and Tobago. It has also been declared applicable by the Netherlands and the U.K. to a number of their dependent territories in the Caribbean. But neither the United States nor Canada has ratified the convention, unlike several of the major receiving countries in Europe, specifically France, Germany, Italy, Spain, and the United Kingdom.

The second relevant convention, adopted by the ILO in 1975, has attracted few ratifications. This is Convention No. 143 which deals with abuse of migrants and the promotion of equality of opportunity and treatment of migrant workers. Basing itself on what had then become a common experience in Europe, particularly with regard to clandestine migrations from northern Africa, it sets an obligation to respect the basic human rights of all migrant workers. Ratifying states are required by the convention to suppress clandestine movements of migrants for employment and illegal employment of migrants. Measures are also specified against the organizers of illicit or clandestine movements of migrants for employment, and against those who employ workers who have immigrated in illegal conditions. The convention also has a number of provisions inspired by the ILO's Discrimination Convention (No. 111) and designed to promote and guarantee equality of treatment for migrants in respect of employment and occupation, social security, trade union and cultural rights, and individual and collective freedoms. The accompanying recommendation defines the principles of social policy that will enable migrant workers and their families to share in the advantages enjoyed by nationals, and suggests a number of measures with regard to the reunification of families, protection of the health of migrant workers, and the establishment of social services.

Two other conventions adopted twenty years apart (1962 and 1982) have to do specifically with social security, always a difficult issue to regulate internationally but one that can acutely affect the welfare of migrant workers and their families. Under the terms of Convention No. 118 on equality of treatment (social security), ratifying states undertake to grant reciprocally to nationals of other states, including refugees, equality of treatment with their own nationals in respect of social security without any condition of residence. Such equality applies to medical care and to sickness, maternity, invalidity, old-age and survivors' benefits, employment injury, unemployment relief, and family benefits. Convention No.118 has so far received 37 ratifications, including ratifications from Barbados and Suriname and, among the major receiving countries, from France, Germany, Italy, and Sweden.

As of the mid 1990s, there are only two ratifications registered with respect to the most recent convention, Convention No. 157 (1982) concerning the maintenance of social security rights. This perhaps reflects the difficulties involved in applying such a complex and technical convention, one that sets out to ensure wide-ranging but flexible coordination among national social security schemes. Members of migrant workers' families are specifically covered. Certain provisions allow for adding together periods of insurance, employment, or residence, and others set out conditions for the maintenance of acquired rights. The accompanying recommendation, No. 167, gives model provisions for the conclusion of bilateral or multilateral social security agreements.

The United Nations Contribution

In addition to the ILO conventions mentioned, reference should be made to the United Nations International Convention on the Protection of the Rights of all Migrant Workers and Members of their Families, adopted by the General Assembly by resolution 45/158 of 18 December 1990. Unlike the ILO standards that evolved through a conventional process of two years of elaboration, discussion, and adoption at the International Labor Conference, the U.N. Convention had a chequered history of ten years of drafting at no less than nineteen sessions of an open-ended working group. It is an ambitious and comprehensive document that dramatizes in the international arena the situation of the Mexican and other immigrants from Latin America to the United States, and that would not have seen the light of day without intense diplomatic effort.

The U.N. Convention is interesting not only in the breadth of its coverage but in the fact that it seeks to incorporate, or at least not to contradict, the ILO's own principles, and even follows the model of its mechanisms for ensuring international compliance. This is not surprising, since the ILO was involved from the start in the drafting process and is now part of the supervisory machinery established by the U.N. convention.

The core of this very long text spells out the rights and freedoms that all migrant workers and members of their families should have, even if their situation is not regularized. These include basic human rights such as the right not to be subjected to torture or to degrading treatment, and the right to be treated no less favorably than national workers in respect of conditions of work and terms of employment. Other rights spelled out by the U.N. convention apply only to migrant workers in a regular situation; they include rights to political participation and to equality of opportunity and treatment with respect to many economic and social matters (for example, the right to form unions). Irregular migrants are additionally entitled to take part in trade union meetings, to join unions, and to seek their assistance. The U.N. convention also sets limits to the authority of the states to expel non-nationals. Part VI of the convention, in the drafting of which the ILO had a crucial role, includes provisions designed mainly to combat illegal movements and illegal employment of non-nationals who are invariably open to abuse.

This discussion of the range of international labor standards relating to migrants, the record of their ratification by member countries, and the principles involved in the U.N. convention on the rights of migrants, is motivated by the hope that new perspectives and new practices may be evolved in the western hemisphere. In this regard, it may be said that ILO standards with respect to migrant workers have failed so far to make a significant dent on legislation, and it can be argued that this creates a large gap in human rights observance. Collaboration between sending and receiving countries is needed to correct this situation.

Note

1. There are numerous works available on migration and its economic and social effects on both host and sending societies. With respect particularly to the relationship between migration and development, see Pastor (1985; 1990).

Bibliography

Bouvier, Leon F. 1986. *Many Hands, Few Jobs: Population, Employment and Emigration in Mexico and the Caribbean.* Washington, D.C.: Center for Immigration Studies.

Bonadie, J. Burns, compiler. 1977. *Trends in Labor Legislation in the Caribbean.* Barbados: Caribbean Labor Economics Research Training Program.

International Labor Office (ILO). 1995. *The International Labor Organization in the Service of Social Progress: Worker's Education Manual.* Geneva: ILO.

Lemoine, Maurice. 1985. *Bitter Sugar: Slaves Today in the Caribbean.* Chicago: Banner Press.

Maingot, Anthony P., ed. 1991. *Small Country Development and International Labor Flows: Experiences in the Caribbean.* Boulder, CO: Westview.

Pastor, Robert. ed. 1985. *Migration and Development in the Caribbean.* Boulder, CO: Westview.

———. 1989–1990. "Migration and Development: Implications and Recommendations for Policy." *Studies in Comparative International Development* 24, Winter: 46–64.

Sassen, Saskia. 1981. *Exporting Capital and Importing Labor.* New York, N.Y.: New York University, Faculty of Arts and Science, Center for Latin American and Caribbean Studies.

Sirianni, Carmen, ed. 1987. *Worker Participation and the Politics of Reform.* Philadelphia: Temple University.

17

Caribbean Migrations in the 1990s: Some Policy Implications

Monica H. Gordon

Anti-Immigrant Sentiment

The turmoil occurring in many countries in the 1990s suggests that asylum seekers will pose a major global immigration problem in the future. But even before this, immigrant-receiving countries were expressing concern or contemplating restrictions to their liberal immigration policies of the past decades. Increasingly, the objections to continuous immigrant inflow have taken on racial overtones accompanied by strong nationalist sentiments. It has become evident that states will institute more stringent and punitive measures in an attempt to control and restrict the flow of immigrants, both as legal and illegal entrants across their borders. Caribbean countries that have benefited from the liberal postwar immigration policies of Europe and North America are now caught in the politics of the post–Cold War era with emphasis on limits and restraints combined with internal anti-immigrant activism. The indicators and actions of the past decade demonstrate that the United States, the only major receiving country for Caribbean immigrants, will not for the foreseeable future expand any existing limits on immigration from the Caribbean.

Influences on Migration Patterns

Political upheavals in this century have been the prime contributor to international migration. Hollifield (1992) has reminded us that the great migratory waves were closely tied to war, politics, and the economic order. The first great wave of international migration, Hollifield argues, ground to a halt in the 1920s and 1930s, first because of the first World War and subsequent restrictive policies, then because of the Great Depression, the collapse of the international economic order, and the impending second World War. The second great wave took place in the post-World War II period beginning with the exodus of refugees from Europe to the Americas in the 1940s. The emergence of the Cold War in the 1950s imposed constraints on east-west migration and stimulated the south-north migration.

The Cold War initiated the first large-scale unrestricted migration from the English-speaking Caribbean to Great Britain starting in the late 1940s and lasting until 1962 when Britain imposed restrictions limiting migration to selected categories of immigrants (Thompson 1990: 39–70). The Cold War also sparked the exodus from Cuba, creating the first major refugee influx within the western hemisphere.

While the Cold War can be cited as the primary cause for Caribbean emigration in the 1950s and 1960s, the circumstances that promoted emigration varied. The migration to Britain can be characterized as economic for both the sending and receiving societies. The Caribbean had surplus labor and Britain needed semi-skilled and unskilled workers in strategic infrastructural areas (McLean Petras 1983). The migration from Cuba, on the other hand, was primarily political—the flight (and push) from communism. Subsequent departures from Cuba have blurred the distinction between economic and political immigrants although there has been no policy change toward restriction from that country. The Cold War also led to changes in U.S. immigration policies leading to significant legal migration from non-European countries, including the Caribbean.

The third factor impacting on international migration is the end of the Cold War and the dissolution of the Soviet Union. The general consensus is that international migration will become a more important issue into the next century. The problem is centered around rising supply of immigrants at a time when industrial nations want to reduce unskilled worker immigration. The south to north migration encouraged by recruitment in the 1960s is now considered unnecessary because these countries are experiencing high rates of unemployment. The immediate repercussion of this momentous event was the deluge of asylum seekers invading the Western European countries.

Martin (1992), commenting at a conference held to mark the opening of the European Forum for Migration Studies, observed that confusion over the best immigration and integration policies for the 1990s is most obvious in Germany, the country with one-third of Europe's foreigners. Another observer (Freeman 1992) has noted that if the refugee-processing mechanism has not yet collapsed, it is because every state and numerous intergovernmental agencies have been revamping their procedures at warp speed. Indications are that the system is ineffectual and that there is growing cynicism about the asylum system among officials who are finding it more difficult to maintain the distinction between economic migrants and political refugees, a confusion that Haitians trying to enter the United States as refugees have certainly encountered.

The refugee problem is only the most recent immigration dilemma in Europe. According to Freeman (1992: 1145):

> Immigration policy is at the intersection of domestic and international politics. It reflects national political coalitions committed to one policy or another, the structure of the state institutions responsible for making the policy, and a host of extranational factors such as geopolitical obligations, accession to international accords, membership in transnational organizations, and strategic trading relationships.

Freeman asks pertinent questions about the seriousness of the immigration issues of the 1990s. How general is the trend toward restrictive immigration policies? How has the crisis manifested itself in individual states? Do prospects exist for moderate and orderly reform or a more radical backlash against migration pressures? He identifies two categories of receiving states: those still operating mass migration programs (for example, the United States, Canada, and Australia) and those trying, unsuccessfully, to restrict new migration for settlement and work (for example, Western Europe).

Rystad (1992) concluded, after overviewing the history of international migration, that open and unrestricted migration is a thing of the past. In his opinion, the selective recruitment of individuals deemed as valuable additions to the existing labor force will take place. At the same time, illegal immigration will continue and possibly increase, and Europe will be confronted with an onslaught of refugees as a consequence of "ethnic cleansing," political conflicts, and economic and social paroxysms in the countries that were once part of the Soviet empire.

Although the concerns addressed above are specific to Europe and migration from the Caribbean to Europe has diminished to insignificance, there is the probability that the pressure for asylum in Europe will spill over to the United States. Given the emphasis on skills as means for entry, migration from the east may well supersede migration from the south, including the Caribbean.

The question is whether the rapid increase in the number of persons needing political asylum will cancel other forms of permanent migration. More importantly, the question arises as to whether other countries will follow the example of Germany and close their borders in response to the backlash against immigrants.

Caribbean Immigration Issues

The *New York Times* (May 6, 1992: A1, A2) reported that the Caribbean, with a total population of only 33 million, exports a greater percentage of its people than any area of the world. Tiny states like St. Kitts and Nevis, Grenada, and Belize are exporting 1–2 percent of their population every year, while the Dominican Republic, Jamaica, Haiti, and Guyana accounted for nearly 12 percent of all legal immigrants to the United States between 1981 and 1990. The Caribbean countries have become dependent on migration both as an outlet for surplus labor and for the remittances sent home by immigrants.

Up to this point, English-speaking Caribbean people have used emigration to achieve social and economic mobility. Even the refugees are not merely seeking political asylum but also the opportunity for economic and social predictability and viability. This raises the issue of whether the traditional absorbing countries can afford to absorb both planned immigration and the intermittent influx of persons seeking political asylum.

It has been this freedom to move to whichever market was able and willing to absorb Caribbean labor that has mitigated some of the more extreme social conditions in the various countries. Will emigration continue to be an option for the Caribbean in the future? Labor needs, the driving force in the migration process, are not constant. There are many available labor pools to choose from, and there has been a decline in the demand for labor, engendered by the shift from human to technological means of production. Moreover, this shift has led to an inability to absorb the labor already available in the traditional labor-absorbing societies. These factors are exacerbated by increasing antagonistic behavior toward immigrants (especially guest workers, permanent residents, and refugees). Politicians, alienated groups, and workers feel, rightly or wrongly, that their jobs and well-being are threatened by immigrants. However, the United States, which has been the primary absorber of Caribbean immigrants for the last three decades, has maintained its immigration policies of recent decades, albeit with some changes.

U.S. Immigration Policy

The United States has been confronted with new issues that impel periodic amendments to its major revised immigration legislation of 1965. First, the revised legislation, liberal on issues of race and ethnicity, had not anticipated the magnitude of the immigration from non-European countries. The unprecedented influx of non-European immigrants generated the 1976 amendment which imposed hemispheric quotas of 120,000 from the west and 170,000 from the east per country limit of 20,000. Again, in 1978, the 1965 act was amended to impose a worldwide limit of 290,000. As numbers go, this is not large for the United States; the potential problem has been the family reunification clause which affected 80 percent of immigrants, many of whom were dependent persons.

The Refugee Act, passed in 1980, separated refugees from the worldwide limit of 290,000 which was reduced to 270,000 to accommodate this separate category. Refugees and asylees—those already living in the United States as opposed to refugees who are admitted from refugee camps outside the country—are identified on the basis of race, religion, nationality, membership in social groups, or political opinion. They differ from immigrants who, presumably, leave their countries or place of residence voluntarily.

In 1986, the U.S. Congress acted again, this time to pass the Immigration Reform and Control Act (IRCA) in response to increased concerns among Americans about the growing number of undocumented aliens. The purpose of this act, as the name proclaimed, was the control of illegal entry or residence. An amnesty provision gave legal status to those who had lived continuously in the United States since 1982 and to certain agricultural workers. The punitive aspect of the act was the measures against employers who knowingly hire undocumented aliens, and increased border enforcement to prevent illegal entry.

Each amendment to the 1965 Act was made to correct some manifest or perceived deficit in the system, usually to control the numbers and categories of immigrants. The most drastic reorganization, however, has been the Immigration Act of 1990. This Act provided for an annual immigration level of 675,000 worldwide, which represented an overall increase over the approximate 600,000 annually since 1980 (all categories). The three important changes incorporated in this act were: (1) the increase in the number of visas allocated to family reunification; (2) the introduction of a "diversity pool" program; and (3) the expansion in the number of occupational and skill preference visas.

The most significant change in the 1990 amendment was the "diversity pool." The argument for this provision was that the 1965 act had adversely affected immigration from Europe. The emphasis on family reunification had broken the generational chain migration from Europe in favor of Asia, the Caribbean, and Latin America. Thus the diversity pool was a corrective to favor, most specifically, Ireland for the period 1992 to 1994. Thereafter the pool would be open to all countries with fewer than 50,000 immigrants in the preceding few years, with each country limited to 7 percent of the total 55,000. The one condition was that these immigrants had to have a minimum education of high school or equivalent, or training in an occupation.

With respect to the third change mentioned, affecting the third and sixth preferences (employment categories) of the 1965 Act, the number of visas issued in these categories went from a limit of 54,000 to 140,000. The emphasis was very clearly on education, training, and skills.

On the surface, it would appear that the Caribbean has not been adversely affected by the 1990 amendment since the overall numerical provision has been increased. However, a more careful examination indicates problem areas. The amendment reduced the number of first-preference immigrants (unmarried sons and daughters of U.S. citizens and their children) from 54,000 to 23,000, and fourth-preference immigrants (married sons and daughters of U.S. citizens, their spouses, and children) from 27,000 to 23,400. This has had a direct impact on migration from the Caribbean because many Caribbean immigrants have used citizenship as the route to family reunification for adult children. The increase in visas for spouses and unmarried children of *permanent resident aliens* from 70,200 to 114,000 has undoubtedly benefited those immigrants falling under the "diversity pool" more than other categories. But the majority of immigrants from the Caribbean have been in the service and family categories, with the family categories dependent on the employment category. In the long run, the curtailment of the last category, implied by the added educational requirements, will have an overall negative impact on immigration from the region. The one positive aspect is that many Caribbean immigrants are indeed able to meet the 1990 educational requirements. The emigration of such persons, however, will drain the Caribbean of educated and skilled workers.

In 1995, a commission headed by former U.S. congresswoman Barbara Jordan recommended that the U.S. government adopt a more restrictive approach to the granting of family visas, eliminate the annual allotment of 10,000 visas to unskilled foreign workers, and cap legal immigration at 550,000 a year. At the time there was strong sentiment in congress for capping legal immigration. A bill to cap immigration at 595,000 by the year 2001 and to slash the number of visas granted to siblings and parents of citizens or legal residents was placed on the congressional agenda for the 1995–1996 term. After much debate and lobbying by business and pro-immigrant groups, legal immigration levels were preserved for the time being. However, Congress has at the same time moved, through this and other legislation, to deny or restrict certain federal benefits to some legal aliens.

With the exception of Cuba and Haiti, the Caribbean area has not had the refugee problem of other regions of the world, although there has been considerable illegal migration. During the crisis in Haiti, controversy surrounded the treatment of the "Haitian boat people." Unlike Cubans fleeing Castro's regime, Haitians were categorized as economic migrants fleeing poverty and not genuine political refugees. The Bush administration followed a policy of interdiction at sea and return of those who did not qualify for asylum. President Clinton reneged on his campaign promise to reverse the Bush policy toward the Haitians, and most fleeing Haitians were peremptorily returned or left to languish in camps in Cuba and elsewhere. After the U.S. invasion of Haiti, the immigration issue was stabilized as Haitians in refugee camps were either returned to Haiti or accepted in the United States.

Cuban policy has also gone through some changes. A policy of unconditional acceptance of refugees was changed in 1995 to one of not accepting refugees other than the 20,000 allowed to leave legally per year. Cubans already in camps were allowed into the United States.

Conclusion

The impact of the migration crisis generated by the end of the Cold War has been felt largely in Europe. Germany, traditionally the most liberal of the immigrant-receiving states, capitulated under the pressures of asylum seekers and anti-immigrant violence. Hollifield (1992) asks whether there ought to be some international regime to regulate migration comparable to regimes for trade, money, and finance, recognizing that migration is an essential part of international activity. Weintraub (1992) sees Europe heading in this direction as part of the European Community (EC) agreement.

On the other hand, the North American Free Trade Agreement (NAFTA) among the United States, Canada and Mexico made no provision for the free movement of people across borders. The consequences of the end of the Cold War have in fact not yet impacted on the United States significantly enough to require more than modest amendments to its immigration policies in the 1990s. While these amendments favor migration from Europe, they do not indicate significant decrease in the migration from the Caribbean for the rest of this decade. However, increasing anti-immigrant sentiment may yet lead the United States to take measures to close its borders more firmly.

Bibliography

Freeman. Gary P. 1992. "Migration Policy and Politics in the Receiving States." *International Migration Review* 26(4), Winter: 1144–1164.

Gordon, Monica H. 1983. *The Selection of Migrant Categories from the Caribbean to the United States.* New York: Center for Latin American and Caribbean Studies, New York University.

Hollifield, James F. 1992. "Migration and International Relations: Cooperation and Control in the European Community." *International Migration Review* 26(2), Summer: 568–595.

Martin, Philip L. 1992. "Comparative Migration Policies." *International Migration Review* 26(1), Spring: 162–170.

McLean Petras, Elizabeth. 1983. "The Global Labor Market in the Modern World-Economy." Pp. 44–63 in M. Kritz, C.Keely, and S. Tomasi, eds., *Global Trends in Migration*. New York: Center for Migration Studies.

Rystad, Goran. 1992. "Immigration History and the Future of International Migration." *International Migration Review* 26(4), Winter: 1168–1199.

Thompson, Mel. 1990. "Forty-and One Years On: An Overview of Afro-Caribbean Migration to the United Kingdom." Pp. 39–70 in Ransford W. Palmer, ed., *In Search of a Better Life: Perspectives on Migration from the Caribbean*. New York: Praeger.

Weintraub, Sidney. 1992. "North American Free Tree Trade and the European Situation Compared." *International Migration Review* 26(2), Summer: 506–524.

18

Telecommunications Policy in the Caribbean: From Tele-Colonialism to Sustainable Development?

Felipe Noguera

Divestment and Regulation

Just as the agrarian revolution and the succeeding industrial revolution produced epoch-making changes in social formations and modes of production, so too the Information Revolution is producing a profound global transformation today. In the context of post-industrial or information-based society, it is hardly debatable that telecommunications, as the service of services, has become the motor force, the arterial nervous system for the information economy (Willenius and Saunders 1989; Sapolsky, Crane, Neumann, and Noam 1992). The Caribbean has not, as a region, been bypassed by the technological wave of communications and its concomitant products and services. Indeed, the legislation that regulates telecommunications in the English, Spanish, French, and Dutch-speaking Caribbean is now being appropriately redrafted from policies that date back to the early part of this century.

A number of English-speaking Caribbean territories have recently undertaken exercises intended to upgrade and modernize their telecommunications legislation, and one can discern a pattern of deregulation consistent with the divestment and privatization policies embraced by post-colonial Caribbean governments as part of their structural adjustment programs. Lamentably, there seems to be a non-discriminatory approach to adapting these structural adjustment programs: Not only have governments divested state shares in what were formally regarded as telecommunications public utilities, but also they have divested responsibility for regulating the sector in a manner consistent with the public interest and the strategic development trajectory of Caribbean society. Furthermore, foreign private investors are usually loath to accept the phrase "public interest," which they interpret as state interference in their business operations. On the other hand, the experience of countries such as Mexico and Venezuela indicates that foreign capital is much more likely to make a substantial investment in an environment in which criteria and conditions of investment are clearly articulated in advance as public policy than one in which government priorities are unknown or unstated. It is interesting to note that in the United States and the United Kingdom, both considered leaders in free market privatization policies, the (U.S.) Federal Communications Commission (FCC) and the (U.K.) Office of Telecommunications (OFTEL) are the most elaborate and sophisticated regulatory telecommunications authorities that exist today.

What do we conclude from this phenomenon? For competition to serve the economic and social interests of developing countries, an expansive public policy is needed to guide a competent and effective telecommunications regulatory authority. When a public or government monopoly is privatized, an independent government authority is necessary to ensure that certain explicitly-stated corporate policy aims and public policy objectives are articulated and achieved. Failure on the part of the private investor to achieve these objectives might result in penalties being imposed or in the opening up to competition of sectors that were formally the exclusive purview of the telephone monopoly.

There is, however, a disturbing tendency among governments in the developing countries generally, and in the Caribbean in particular, to shy away from confronting the perplexing regulatory issues in telecommunications. This can be attributed to a number of factors. First, there is the proverbial and perennial "brain drain." Like many developing regions, particularly in the 1980s, the Caribbean suffered the structurally and psychologically debilitative consequences of a steady flow of its talented sons and daughters to the industrialized nations. The valuable skilled human resources, often trained at the expense of taxpayers, are lured into leaving the country to work for higher-paying transnational corporations (TNCs), either in the metropole or elsewhere in the service of one of the TNC's subsidiaries. Second, the global character of telecommunications manufacturers and carriers makes small island states highly vulnerable and easily susceptible to the deep pockets and lofty promises of investors and vendors, resulting in a total loss of initiative and creativity by local managers and bureaucrats in the face of "foreign experts." Third, there is a lack of political will, an ostrich-like, head-in-the-sand syndrome, which feeds technophobia and perpetuates the myth of the high-tech "informatics mystique."

This chapter examines the regulatory regimes of several Caribbean countries, assesses the environmental impact of space exploration for telecommunications, analyzes the economic, social, and cultural dimensions of existing telecommunications public policy in the Caribbean (or lack thereof), and projects possibilities for progress beyond the parameters of tele-colonialism.

Regulation as Public Policy

Table 18.1 suggests that privatization is an irreversible trend in the region.[1] Across the English-speaking Caribbean, only the Bahamas Telecommunications Corporation remained a wholly-owned national telephone company in the mid-1990s. In the Spanish-speaking countries, Cuba's telecom company is state-owned, and Mexico (not in table), like Trinidad and Tobago, retains a substantial interest in the sector through the state-owned Telecom de México which has full and exclusive authority over international telecommunications.[2]

Given the dearth of regulatory apparatuses for telecoms in the region and the overwhelming trend toward state divestment, the public policy implications are quite alarming. Critical and strategic policy decisions for the development of the Caribbean telecom sector are being made in London (by Cable & Wireless), France (by France Telecom), Spain (by Telefónica de España), Holland (by Dutch PTT), and the United States (by Atlantic Telenetwork and AT&T). Because of interlocking corporate directorates, even when governments like that of Trinidad and Tobago retain majority shares, the lack of access to global telecom data and a clear policy framework means that these nations are at a severe disadvantage when they sit at the negotiating table. They have neither the knowledge (that is, information and expertise) nor the infrastructural mechanisms and mandate to effectively broker their strategic interests vis-à-vis global competitors. Of course, to say that there is no public policy for telecommunications in the Caribbean would not be entirely correct. Simply because a policy is not written or articulated as a set of regulations does not mean that one does not exist. But the existence or non-existence of clearly-defined rules and regulations, beyond licensing, is a policy condition that reinforces the status quo, whether or not this is the intention.

Embrace of the ideology of privatization of telecoms by Caribbean governments resembles much less a case of prudent exercise of policy options than a neo-liberal, pseudo-religious crusade in which privatization or the replacement of government monopoly by foreign private monopoly is touted as the only option. Once structural adjustment programs became fashionable, few governments in the region were able to resist their

Table 18.1 Structure of Telecommunications Companies in the Caribbean

Country	Company	Sector of Operation		Governmental Participation in Shares	Foreign Company's Name	Foreign Company's Nationality	Sector of Operation	
		National	International				National	International
Antigua/Barbuda	A.P.U.A.	✓	—	100%	C&W	UK	—	✓
Aruba	Setar	✓	✓	100%	—	—	—	—
Bahamas	Batelco	✓	✓	100%	—	—	—	—
Barbados	Bartelco	✓	✓	35%	C&W	UK	✓	✓
Belize	B.T.L.	✓	✓	51%	Brt. Telecom	UK	✓	✓
Curaçao	Setel	✓	—	100%	Lands Radio	Neth. Antilles	—	✓
Cuba	Telco	✓	✓	100%	—	—	—	—
Dominican Republic	Codetel	—	—	—	GTE	USA	✓	✓
Grenada	Grentel	✓	✓	30%	C&W	UK	✓	✓
Guyana	Guytelco	✓	✓	20%	Atlantic Net	USA	✓	✓
Guadeloupe/Martinique	DGT	✓	✓	100%	Fr. Telecom	France	—	✓
Haiti	Telco	✓	✓	100%	—	—	—	—
Jamaica	T.O.J.	✓	✓	20%	C&W	UK	✓	✓
Puerto Rico	P.R.T.C.	✓	✓	100%	—	—	—	—
Montserrat	Telco	—	—	—	C&W	UK	✓	✓
St. Vincent & Grenadines	Telcos	—	—	—	C&W	UK	✓	✓
St. Kitts/St. Lucia	Skantel	—	—	—	C&W	UK	✓	✓
Suriname	Telesur	✓	✓	100%	—	—	✓	—
Trinidad & Tobago	T.S.T.T.	✓	✓	51%	C&W	UK	✓	✓
U.S. Virgin Islands	U.S. Vitelco	—	—	—	Atlantic Net	USA	✓	✓

Source: Caribbean Association of National Telecommunications Organizations (CANTO), Library Education Resource Center (CLERC), Port-of-Spain, Trinidad, 1991.

appeal. Decisions to privatize, taken by cabinets of Caribbean governments counter to the wishes of large segments of the electorate, were enthusiastically supported by foreign consultants, who helped to rationalize the selection of investors.

Many arguments were advanced, including the promise of competition and its virtues, as the basis to underscore state divestment of telecom interests. Another aspect of the impact of exogenous and international variables on national and regional decision-making with respect to privatization, was the desire for foreign investment and access to state-of-the-art technology. In particular, Barbados, Belize, Curaçao, Bahamas, Puerto Rico, Jamaica, Guyana, Trinidad and Tobago, and Grenada either made the decision or are likely (in the mid-1990s) to make the decision to divest state shares in telecoms based in part on foreign investment and access to technology criteria. The belief was widespread that rapid changes in technology would result from privatization, and there was a felt need to "catch up" with international trends and forecast demand for competitive services.

These are understandable motivating factors. If the region does not remain abreast of innovations in telecom technology, the implications for its dependence are staggering. Investment in the switch and data networks, along with value-added or enhanced services for data and mobile telephony, could act as a stimulus for further development of basic services. This prospect was far more decisive than a modern regulatory policy or telecom legislation in influencing the decision and timing of privatization of Caribbean telecommunications.

Prior to 1985, when the general trend toward privatization began in response to the international patterns observed in the breakup of AT&T in the United States and British Telecom in the United Kingdom, external telecommunications were already privately owned in Antigua and Barbuda, as were both internal and external telecommunications in Dominica, the Dominican Republic, Saint Lucia, St. Kitts/Nevis, Montserrat, and St. Vincent and the Grenadines. Plans forecasting the capability of offering a wide array of services resulting from the digitalization of Caribbean networks had already been undertaken by most Caribbean telephone companies and telecommunication organizations prior to the advent of privatization and the introduction of large-scale foreign investment in regional telecommunications systems.

This is important in conveying a realistic picture of the evolving scenario of Caribbean telecommunications. While it is true that such services as fixed and mobile cellular telephony or packet switching have come "on stream" as customer service offerings since the privatization of some of the Caribbean telecommunications, investment in the basic digital infrastructure (that is, switching and transmission) had already been made by many Caribbean states. A glimpse at Table 18.2 indicates that in terms of tele-densities, the Caribbean compares favorably with other developing regions and even many developed nations. Africa, for example, has less than one telephone per hundred population, or fewer telephones than the city of Paris.

Table 18.2 also reveals the wide disparities among Caribbean states in population size, total number of telephone lines, and tele-densities. With the exception of Guadeloupe (a department of France), there is generally a proportional relationship between population size and total number of lines. But it should be noted that telephone density is becoming less important as an indicator of economic development than telephone *accessibility*. In a Caribbean country like Barbados, whose economy is based on tourism, the telephone density or penetration rate may be 30 percent or 30 telephones per 100 population. But this statistic does not explain how widely telephone services are diffused or how available telephones are to the public, whether they are located in urban or rural areas, how they are maintained, and other important indicators. Greater statistical detail is especially important when one considers that there is a high concentration of telephones in hotels to service foreign tourist subscribers whereas phone service may not be widely available or accessible to low-income or sparsely populated communities. Thus indices such as telephone accessibility are more helpful in assessing issues of economic development and "social justice." Whereas tele-density is measured by a per capita index that reflects the absolute number of telephone lines per 100 population, regardless of how these telephone lines are distributed across the population, tele-accessibility deals with demographic, geographic, and economic factors. For example, whereas the tele-densities would not indicate how telephones are distributed along class and geographic lines, tele-accessibility addresses telephone penetration to economically marginal and rural areas. Further, tele-accessibility deals with the issue of maintenance of infrastructure, central office, transmission systems, outside plant, and subscriber terminal equipment. As many in the Caribbean have lamented, it does no good to have a telephone that does not work. In sum, measures of tele-accessibility are highly useful in evaluating the success of public policy in the telecommunications sector.

In privatizing their telecoms, Caribbean governments have generally taken steps during the negotiation process to ensure that management control of the carrier remains in local hands. Belize, Jamaica, and Puerto Rico exemplify this approach. In Trinidad and Tobago, on the other hand, management has been conceded to new owners, even when they are not majority shareholders. In still other cases, for example in Grenada, Guyana, and Venezuela, executives both at the level of the board of directors and line management have been appointed by new majority shareholders.

Table 18.2 Tele-Profiles of Caribbean States

Country	Population	Total No. Main Lines	Telephones Per 100 Population	Total No. of PABIs[a]	Total Public Phones
Antigua and Barbuda	70,000	10,870	15.5	91	108
Bahamas	254,685	65,009	25.5	316	573
Barbados	250,000	76,478	30.6	240	365
Belize	160,000	21,320	13.3	98	35
Bermuda	57,784	37,142	64.3	229	704
Curaçao	171,000	42,116	24.6	316	235
Dominican Republic	6,500,000	442,521	6.8	801	2,655
Grenada	90,000	13,634	15.1	43	139
Guadeloupe	330,000	119,445	36.2	1,765	622
Haiti	6,000,000	45,000	0.8	141	42
Jamaica	2,360,000	8,348	3.7	1,004	1,006
Puerto Rico	3,254,000	815,898	25.1	19,530	15,997
Suriname	400,000	36,714	9.2	731	175
Trinidad and Tobago	1,234,388	216,040	17.5	5,586	699
U.S. Virgin Islands	112,000	46,769	41.8	1,136	615
Total/Average	21,243,857	2,077,304	9.77	32,027	23,940

[a]Publicly accessible branch interchanges.
Source: Information from CANTO Library Education Resource Center (CLERC). Port-of-Spain, Trinidad, 1991.

In all cases, regulation is now being recognized as a vital component of public policy, although such regulation is still not in place in many countries (notably, Antigua and Barbuda, Belize, Cuba, Dominican Republic, Grenada, Jamaica, and Trinidad and Tobago). Whether monopoly protection will persist in the privatized environment, to what extent and in which markets competition will be allowed, which technical standards are being adopted, which licenses are being granted, what rates are being charged by the carrier for what services, what penalties are imposed for which infractions, what rate of return is allowable by the private investor as distinct from that previously enjoyed by the state monopoly, and how the frequencies of the electromagnetic spectrum are to be apportioned— all these are urgent and important questions begging for the attention and response of competent government regulators of telecommunications in the Caribbean as we approach the twenty-first century.

Regional Initiatives

In the aftermath of extensive privatizations in the region, it is important to note that efforts have been underway in the Caribbean to articulate public policy objectives and influence policy-makers in a manner that can lead to the identification and defense of a public interest in regional telecoms. Among those agencies that have influenced the telecommunications policy process are: the regional office of the International Telecommunications Union (ITU), the Institute of Mass Communications (CARIMAC) at the University of the West Indies in Jamaica, the Caribbean Telecommunications Union (CTU) based in Trinidad, the Caribbean Association of National Telecommunications Organizations (CANTO) which is a 33-member non-governmental organization headquartered in Trinidad, the Caribbean Broadcasting Union (CBU), and Caribbean News Agency (CANA). These agencies have had an input by way of the public airing of issues once considered arcane and esoteric, through lobbying in Caribbean and international fora, and through various technical initiatives. But notwithstanding the attempts of all these organizations, individuals, and groups functioning in various niches of regional communications to fill the public policy void, there remain key areas that require the active attention and formal public policy of regional governments.

A recent development in the region is the implementation of bypass network inter-connection by unlicensed international carriers operating nationally, as well as international call back services, resulting in up to 75 percent reductions in overseas telephone billings of subscribers. Licensed carriers complain that the operations of these carriers are having deleterious effects on their revenues and, consequently, their networks.

Competent government regulatory authorities at both national and regional levels will have to intervene to provide clear rules for participation or competition as determined by public policy objectives. If not, then both legal and technological deterrents to unauthorized access to the Public Switched Telephone Network (PSTN) will need to be devised and enforced.

The impact of telecom development on the environment is another area that requires public policy attention. Scientists have shown a correlation between high voltage electrical wires in residential areas and leukemia among children. Is such a trend possible with a proliferation of microwave signals in heavily populated areas? To what extent can copper and fiber optic cable be recycled to avoid waste and environmental pollution? With environmental sensitivity and sustainable development assuming a higher priority on the agenda of global policy-makers, it is only natural that this concern in the field of telecoms and broadcasting should be placed on the agenda of the regional governments.

The technological convergence of telecommunications, computers, and broadcasting referred to now as the "multimedia wave" is occurring simultaneously with mega-mergers of telecom suppliers and carriers, software and hardware manufacturers, and video and film broadcasting and production houses. The gargantuan deals between Bell Atlantic and Telecommunications Incorporated (TCI), Viacom or QVC (Quality Value and Convenience Network) and Paramount, U.S. West and Time-Warner, Bell Atlantic and the Mexican cellular giant IUSA-CELL, are already legendary in the history of international business. In this context, how does the Caribbean defend its interests and best prepare itself to deal and negotiate with these global multimedia power brokers?

Fortunately, certain democratic principles such as "one country, one vote" still apply in the ITU as in the United Nations. For example, at the World Administrative Radio Conference (WARC), convened in Málaga, Spain, in January to February 1992, developing countries were able to establish a formidable coalition because the electromagnetic spectrum is considered, like the sea, to be part of the common heritage and patrimony of humankind. Regardless of the level of technological development or economic and financial resources of a nation, each country has the right to exploit, or lease, or leave idle this limited but renewable resource. At the WARC conference, developing countries were able to exploit differences among industrialized nations to their advantage and secure access to frequencies for digital radio, an appropriate technology for many developing countries. This augers well for multilateral cooperation in North-South negotiations and can teach the Caribbean a great deal.

Concluding Suggestions

An important focus of the region's public policy should be the area of international calling rates. The CARICOM region has put much emphasis on possible comparative advantages and economies of scope and scale which the Caribbean could realize as a result of strategically strengthening the region's bargaining position in trade in services. But where resolve has been lacking, not only within CARICOM but also within individual Caribbean governments, has been in the enormously lucrative but little known and therefore highly mysterious realm of international call accounting rates.

Studies by the ITU and World Bank have shown conclusively that contemporary social, economic, and cultural development is contingent upon a consistently modernizing telecommunications network (see, for example, Willenius and Sanders 1989). Where, however, both the World Bank and ITU as well as governments have been conspicuously silent has been on the issue of the specific, tremendous contribution of international call accounting rates to the revenues of developing countries. The accounting rate is the settlement payment agreed to bilaterally by correspondent telecom carriers. In the case of existing agreements between U.S. and Caribbean carriers, because Caribbean subscribers are called overwhelmingly more by U.S. subscribers than vice versa, the U.S. carriers make significant outpayments to the local carriers and other foreign correspondents. AT&T's submissions to the U.S. FCC suggest that these outpayments contribute approximately $3 billion dollars per year to the U.S. trade deficit (United States 1994).

AT&T has declined, however, to provide the FCC with information about the impact of its Country Direct (800 #) and other U.S.-billed, foreign-based calling services on the U.S. telecom services balance of payments deficit. Apart from a few highly specialized technocrats in the employ of carriers such as AT&T and Cable and Wireless, Caribbean telecom regulators, ministries of finance, and certainly the public are totally oblivious to the financial stakes and economic implications of international call accounting rates as regards public policy. This is a dimension of the telecom public policy debate in the region that is being ignored to the strategic disadvantage and peril of Caribbean economies. Just as the giant AT&T can seek regulatory redress and intervention from the FCC to pressure developing countries to lower their accounting rates (that is, AT&T's outpayments) with U.S. carriers, so too governments of the Caribbean region must intervene to safeguard their strategic economic interests. The problem is that private foreign carriers with monopoly franchises in the Caribbean have already shown themselves willing to take actions that make Caribbean countries vulnerable, by virtue of their ignorance and apparent powerlessness in this issue, and that sacrifice Caribbean interests in exchange for strategic quid pro quo advantages for these carriers' investments elsewhere in the world.[3]

Another important issue demanding public policy attention is that of telecommuniations education. Apart from the electronic engineering faculty and the Caribbean Institute of Mass Communications at the University of the West Indies, there is an alarming dearth of training or educational opportunities in this vital sector. This is particularly so in the areas of strategic and financial planning, management, software development, and telecom technology development policy. CANTO has filled the gap by offering a few well-attended public training courses, but this training is outside of CANTO's mandate or core business activity. While the Caribbean is not unique in omitting this crucial dimension from the educational curriculum (even Harvard University offers no telecom courses), among the numerous pressing social issues of telecom that need to be seriously addressed from a public policy perspective, no void is more dangerous for society's future than the one that exists in the pedagogical or educational sphere.

While there is still a prevailing tendency of policy-makers and planners to operate within sectoral confines, this treatment of telecommunications is not conducive to sustainable development. Telecoms are comprehensive, multifaceted systems comprising elements that represent essential public infrastructure, vital links among various markets for goods, services, and finance, safety structures for social needs and national security requirements, and the conduits for the preservation and projection or eradication and dissolution of indigenous Caribbean culture.

It may be true that with the dissolution of the East-West schism, the North-South dichotomy in relation to "development" is also fading. Nevertheless, telecommunications has to be a focal point of public policy in order to ensure that it is a means of facilitating south to south cooperation and exchange, and south to north export of cultural material and entertainment. Negligence by Caribbean policy-makers of this key application of telecoms will result in a deepening dependence and underdevelopment associated with tele-colonial domination by metropolitan telecom carriers and suppliers, and with the debilitating and pernicious psychological and spiritual impact of cultural (electronic) imperialism. Conversely, careful, strategic deployment of telecoms to bolster and support local production of Caribbean cultural and entertainment programs can help to create an authentic and equitable Caribbean role in the global village.

Notes

1. In the 1960s, Continental Telephones and Cable and Wireless owned the telephone companies throughout the English-speaking Caribbean, with the exceptions of Guyana and the Bahamas. This period was followed by a trend of na-

tionalization of the economies' "commanding heights" (including telecommunications), largely in response to demands for reform emanating from militant trade
unions. The unions were supported by a very vocal "Black Power" movement
that agitated for increased "Caribbeanization" of the regional economy.

2. Telmex, the national telephone company of Mexico, was privatized in 1990.
Southwestern Bell of the United States, France Telecom, and a group of Mexican
private investors formed the consortium that won the investment bid for Telmex.
In Trinidad and Tobago, the government sold 4 percent of the shares in the Telephone Company in 1991 to Cable and Wireless, retaining 51 percent of the shares
itself. Haiti, Guadeloupe, Martinique, and French Guiana all have state-owned
telecom entities. While Curaçao and the other Netherlands Antilles (but not
Aruba) are considering privatization options with the Dutch PTT being the best-
placed candidate to acquire shares, Suriname is the only independent Dutch-
speaking territory that continues to articulate as public policy a position that has
not yet embraced privatization of telecoms.

3. When CANTO was negotiating with the FCC on behalf of its members,
Cable and Wireless' London office worried intensively that attention to the
Caribbean by the FCC might adversely affect the company's efforts to compete in
the U.S. market.

Bibliography

Blatherwick, David E.S. 1987. *The International Politics of Telecommunications*.
Berkeley, Calif.: Institute of International Studies, University of California,
Berkeley.

Duch, Raymond M. 1991. *Privatizing the Economy: Telecommunications Policy in
Comparative Perspective*. Ann Arbor: University of Michigan Press.

Hobday, Michael. 1990. *Telecommunications in Developing Countries*. New York:
Routledge.

Sapolsky, H. M., R. J. Crane, W. R. Newmann and E. M. Noam. 1992. *The Telecommunications Revolution: Past, Present and Future*. New York: Routledge.

United States Congress. Committee on Energy and Commerce. 1990. *Globalization
of the Media*. Washington: U.S. Government Printing Office.

United States Department of Commerce. 1986. *Caribbean Telecommunications Infrastructure Development Project*. Washington D.C.: National Telecommunications
and Information Administration. Caribbean Basin Division.

United States. Federal Communications Commission. 1994. *AT&T Accounting
Rate Progress Report*. CC Docket No. 90-337 (Phase II). January 6.

Wenders, John T. 1987. *The Economics of Telecommunications: Theory and Policy*.
Cambridge, Mass.: Ballinger.

Willenius, Bjorn and Robert J. Saunders. 1989. *Telecommunications and Economic
Development*. Washington D.C.: World Bank.

19

Telecommunications Policy: Philosophical Issues, Creative Prescriptions

Ewart Skinner

The Problem

Three structural problematiques characterize the discussion of the state of telecommunications policy in the Caribbean: (1) a psychological problematique, that is, political lethargy, lack of will, and technophobia; (2) a demographic problematique, or a loss of development talent via the brain drain; and (3) a world-system problematique, expressed in terms of the asymmetrical relationship between global telecom actors and local business and political actors. In this chapter, some comments are made about the implications of these problematiques, and these are accompanied by some suggestions for the adoption of creative strategies in the enhancement of policy in the telecom sector.

Policy Issues and Theory

The general endorsement of regional initiatives in the Caribbean as the appropriate strategy for the telecom sector and the uncritical acceptance of the principle of privatization raise the issue of how emergent policy will address competing state, regional, and multinational corporate interests. In the last chapter, Felipe Noguera offered what can be read simultaneously as critique of and apology for strong localized regulation, elite design of the telecommunications future, and an "industrialization by invitation" approach to multinational business dealings. It is difficult, however, to distinguish this policy as a philosophy of regulation from the actual regulation as process in praxis.

Numerous relevant questions can be raised but not immediately answered: Who benefits from the lack of a Caribbean telecoms policy? What does "competition" mean in the Caribbean environment? Which Caribbean entities enjoy, or may come to enjoy, that status (as competitors)? How can competition serve the interests of the host nations? Is the psychological issue a structural one, or is government inaction merely a "straw man" that masks a stiffer critique of Caribbean politics? Which socio-economic and cultural groups within nations stand to benefit and which stand to lose as the new system emerges? How does the fact that some Caribbean nations have already begun to modernize affect the ordinary citizen? Where will the space for dissent and public empowerment be created within the system? Which impacting exogenous, international variables can be intercepted and diverted by indigenous policy? What areas of development would be enhanced by investment in the telecommunications future? How effective or independently constructed can monopoly protection and attendant indigenous prerogatives be if the regional tie-in to international systems is already a *fait accompli?*

From a theoretical perspective, the classic agency-structure dialectic brings an informative tension to the analysis. It suggests, perhaps unwittingly, the relevance to telecommunications development of the general sociology of the 1980s and 1990s dealing with micro and macro integration and agency-structure integration. However, theoretical perspectives tell us little about the underlying issue which centers on the ability of local actors to make their telecom systems effective instruments of positive change.

A central and unresolved theme in Caribbean sociology has been Caribbean consciousness and its representation in regional institutions (Manley 1975; Nettleford 1978). The telecommunications institutions, as systems of imaging and meaning, of information and formation, embody the twenty-first century challenge to culture, that is to say, "identity," in that they impact equally on leisure as on labor, on our symbolic world of games and play and on our pragmatic world of jobs and work; hence the seriousness of the implicit observation that policy must represent a liberating consciousness (agency, as it were) through its influence on information systems and the regulatory apparatus that organically represents them. The difficulty is that both "identity" and "institution" in the Caribbean are represented by real histories and real people who constitute and have been constituted by the impact of imperialism and colonialism. Thus they are constrained by the frameworks inherited from those histories. In structural terms, those histories have bequeathed to the region a legacy of political fragmentation and economic uniformity (Payne and Sutton 1993: 4) which in very specific and selected areas constrain individual agency and institutional flexibility. The prescriptions of the World Bank and International Monetary Fund serve as examples.

Caribbean states have sought in recent years to invert fragmentation in politics and uniformity in economics by engendering political solidarity—with all that implies for the psychology of the region—and enhancing economic diversity—with all that implies for regional political-economic cooperation. From a communications policy perspective two models of development have been available. During the 1950s and 1960s metropolitan theorists linked characteristics of the person to the characteristics of the media institutions. They then ascribed transformative attributes to media institutions via the affective "consciousness" they would engender. Middle-range theories such as Lerner's (1958) subsequently fueled the drive evident in most post-colonial, postwar societies to put faith in traditional communication media as catalysts for development. The vehicle of this promise today, according to the prevailing orthodoxy, is the telecommunication industry, privatized, regionalized, and well regulated. Its inspiration stems from the work of Ithiel de Sola Pool (1977) and others working in Egypt in the 1970s, and from subsequent World Bank studies in Kenya and other places. Agency/structure problematiques appear in both models at the expense of cultural and historical depth.

Telecommunications policy falls directly into the larger province of "development" and is, in fact, socio-economic policy. It can be explained by analysis of one basic question: telecommunications for whom, by whom? This questions underlies all fundamental policy and regulatory issues of the 1990s. Its relevance becomes clear when one reviews the "forgotten genealogy" of the information revolution and its impact upon Caribbean communication. That revolution was never meant for general Caribbean development. Its impact has been selective, unequal, and uneven, according to Cuban historian Moreno Fraginals, one of the few and first Caribbeanists to provide an analysis of information and telegraph networks in the configuration of a local economy (see Mattelart 1985: 42). Thus the structural problematics identified in the last chapter could be usefully informed by a review of cultural, developmental, and historical events.

Opportunities and Challenges

From a technological/economic perspective, one might ask: Given the Caribbean's current status in the global marketplace, why (and how) has the region been specifically selected for incorporation in the international telecommunication economy? Does incorporation represent a new opportunity? If so, what are the advantages and disadvantages for the

overall Caribbean political economy? Superficially at least, there appear
to be opportunities for employment in offshore activities, banking, insurance, data processing, and other areas. The potential for civic empowerment, democratization, and emancipation is less frequently promoted. Does the ordinary Caribbean citizen, either as potential investor
or consumer, truly understand the important ramifications of cable? The
assumption is that privatization itself is liberating and therefore constitutes emancipation. Nothing can be further from the truth. Ostensible
employment opportunities in telecommunications often hide pernicious
structural relationships. Like the older "industrialization by invitation,"
it may in the long term deliver neither the economic payoffs so desper-
ately needed by the Caribbean people nor any but the most narrow
gauges of civic empowerment.

It is therefore incumbent on those with discretionary power to ensure
that Caribbean people are not mystified accomplices to their subordinate
incorporation in the global tele-economy. Micro-processing and comput-
ing technology do not represent new forces recently unleashed on an unprepared society. Rather, they are merely the most recent instalment in
the continuing development of the "control revolution" (Hepworth 1990:
9). They represent simply another phase of dependent incorporation
which allows only the narrowest range of discretion in policy matters.

The Caribbean experience specifically demonstrates that the region is
no stranger to machinations of the telecommunications control revolution. Regional leadership has had a long enough time in which to incorporate structural change in the telecommunications industry. Quintes-
sentially and characteristically colonial, those systems were reified
(questionably so) until very recently. They simply reproduced ethnic and
socio-economic patterns of dominance. Over 125 years ago, the introduction of telecommunications to the Caribbean coincided with significant
readjustments in Caribbean labor, the start of Caribbean out-migration,
and the first program of proposals for a West Indian federation. Yet
telecommunication systems as tools of development never effectively in-
terfaced with ordinary Caribbean life. To Europe, Caribbean life represented labor, telecommunications, and technologies of management and
control. Today, as the oldest "industrial" colonies of Europe outside of
Europe (Lewis 1983: 4), Caribbean labor is still fitted to metropolitan
needs. Therefore telecom policy as both policy and philosophy must be
distinguished from regulation in the sense of rules of management because the industry carries enormous structural potential but significant
structural inequalities as well. Policy-makers must beware the temptation
of putting new wine into old bottles.

How much leeway telecom organizations have in making policy is another issue of significance. Telecom institutions are constrained by their

limited portfolios, and non-governmental organizations cannot dictate national policy. Any critique of telecommunications policy must therefore also be a critique of governmental philosophy. It may be that it is already determined that telecom administrators will be putting new telecom policy into old Caribbean socio-economic structures since the responsibility for comprehensive restructuring lies securely still at the national level of government policy.

Success will be determined only by how well disposed and willing states are to adapt state ideology to pressures arising from the international telecom movement, how seriously they listen to their intelligentsia (as social science theorists), and how effectively they engage the actual industrial communities in the praxis of localized work. The appeals by one Caribbean government to "Caribbean scholars to volunteer their summers and sabbaticals" (Brotherson 1993: 20), the focus of New World/post-New World political economists on telecommunications and labor, and the effort by the Caribbean Association of National Telecommunication Organizations (CANTO) and associated NGOs to link national and regional initiatives, all are movements in the right direction. Only through full integration at these levels can the region achieve a stronger position within the global economy. Effective integration would involve perhaps cooperative analysis of the impact of offshore data services—data processing, banking, insurance, and so on—on the Caribbean citizen.

Effective involvement in the international environment is affected not only by the level of training provided in telecommunications but also by the flight of talent from the Caribbean. Failure to effect the first may be seen as a lost opportunity in cultural capital formation; failure to effect the second can result in a flight of capital. In either case a determination of what constitutes Caribbean resources or capital has to be made at some level. Sensitivity to the insights of Caribbean scholarship, regardless of its point of origin, could put a different spin on how we look at these issues. Is it not possible, for example, to see the "brain drain" as a dispersal of capital rather than a flight of capital? According to Trinidadian anthropologist Christine Ho, Caribbean immigrants could be seen as forming a cultural matrix, a Caribbean extension through "international linkages in the form of transnational social networks" (Ho 1991: 175). She implies that we fail to make these favorable distinctions because of the "dualist" way we think about science. Ho calls for a critical reappraisal of analytical frameworks in the social sciences, one that would replace the "dichotomous distinctions of brain drain resources with a concept of interdependence that does more justice to the empirical realities of the West Indian migration patterns" (p. 175). Extending the assessment, it is perfectly acceptable to look at the problem of telephone accounting rates (personal and business calls back to the Caribbean, a deficit in the U.S. view) as repatriation of capital, driven by a cultural imperative, rather than merely a statistic of interest to the Federal Communications Commission (FCC), AT&T, or regional telephone companies.

The problem of asymmetry among states in the international community is yet another basic structural issue related to the new telecom global economy. Caribbean efforts to negotiate with multinationals and catch up technologically with the developed nations are driven by a momentum that comes, not from the Caribbean, but from outside forces. Foreign investors believe that:

> The requirements for foreign capital will drive an ongoing phenomenon much like that seen in Asia-Pacific, with services and equipment vendors from the developed world vying to create strategic alliances with strong in-country partners. The relentless process of privatization, deregulation and liberalization should eliminate all but the most arcane—and unimportant—barriers to doing business in the region (Chase 1994: 38).

Thus the power, scope, drive, purpose, indeed the hegemony of multinational firms in alliance with their home governments demonstrate the futility of economic and technological parity. For example, the FCC initiatives that have allowed Bill Gates and Craig McCaw to "create a global information network with a ring of 840 [low earth orbit] satellites" by the year 2001—note that three geosynchronous orbital satellites of a certain size and power are sufficient to cover the globe—will set the pace for the twenty-first century ("Telemedia Watch" in *Broadcasting and Cable* 1994: 18). Is it reasonable to assume that Caribbean states can be equal competitors in this environment? Quite clearly, compared with multinational corporate budgets, Caribbean capital is primarily geographic and cultural, broadly defined. Although touted as "the most digitalized region" in the world (according to an eight-variable index of technological development), Latin America and the Caribbean have not achieved an internationally competitive level of computerization (Mattelart 1985: p. 69). Indeed the index could be taken as a measure of potential effectiveness in negotiating in the global economy.

Some Suggestions

What, then, are the options of the telecommunications policy-maker in this global tele-economy? It is clear that the policy-maker must be prepared to treat with the psychological effects of colonialism by: (1) bringing history back into analysis of technology; (2) developing new ways of approaching regional consciousness and defining national spaces within it; (3) finding common ground with regional social scientists, including development of programs for scholarship on the socio-cultural and economic implications of these technologies; (4) initiating programs to bring hands-on telecom network (e-mail, for instance) experience to the ordinary citizen; (5) exploring and publicizing the implications of all aspects of privatization to Caribbean publics; and (6) developing strategies for wide dissemination of information about new information technologies and their implications for Caribbean citizens.

In the end, Caribbean success in the mission of political solidarity and economic diversity depends on how comprehensively the impact of telecommunication on society is understood by all members of society, and how well the Caribbean community achieves what may be called, for lack of a better term, a *post-metropolitan imagination,* by which is meant a radical reformulation of Caribbean relationships vis-à-vis the metropolis. It is an imagination that drives the community itself to *define its own terms of work* within the world of work or the New International Division of Labor (NIDL). It would be an "imagination" that would anticipate rather than follow metropolitan thought and material progress in telecommunications; an imagination lodged in the history and cultural geography of the region. This is not a novel observation. It issues directly from the English-speaking Caribbean's "New World" movement of the 1960s, in which "development" itself was perceived as equivalent to just such an "imagination" (Best 1967). This challenge is not unique to developing nations. Internationalization of telecommunication technology changes the implications for all actors in the global marketplace, including the industrial countries. In fact, success in the NIDL and in the rapid globalization and internationalization of work and services driven by "digital telecommunication highways" demands at least some new "imagination" of self and community by all such players.

For Caribbean planners, this "new imagination" might involve promoting relationships via telecommunication technologies. Thus for example, a fishing proprietor in Trinidad could close a sale of a tuna catch to a European buyer while her boat was still at sea; a farmer in Saint Lucia could get up-to-the-minute information on market prices and conditions from agents in Belize; students in Grenada could engage in teleconferences with counterparts in Jamaica; Dominica's Caribs could link up via a post office "communications center" to a world symposium on "Caribbean and Third World Indigenous Peoples" being held in the United States or the Dominican Republic; children in Barbados could discuss scientific research papers with their Puerto Rican counterparts using e-mail; and physicians in Jamaica could conduct complex medical operations with colleagues from Venezuela using tele-medical technology. The task here is for Caribbean governments to reconsider the role of the old post offices and other such agencies. In this "new imagination," these facilities would be refurbished and re-designed as "communications centers" or "communication network facilities" hooked into the information super-highway as well as to local schools and civic institutions. Significant benefits could be derived from such investments. And so, in answer to the question of how can communications policy lead to "people empowerment," the reply can be given: It can do so when ordinary people are the users of this technology.

Conclusion

The perspective followed here is simply a reflection on some of the important issues involved in telecommunications today. It has attempted a reflection on these issues with attention given to various discourses of social science theory, history, and political economy. Indeed, it is hard to deny or resist globalization and privatization trends, and the attendant structural determinants that impact and structure telecommunications policy. Hopefully, this perspective provides a parallel framework that can push analyses of telecommunication policy-making to a critique of more theoretical consequence. It is not meant to proscribe options but to lead to creative prescriptions for new, imaginative, emancipatory ones.

Bibliography

Best, L. 1967. "Independent Thought and Caribbean Freedom." *New World Quarterly* 3(4): 22–23.

Brotherson, Festus. 1993. "Caribbean Scholars Needed in Guyana." *Caribbean Studies Newsletter* 20(4), Fall: 20.

Chase, S. 1994. "Private Networks in Latin America: Building Steam for the Satellite Solution." *Via Satellite* 11(3), March: 38.

Hepworth, M. 1990. Geography *of the Information Economy.* New York: The Guilford Press.

Ho, C. 1991. Salt *Water Trinnies: Afro-Trinidadian Immigrant Networks and Non-Assimilation in Los Angeles.* New York: AMS Press.

Lerner, Daniel. 1958. The *Passing of Traditional Society: Modernizing the Middle East.* Glencoe, Ill.: Free Press.

Lewis, G. 1983. Main *Currents in Caribbean Thought: The Historical Evolution of Caribbean Society in its Ideological Aspects, 1492–1900.* Kingston, Jamaica: Heinemann Educational Books (Caribbean) Ltd.

Manley, M. 1975. The *Politics of Change: A Jamaican Testament.* Washington D.C.: André Deutsch. Howard University Press.

Mattelart, A. and H. Schmucler. 1985. *Communication and Information Technologies: Freedom of Choice for Latin America.* Norwood, N.J.: Ablex Publishing Corporation.

Nettleford, R. 1978. Caribbean *Cultural Identity: The Case of Jamaica.* Kingston: Institute of Jamaica.

Payne, A. and Paul Sutton, eds. 1993. *Modern Caribbean Politics.* Baltimore: The Johns Hopkins University Press.

Pool, Ithiel de Sola. 1977. The *Social Impact of the Telephone.* Cambridge, MA: MIT Press.

"Telemedia." 1994. *Broadcasting and Cable* 124(13), March.

20

Environmental Policy: Changing Patterns of Coastal Eco-Development

Alfredo César Dachary and Stella Maris Arnaíz Burne
(translated by J. Braveboy-Wagner)

The Fragility of the Natural Environment

In the last unstable decades of this century, global society is being confronted with profound changes stemming from the new technological revolution and the intensive use of the planet's natural resources. As a result, societies have had to face up to the fragility of mankind's relationship to nature. Major changes have reduced global distances, and the revolution in communications and transportation now allows for the expansion of influence to even the most isolated zones, those regions where a balanced relationship between humans and the environment still exists.

The process of expansion of the borders of the capitalist world-system informs this chapter's reflections on the socio-economic changes that are occurring along the coast of the continental western Caribbean. Historic changes have occurred in land use in this zone, generating problems that are also being experienced in varying degree in other areas of the Caribbean. Appropriate policy changes need to be made by the governments of the region to ensure the preservation of the region's fragile ecological environments.

Geographical Scope

Since geopolitics does not always coincide with physical geography, the first task is to determine the study universe, in this case a large band of more than seven hundred kilometers of beaches (four hundred if measured in linear form) that begins in the north of the Yucatan Channel and ends in Ambergris in the south see Figure 20.1). Key Ambergris is included because it is geographically a part of the region, though separated artificially by human action. Ambergris is not in fact a key (or cay), but the continuation of the south coast of the Peninsula of Yucatan. In the middle of the nineteenth century a group of fishermen, exiled as a result of the tribal wars, built a little channel to unite Ambergris with Chetumal Bay and named it Bacalar Chico (Rebolledo 1946). When the English, who were perfectly familiar with the coasts of the region through their studies and through the already classic coastal surveys made by the French at the beginning of the nineteenth century, decided to sign the Spencer-Mariscal Boundary Treaty (1893), they transformed the fishermen's work into a geographical accident that became Ambergris Island, thus breaking the continuity of the coast. Because of this, Mexico lost its outlet to the sea in the south (César Dachary and Arnaíz Burne 1993b). Thus the entire continental coast of the Mexican Caribbean, including Ambergris, shares the same coastal ecosystem.

According to Yañez Arancibia, the coastal zone, including marshes, lagoons, estuaries, connecting mouths, and the continental platform immediately adjacent, is a wide space where the sea, the earth, the atmosphere, and the epicontinental waters interact (Yañez Arancibia 1986). This complex coastal ecosystem does not have functional and finite frontiers and its characteristics are frequently influenced by factors external to the system. This is so in the case of the Mexican Caribbean coast, a young coastal system. The main geo-biomorphological characteristics of the land and sea zone of this system are as follows:

The land zone, from the continent to the sea, includes: (a) berms that cordon off the old coastlines; (b) a fossil lagoon, a depression flooded most of the year, where mangroves dominate; and (c) a sandy bar, part of the coastline, an area of population settlement that varies in width from 100 to 300 meters along most of the Mexican Caribbean coast (Ibarra and Dávalos 1991).

The marine zone comprises the marine territory from the sandy bar to the sea, and contains the following environments: (a) the reef lagoon, a depression that averages 350 to 1,600 meters in width and lies between the coast and the barrier reef; its depth is a shallow 3 to 8 meters on average; (b) the barrier reef, second largest in the world, beginning in Cabo Catoche and ending in the Gulf of Honduras and divided into three zones: the back reef, 50 to 200 meters wide; a very narrow crest that crowns on the surface; and, stretching from there to the open sea, the frontal reef that sinks to a depth of 20 meters; (c) the sandy platform, a slim overhang 20 to 60 meters deep and between 2 and 7 kilometers wide, where the cliff begins. These environments are found along the whole

Figure 20.1   Map Showing Yucatan Area of Mexico

coast with some differences that will allow us a little later in this chapter to analyze the area by zones.

The width of this region, up to where the interaction of the different ecosystems occurs, has been an issue of great debate among specialists in the field. The wetlands boundary widens the region and unites the coast with the continental zones that are undoubtedly highly interdependent.

In Central America, a series of characteristics of the coastal region have been defined and these can be used here as a point of reference. This definition takes a broad perspective by including four areas of interest to the analyst (see Gordon and Olsen 1992): (1) the territorial sea zone (3 to 12 miles) and exclusive economic zone (200 miles); (2) keys, atolls, and islands; (3) the area adjacent to the coast; and (4) coastal plains and small basins directly relevant to human activity. This definition, widely accepted in the region, can provide a frame of reference for analyzing the use and the associated derivative problems of this complex region which, in recent decades, has experienced high demographic and economic growth, transforming it into an area with major problems and challenges.

In recent times, the authors of this chapter have witnessed and analyzed these changes from a socio-environmental perspective. Thus in order to deal with the problems of today, we offer here a historical perspective that begins with the traditional models of coastal settlement and exploitation and ends with the model being employed today in the 1990s, one characterized by the dominance of tourism complemented by offshore fishing.

Traditional Models of Settlement and Exploitation

Because this vast region has a checkered history of human presence interspersed with large periods of de-population, only two historical models can be applied here: first, the Mayan model which is more of an approach since there are not yet any conclusive studies of it; and second, the re-population model characteristic of the forest enclave stage (1850–1950).

The Mayas and the Coasts

The presence of the Mayas in this region dates from the arrival of the Putunes or Mayas Chontales who brought their many arts, including the art of navigation. This allowed them to control the difficult continental Caribbean coast where they established ports and factories such as the ones in Cozumel, Pole (Xcaret), and Xel-ha, and from there they proceeded to the center of the peninsula around the year 918 (Thompson 1979).

The Mayas achieved a balanced development in the peninsula: Considering that they had to sustain huge populations, there is no trace of serious alterations in the environment. The cities were located in the continental zone, except for Tulum, the only exception in the region, but coincidently Tulum was established on the only elevation of the entire coast without a reef barrier, that is to say, it was a natural port.

The coastal population, knowledgeable about the dialectic of nature, found on the coasts fish and salt, which they combined in order to maintain production (Roys 1957). Thus they succeeded in supplying their cities and generating production for exchange with other villages. In order to control the coast for fishing and navigation, they did detailed surveys of all the coasts, placing a long line of lighthouses fed by fires that by night lighted up the entrance of the uneven straits of the dangerous coral barrier that sheltered their boats. Mayan management of both the tropical forest and the coasts deserves further study, considering that at its height the Mayan population was greater than the present population of the area.

The Forest Enclave: Coast-Continent Articulation

During colonial times, this vast region was unoccupied except for occasional exploitations of dye, fishing, and the capture of turtles and manatee by pirates and other sailors of the era. In the middle of the nineteenth century, this zone began to be resettled definitively by the yucatecos as a result of tribal wars, beginning with the islands and moving to the occupation of the coastal zones in the last decades of the century (César Dachary and Arnaíz Burne 1984). When the war with the Mayas ended, the Federal Territory of Quintana Roo was created and the region began to draw people, given its rich forestry resources that were granted as concessions to the big regional and foreign companies. Thus, in the first fifty years of this century, the model of occupation-exploitation was established, a model we call the "forest enclave" because the exploitation of the tropical forest was the principal activity in the region and the profits went abroad. And when reserves were exhausted, the region remained deeply isolated, unpopulated, and lacking in infrastructure and without other productive options (César Dachary and Arnaíz Burne 1983).

During this period there emerged a clear division of the productive areas: In the continental zone the high forest facilitated exploitation of gum and precious woods, and the local Mayan population combined this activity with the itinerant milpa (small plot) cultivation for individual consumption. The coastal zone, being so fragile, fulfilled two functions: first, to facilitate settlement of the small ports for the extraction of gum; and second, to become a zone of fruitculture, based initially on the export of coconut water, the only possible production in this zone given the sandy soil. The establishment of copra ranches, common to most of the continental Caribbean coasts, was one of the most appropriate uses of these fragile soils which, many years later, would make the landscape of the region famous: that is, the palm trees, sand, and sea.

Thus a model was developed, based on low population density and a combination of offshore fishing and copra production. This generated a peasant economy that we can call "copra-coastal economy," which would last more than seventy years, after which it began to be replaced by tourism which radically changed the use of this zone (César Dachary and Arnaíz Burne 1986).

In this zone a coastal culture originated, conducted chiefly in solitary settlements populated by copra ranchers, lighthouse keepers, carpenters, fishermen, and sailors, although in most cases everyone sailed. This was a society of people isolated for long lonely periods but joined completely to the sea (César Dachary and Arnaíz Burne 1985). During this period, the region became part of international commerce, an integration brought about by the great fleets of the United States, among which the white fleet of the United Fruit Company stood out, anchored in Cozumel to load gum and the famous island pineapple, and in Belize, gum and precious woods. Relations with Belize, Cuba, and the United States, as well as Jamaica and Honduras, grew by way of the navigation that had been historically developed by seasonal fishermen. The Cuban fleet was authorized since 1848 by the Governor of Yucatan, Miguel Barbachano, to fish in Yucatan. Cuban ships arrived at Isla Mujeres at the end of every November in order to avoid the first north winds of the season (César Dachary and Arnaíz Burne 1992a).

The isolation of this area was reduced in 1927 when Charles Lindberg arrived in Cozumel. Two years later, an air route from Miami to Panama, passing by Cozumel and Belize, was opened. This continental Caribbean route was the pioneering route of the now-defunct Pan-American Airways (Vásquez Monsreal 1984). Then, during World War II, the United States built the first important airport of the Mexican Caribbean in Cozumel, with the aim of controlling the maritime route of the western Caribbean, destroyed by German submarines.

But despite these advances, the region continued to be isolated internally as well as from the rest of the peninsula and, especially, the rest of the country. At the end of the forest enclave period in the 1960s, the whole Federal Territory of Quintana Roo, 50,000 square kilometers in area and 800 kilometers of littoral, had a population of only 50,000 inhabitants. The coasts, after Hurricane Janet (1955), were practically deserted, entire villages and copra ranches having disappeared.

In Ambergris, Belize, the coastal zone had a similar pattern of development during this period. Copra-fishing was the dominant economic activity in this semi-populated island. Ambergris did manage to increase its population in the 1950s through the emigration of Mexicans from Xcalac to San Pedro, the only town in the zone. However, the abandonment of the coasts was the point of departure for the major change in land use and the opening to tourist development.

Tourism and Rediscovery

It could be said that the models employed prior to the tourism boom were based on sustainable development, even if one includes copra production, since this production was integrated into the capitalist economy *in combination* with production for subsistence, that is to say, in such a way that the relationship with the market was rather limited. But the changes that took place in the coastal region correspond to a deep transformation in the geopolitical and socio-economic order.

In the 1960s, Mexico began its return to the sea, to coastal settlement and development. In the Mexican Caribbean, the population had been reduced because of the decline of the forest enclave and the lack of alternatives, given the small domestic market and the deep isolation of the region. The development plan devised for the Mexican Caribbean went beyond tourism because it involved a historical recovery of the presence of Mexico in this region, that is, an act of sovereignty. In the Mexican southeast lie all the oil reserves and 70 percent of the hydroelectric capacity of the country. Moreover, the Yucatan canal zone is a strategic area where the main U.S. fleet is deployed and also constitutes the border with conflict-prone Cuba.

The exhaustion of the export model based on gum-forestry and sisal in Yucatan forced the formulation of a new strategy of development based on three projects located on three frontiers:

(a) A plan to resettle the fluvial frontier with Belize, beginning with the settlement of people brought from the interior to promote sugar cane cultivation and on-site industrialization. This project has succeeded and today the Álvaro Obregón sugar refinery is an important source of employment and wealth for the border zone.

(b) A fishing development project, oriented in principle to the following: re-populating the Caribbean coast, de-populated since Hurricane Janet and the decline of the forest enclave; resettling the population on the basis of an activity that would bring immediate results; and creating the minimum infrastructure needed to facilitate primarily export-oriented fishing activity. On the basis of this plan, in two decades of development, population was successfully resettled on the coast, distributed in twenty cooperatives of more than 2,000 fishermen. Including the families of these fishermen, the population increased to around 10,000 persons.

The modernization and the diversification of production brought a sharp change from the original technology of wooden sail boats to fiberglass and outboard motor boats, but the results were less beneficial than expected. Offshore fishing, dedicated mostly to more valuable species such as lobsters, was very successful until the mid 1980s when production began to fall, coinciding with Hurricane Gilbert in 1988.

The social problems caused by the now-exhausted cooperativist model and the over-exploitation of the area's resources combined to reduce fish production and led to a call for a diversification of the industry to include scale fish (which had barely been exploited) and new alternatives such as aquaculture. The decline in production is also reflected in exports which in 1987 were valued at $7.4 million and in 1991 were down to $2.6 million (figures obtained from the Federal Delegation of the Secretary of Commerce and Industrial Growth, Quintano Roo, 1993).

(c) A tourism project, the most ambitious of the three plans. The results, insofar as employment generation and the regional economic dynamic are concerned, are satisfactory but in terms of sustainable development and environmental costs the project has caused serious alterations to the north coasts of the state of Quintana Roo. This project generated a great demographic change as well as increased spatial occupation, in that the population grew from 70,000 inhabitants in the 1970s to 500,000 according to the census of 1990. Today, the figure is closer to 700,000 inhabitants. This population is concentrated on the north coast of the state where 28.3 percent of the total population resided in 1980 and 47.1 percent in the 1990s (see César Dachary and Arnaíz Burne 1992 for details).

Economically, the coastal zone generates 75 percent of the gross domestic product of the state and 25 percent of the gross product emanating from tourism (César Dachary, Navarro, and Arnaíz Burne 1992). For 1992 the hotel capacity of the Cancun-Cozumel and Isla Mujeres triangle surpassed 22,000 rooms and there were more than 2 million tourists, excluding the visitors coming on the 500 cruise ships that arrive every year. With the growth in tourism, the impact of the profound socio-economic changes and the intensive and uncontrolled use of the ecosystems is highly significant and will be even more so in future, given plans for the unregulated growth of this macro project, a project that has placed Mexico in the top tier of tourist destinations based on hotel capacity.

The Coastal Region Today: Problems and Issues

In this section, a zoning approach is taken, one that will allow us to ascertain the characteristics and possible uses of the zones and at the same time evaluate the impact of these uses.

North Zone

The north zone is a long strip that runs from Cabo Catoche to Tulum. This is the zone where current tourist development is concentrated and there is also a high concentration of people. The area can be divided into three sub-zones:

(a) A reserve and potential expansion zone stretching from Cabo Catoche to Isla Blanca in the south; this is an extremely fragile zone where one can find both the aforementioned reserve with potential zones of tourist expansion, and, in its midst, an intensive fishing zone that is also subject to review. In this area one can find "The Reserve and Refuge for Contoy Island National Fauna," created by a presidential resolution of 1961 and covering the complete island. The zone is a nesting ground for birds and a shelter for egg-laying turtles. Until February 1993, it was also a temporary camp for fishermen but, in view of the introduction of extraneous species and the irrational use of the land, the island has now been closed to the fishermen and also closed down as an eco-tourist site, for an unlimited period, until the habitat can recover.

The continental zone, which belongs to the community of Isla Mujeres, and the Isla Blanca peninsula itself are already being parceled up, contrary to a ruling that designated the zone an area of great fragility not conducive to intensive tourist activities. This region is likewise subject to overuse by fast launches and by the four cooperatives that operate in the zone, not to mention the carters working on the coast and the shrimp fishermen operating in the bank in front of Contoy Island. This situation is bound to bring environmental problems to this zone in the medium term, especially in the wetlands that are the water capture zones of the pole of Cancun. Deforestation, reclamations, and other altering activities in these coastal areas will surely have an adverse impact on the hydrologic balance of the ecosystems of the wetlands. Also in this zone there is a confrontation between the tourism developers and the immigrant workers who are looking to expand the periphery of Cancun in order to have their own piece of land. But only by transforming the zone into a reserve can the large-scale environmental impact for Cancun and Isla Mujeres be lessened.

(b) Cancun-Isla Mujeres and suburban zones: From the center of Cancun, 20 kilometers to the south and 15 kilometers to the north, the suburban zone of Cancun has been established, linked to Isla Mujeres but separated from it by Meco Bay. This is an area of maximum land use where the densities exceed the limits of medium-sized Mexican cities. The coasts, which maintain the same characteristics as the general region, join with Cancun Island, which forms a horseshoe anchored to the continent by two bridges, enclosing the Nichpté-Bojorquez lagoon system. The following socio-environmental changes, broadly speaking, characterize this urban area that did not exist two decades ago and today has a floating population of more than 300,000 inhabitants:

• Overdensity of population due to a speculative building boom, in itself based on land values. The original tourist development project was limited to no more than 10,000 rooms, which have now been doubled and will keep on growing, using the sites below.

- Development of the area around Morales lagoon (specifically, there are plans for Puerto Cancun's development as a top-notch marina with a maximum of 5,000 rooms), and the mangrove zone at the extreme west of the lagoon, bordering the city (Project Buenaventura);
- Reclamation of a part (about 20 percent) of Nichupté lagoon, for residential and hotel zones;
- Reclamation of semi-flood zones of Nichupté lagoon for building a residential area and a golf club;
- The use of green zones, reserve areas, and other protected zones for commercial use.

All this has succeeded in transforming the region from a tourist area of excellence to a zone of mass tourism, a process that has produced the inherent deterioration of the conditions of both population and tourists, a deterioration known as "Acapulquization," in reference to the case of Acapulco.

In this zone there is a refuge of marine flora and fauna in the western area of Isla Mujeres, Punta Cancun, and Punta Nizuc, created by presidential decree of February 1973. The indiscriminate and large-scale diving activity, the transit of launches, and the discharge of sewerage have caused significant damage to the zone known as the Garrafón and to other protected areas.

Other problems in this zone include:

- The lack of effective controls for construction projects undertaken on the coasts, piers, drains, and other areas, despite the existence of an important regulation dealing with this issue; this benefits the big enterprises at the expense of the environment and the tourists.
- Sewerage plant saturation that has led to the emptying of a significant volume of sewerage into absorption wells without regard to the subsequent effects.
- The lack of proper drainage in 75 percent of the city, the suburban community of Puerto Juarez, and the nearby regions, causes fecal residues to be vented in the open air, the effects of which have not yet been studied.
- The garbage problem and the related problem of the sanitary landfill in the lowest zone near the Nichupté lagoon, are still not effectively controlled.

In Isla Mujeres there are the same problems, made worse by the fact that the two salt pits in the interior of the island are filled with garbage and all kind of wastes, including sewerage and detergent effluent. This situation places this little island (8 kilometers long, 1.5 kilometers wide) in an environmental emergency because pollution is now extending beyond the groundwater to the marine zone.

To add to this complex and accelerated process, there is a construction industry boom that is attracting large groups of peasants who are settling around the suburban zone. At the other end of the scale, the fishermen, also impacted by the magic of tourism, are reducing their numbers and transforming their equipment into sport equipment for tourists.

Finally (with respect to this zone), with the aim of accommodating the growing population of Cancun, there is a plan for a city to be built to the south of the continental zone. This is a zone of wetlands that would have to be reclaimed for construction of this new city (to be called Nizuc City).

(c) Cancun-Tulum corridor: This corridor, 120 kilometers long, is being developed along lines similar to the suburban area of Miami (Boca Raton or similar areas). To accomplish that, development is beginning around five villages that in a decade will be transformed into cities. These villages are from north to south: Puerto Morelos, Playa del Carmen, Puerto Aventuras, Akumal, and Tulum. The official plan at first referred to a capacity of about 90,000 hotel rooms, but now that has been changed and development has been re-oriented toward eco-tourism, which is already a utopia.

All the coastal land has been divided up and the big developers will surely once again engage in speculation. Currently there are mega projects such as those in Playacar and in Puerto Aventura, already a mini-city though built only four years ago. Puerto Aventuras has a town link on its continental side where there are already 10,000 inhabitants. Along with these projects, there are similar projects in various stages of development. In Playa del Carmen the state distributed 600 lots, aggravating the problem of uncontrolled growth that threatens to transform this village into a city of 50,000 inhabitants by the end of the century (César Dachary and Arnaíz Burne 1992b).

In this region there is Cozumel, the largest island in Mexico, which, with a capacity of 3,000 hotel rooms, is an important center for cruise ship tourism. The 500 cruises that come to this port every year contribute to a serious problem of contamination because they discharge detergent waste and sewerage, kitchen and service effluents with organic and chemical compounds, and leftover motor wastes; they throw ballast and garbage equal to 80 tons per every 1,000 passengers, the average number of passengers and crew being 1,500 persons per cruise. And this does not take into account the damage done by propellers, anchors being dragged, and other kind of operations associated with ship movements, all actions that adversely affect different natural species.

Despite the existence of international conventions governing disposal of ballast and wastes in high sea zones, the maintenance and storage facilities of the large ships are very limited. For example, drinking water has to be re-loaded every two days in different ports. This tourism, common to the small Caribbean islands, has a negative impact, but in the third-world scheme of things, its consequences are not treated as part of the analysis of problems affecting port systems.

Cozumel has until now experienced relatively balanced development. Its major environmental challenge is protection of its famous reefs that have sustained significant damage through overuse and traffic. The Calica project, also in this region, is an open air mine where various kinds of calcined material is extracted for export to the southeast of the United States, since in the United States it is prohibited to extract this material from the coastal zones that are similar to the coasts of the peninsula of Yucatan. This is part of the process of transfer of the highly polluting activities from the first to the third world.

The various environmental problems in this zone have been studied but there is no readily available information apart from the critiques of academics and ecological groups concerned about these offenses to environmental sovereignty. The very first offense was the construction of a deep-water harbor which involved the destruction of an area of the barrier reef.

In the south of the corridor is Tulum, a national park by presidential decree of 1981, home of the ruins of the same name. This park is in turn the southern border between the Cancun-Tulum corridor and the Sian Ka'an Biophere Reserve.

The Sian Ka'an Biosphere Reserve

This reserve, the largest in the Mexican Caribbean and one of the most important in the tropics, is located on the central coast of the state, bordering the southern coasts of the municipalities of Cozumel and Felipe Carrillo Puerto. This reserve was formed by presidential decree in January 1986, after earlier research done by the Center for Investigations of Quintana Roo (CIQRO) (CIQRO 1983). In this extensive zone of more than 200 kilometers in length, there are two large bays, Espíritu Santo and Ascención, and a series of keys in the bays, all bordered by a reef barrier.

On these coasts there is underway a process of reconversion of copra ranches to tourist development. Despite the fact that the development envisaged is low density, changes are already occurring in the region. The principal productive activity is lobster fishing from July to March, and this activity is incompatible with tourism and its nautical activities because these disturb the fishing grounds. The confrontation between the different economic activities is beginning to be resolved in favor of tourism, and many fish producers are turning to services and reducing their catches.

This situation, uncontrolled to date, is disguised in different robes, from eco-tourism to cultural or environmental tourism—all activities that initially are low intensity but soon multiply with adverse effects to the region. The introduction of roads on the narrow strip of land, the introduction of electricity, the intensive traffic, and the construction industry that is advancing from Tulum to Punta Allen, all raise questions as to the future of this reserve zone.

In the bays, fishing production has declined significantly, presumably because of intensive exploitation by the biggest cooperative of the state, Vigia Chico. Meanwhile, land speculation in all the coastal areas points to the need for a truly centralized administration of the relevant institutions and legislation.

Punta Herrero-Xcalac Corridor

This corridor, which has a similar coastal environment as those previously discussed, extends for 150 kilometers, 30 kilometers of which are within the reserve of Sian Ka'an. This zone has already been defined by the government as the coastal expansion zone for tourism in the south, given its great scenic quality, even though unlike the north zone it does not have a continental support area. The coastal strip is very narrow, on average 150 to 200 meters, and there are extensive mangroves on the continent side.

The government of the state is planning a combined tourism-fishing pattern of development, and with that in mind, wants to build a highway, introduce electricity service, and build support mechanisms for the fishing industry, including facilities for cold storage and processing (Gobierno del Estado de Quintana Roo 1992). This project is technically feasible but from the point of view of sustainable development, it is not viable for the following reasons:

(a) The mainland zone, the coastal dune, is only 150 to 200 meters wide, with 80 percent of it less than 100 meters. If we take into consideration the 20 meters of federal zone, the 15 meters of mangrove border, and the 30 meters minimum needed for the highway and its boundaries, the average lot could not be more than 15 meters, at most 20 meters if the highway is run toward the mangrove, which would mean the reclamation of a part of that area.

(b) Water capacity, which is linked to the salt zone, is minimal, and handling beyond the current limit will lead to its exhaustion or to salination of the well.

(c) The fact that it is not possible to build sanitary landfills or something similar, will lead to the burial of garbage in the mangrove (with all the damage that entails) or else the dumping of waste in the direction of the continental zone only 50 kilometers away.

(d) There are only two zones where the land widens, in Mahahual and Xcalac, and both are natural population centers. Other centers are already forming in the reclaimed mangrove zones.

Thirty kilometers from the coast is the Chinchorro bank, 47 kilometers long and 18 kilometers wide, and 700 square kilometers in area. It is considered the largest in the entire Caribbean. This is an exceptional fishing ground and a potential tourism zone that is linked to the development of the southern zone. The fishing that is done there by three cooperatives has declined significantly, as has occurred in the rest of the state. This decline in fishing has led the states to institute tourist-oriented projects that bring results in the short term—a potential danger for the sustainable development of this vast and fragile southern coast.

Ambergris

Ambergris, 39 kilometers long, 7.9 kilometers wide and 3 meters high, can be considered the prolongation of the Yucatan peninsula (César Dachary and Arnaíz Burne 1993a). The only existing village to date, San Pedro, had similar activities to the rest of the region, namely copra and fishing. The area has also ethnically, socially (via familiar links), and culturally been integrated into the south of Quintana Roo. The tourist development that was begun in the 1970s went through the stage of adventure tourism to mass tourism, and this has brought serious problems to the island, given its fragility. The problems common to the northern zone—overdensity of construction, intensive use of the land, lack of services, and so on—are repeated in the southern zone, with the added factor that this region is more fragile because the dune, except in two places, has a width of less than 100 meters.

The lack of drainage has contaminated the groundwater and the lack of water obliges both the villagers and the tourists to live off water brought from the continent, which limits tourist development. But the lots on the mangroves and the low areas of the coast are growing without reserve areas and in city-like proportions. This will engender a spatial re-accommodation in the short term, for when these lots are occupied the problems will begin and solutions will be difficult.

In view of this situation, through an agreement with the Ministry of Natural Resources, the authors of this chapter researched the issues and generated a proposal for sustainable development of tourism, taking into consideration current conditions in the zone (César Dachary, Arnaíz Burne, and Navarro 1991). The proposal was based on the following criteria: lower densities, the creation of reserve zones, avoidance of roads, limitations on growth of the airport runway as a way to diminish the development of mass tourism, and reformulation of the use of the coasts in town.

Still, the pressure of U.S. investors has been greater than that of the government. Investors succeeded in getting the concession to the north zone of Ambergris for a Cancun-type development. Likewise, they are continuing to reclaim the coastal lands, pulling out marine flora, cutting down mangroves, and engaging in large-scale construction because of the high value of the land on the island. This is happening also to the southern zone of Quintana Roo where U.S. investors, some owning land in both countries, have taken over 50 percent of the zone (César Dachary and Arnaíz Burne 1993a).

Conclusions

The coasts are the new frontiers of capitalist expansion in services associated with tourism, and this has engendered a demographic movement of great proportions along with intensive use of fragile soils, a transformation that presents a great threat to the coastal ecosystems and a challenge to the promotion of sustainable development.

This is the modern contradiction generated by the new process of recolonization brought about by the new conquerors of the coasts. It conceals the double speak of ecologists and investors from the first world. This new international political reality causes problems of international environmental security stemming from the actualization of frontier projects. This is the new model of coastal development where the ethic and criteria of development are superseded by the central logic of capitalism and unreasonable speculation.

In sum, the problems related to coastal development have gone beyond the narrow margins of a region to become part of national development strategy, in a new stage where sovereignty and state seem to be the only limits preventing globalization from fulfilling its commitment to re-colonize the periphery and bring it into a new relationship where the environmental issue is sure to dominate.

Bibliography

Centro de Investigaciones de Quintana Roo (CIQRO). 1983. *Sian Ka'an: Estudios preliminares de una zona en Quintana Roo propuesta como reserva de la biosfera.* Chetumal, Mexico: CIQRO.

César Dachary, A. and S. M. Arnaíz Burne. 1983. *Estudios socioeconómicos preliminares de Quintana Roo.* Tomo 1: Sector agropecuario y forestal. Puerto Morelos, Mexico: Centro de Investigaciones de Quintana Roo (CIQRO).

————. 1994. *Estudios socioeconómicos preliminares de Quintana Roo.* Tomo 2: El territorio y la población. Chetumal, Mexico: CIQRO.

————. 1985. *El Caribe mexicano: Hombres e historias.* Mexico D.F.: Casa Chata/Centro de Investigaciones y Estudios Superiores en Antropología Social.

————. 1986. *Estudios socioeconómicos preliminares de Quintana Roo.* Tomo 5: Sector pesquero. Chetumal, Mexico: Centro de Investigaciones de Quintana Roo (CIQRO).

————. 1992a. *Bitacora de un viaje a la justicia.* Mexico: CIQRO.

————. 1992b. *Estudio integral de Playa del Carmen.* Mexico: CIQRO.

————. 1993a. *Censo costero.* Mexico: CIQRO.

————. 1993b. *El Caribe mexicano: Una introducción a su historia.* Mexico: CIQRO.

César Dachary, A., D. Navarro, and S. M. Arnaíz Burne, eds. 1992. *Quintana Roo: Los retos del fin de siglo.* Mexico: CIQRO.

César Dachary, A., Stella Maris Arnaíz Burne, and Daniel Navarro, eds. 1991. *Los impactos del turismo y sus alternativas.* Mexico: CIQRO.

Gobierno del Estado de Quintana Roo. 1992. *Proyecto Zona Sur.* Mimeo. Chetumal, Mexico.

Gordon, F. and S. Olsen. 1992. *Las costas de Centroamerica: Diagnóstico y agenda para la acción.* Rhode Island: University of Rhode Island.

Ibarra Merino, M. And L. Dávalos Otero. 1991. *Atlas ambiental costero Puerto Morelos, Quintana Roo.* Mexico: CIQRO, 1991.

Rebolledo, J. 1946. *Quintana Roo y Belize.* Mexico: Stylo.

Roys, R. 1957. *Geografía política de los Mayas de Yucatán.* Washington D.C.: Carnegie.

Thompson, E. J. 1979. *Historia y religión de los Mayas.* Mexico: Siglo XXI.

Vásquez Monsreal, A. 1984. *Cimientos.* Cozumel, Mexico: Ediciones del Ayuntamiento de Cozumel.

Yañez Arancibia, A. 1986. *Ecología de las zonas costeras: Análisis de siete tópicos.* Mexico: Editorial AGT, S.A.

21

In Conclusion

Dennis J. Gayle and Jacqueline Anne Braveboy-Wagner

As the Caribbean region struggles to adapt to the changes and challenges of the new global environment, policy-makers and bureaucrats are being forced out of their traditional inertia toward a dynamic reassessment of development strategies. There has been a noticeable increase in the number of commissions, committees, and consultancies devoted to re-evaluation of policies and formulation of forward-looking strategies. In many ways, the new international order, though fraught with problems for small and developing states, also presents a somewhat exciting challenge in that it demands the generation of new ways of thinking and fresh, creative ideas. It also presents an opportunity for academics, traditionally excluded from the inner circles of policy influence, to formulate ideas that can be useful to policy-makers in this more pragmatic and less ideological era.

In the twenty chapters of this book, a wide variety of issues have been discussed by specialists in various fields. Despite the specialized nature of the analyses presented, three common threads run through the discussion: (1) the difficult challenges posed by the globalization process; (2) the need for innovative policies; and (3) the injunction to be cautious about how the region articulates itself into this "global village."

As César Dachary noted, the process of globalization has "reduced global distances, given that the revolution in communications and transportation now allows for the expansion of influence to even those most isolated zones." Noguera affirms that we now have "globalized information, manufacturing, pollution, trade, politics, and western culture." The effects of this globalization are, in fact, the themes of the essays presented. They include: the imposition of norms of liberalization that may not be completely appropriate for the region; environmental problems caused by changes in land use attributable to new economic linkages; and the spread of new information technologies and threat of tele-colonialism.

Global interdependence has also brought trade interdependence (the creation of new blocs and the enhancement of older regional arrangements); narcotics interdependence (the spread of the drug culture and drug trafficking); pressure to end gender inequality; the rapid global spread of new diseases (AIDS in particular); and increased cultural and economic penetration. Looming over the discussion of the effects of globalization is always the issue of marginalization: Can the region survive in an era in which it has little leverage and few competitive resources? The various analyses done here imply that it can, though with difficulty. There is actually an optimistic tone throughout the contributions, a focus on what can be done and what needs to be done, rather than a mere criticism of what has or has not been done.

The need for innovative thinking and policies is highlighted in this book. The creation of the cross-cultural Association of Caribbean States (ACS), for example, is lauded even if there is much skepticism about its effectiveness. In the area of training and education, contributors call for introduction of new management approaches suited to the competitive environment of today. Reference is made to a new, more "hands on" method of training in environmental management. In the cultural arena, a challenge is issued for development strategies that would incorporate plans for cultural institutions and cultural promotion in the interest of national integration. In the field of labor, we are asked to consider an area that is not normally stressed:'the importance of knowing and understanding the international conventions governing labor movements. And on the issue of the Caribbean's participation in the information superhighway, a suggestion is made to transform post offices and other such institutions into "communications centers."

Despite their positive approach, the authors all stress caution as the Caribbean attempts to find a place in the new global order. For example, contributors caution that liberalization does not necessarily imply that the state should take a back seat in development. Some skepticism is also expressed about regional initiatives, specifically the inclusion of the "Group of Three" in regional arrangements involving the very small states of the Caribbean, the potentially-conflictual rapprochement between Cuba and the Caribbean, and the region's forced competition with Mexico that could turn the former into a chain of "boutique economies" by the turn of the century. Other cautionary notes are sounded with respect to possible forced reductions in immigrant outflows from the Caribbean to the traditional receiving countries; the "re-colonization" of the region through misplaced large-scale land development; and the Caribbean's capacity to profit equitably from the telecommunications revolution.

As we draw the analyses together to form an integrated picture, we might well ask: What are the implications of these public policy analyses for the Caribbean region's evolving future as the twenty-first century approaches? Since the 1960s, Caribbean states have adapted their public and foreign policies to fit the changing global environment: the Cold War era, the greater flexibility of the 1970s, the bi-multipolarity of the 1980s, and the post–Cold War uni-multipolar system of the 1990s. Caribbean countries have traditionally conditioned their policies primarily upon their geopolitical and economic linkages to the United States. Given that the strategic value of the Caribbean to the United States has diminished with the demise of the Soviet Union, such an approach is no longer viable.

Caribbean countries that have benefited from the liberal postwar immigration policies of Europe and North America are now confronted with limits and restraints on immigration. The preferred alternative to the export of human capital is the expansion of regional and third-country exports from the Caribbean Basin, including the Caribbean Community (CARICOM), in the interest of providing attractive employment opportunities at home. But the experience of CARICOM illustrates some of the difficulties inherent in the process of regional integration. CARICOM's intra-regional trade increased in the early 1970s but was almost brought to a halt when national trade restrictions were intensified in 1977. Ten years later, CARICOM trade got a boost when the Council of Ministers agreed to introduce a free trade regime on a selected list of products. Then in July 1989, the Heads of Government agreed to the Single Market and Economy (SEM) that would lead to the introduction of a new Common External Tariff (CET) in 1992 and new rules of origin in 1993. But as we head to the end of 1996, the CET has yet to be instituted by all countries, and the SEM remains on the relatively distant horizon!

Nevertheless, increasing regional integration has become a significant trend across the entire Caribbean, impelled by the end of the Cold War, growing global economic interdependence, and the emergence of three major blocs: the European Union/Economic Community (EU), the North American Free Trade Area (NAFTA), and the Asia-Pacific Area dominated by Japan. Internal factors such as debt accumulation and the broadly accepted need for greater international competitiveness have also contributed to the trend. One consequence has been the creation of the ACS, which has a potential membership of thirty-seven independent states and territories, with a market of some 200 million people, and an aggregate gross domestic product approximating $508 billion. This bloc would rank fourth in market size after the three mentioned above.

Interestingly, Cuba has already joined the ACS, eager as it is to promote closer regional relations to counter its diplomatic and economic isolation resulting from the disintegration of the Soviet Union. By June 1992, Cuba had been admitted as a full member of the Caribbean Tourism Organization (CTO) and was participating with CARICOM in a joint commission, formalized in December 1993. The commission is focusing on cooperation in areas such as biotechnology, disaster prevention, tourism, culture, and fishing. This Cuba-CARICOM collaboration is intended to lead to eventual CARICOM observer status for Cuba.

On the domestic front, during the 1990s Caribbean countries have found themselves simultaneously managing structural adjustment, implementing trade and financial liberalization strategies, privatizing state-owned industries, and pursuing deregulation. At the same time, individual countries have to attract both local and foreign investment to fuel diversification, and to support export-led growth strategies in a context in which net resource flows from the advanced industrial countries to such small island developing countries have been declining. Furthermore, the impact of the NAFTA may well force a restructuring of Caribbean economies toward the production of a set of highly specialized export products, in order to maintain some competitive advantage.

Domestic and international economic policies must surely be built on a cultural foundation, that is, a strong sense of national and regional identity. The Caribbean cultural *mélange* results from a dramatic process of cross-fertilization among the European, African, Asian, and Amerindian civilizations. This process has led to the development of distinctive spheres of culture in the Western hemisphere, each claiming its own inner logic and consistency. The articulation of national culture is seen, at the popular level if not always at the governmental level, as a key component of development, and a means of resisting external domination. Furthermore, whereas the process of formal regional integration has moved forward at an excruciatingly slow pace, informal integration, based on regional cultural affirmation by the *people* of the Caribbean, has long been a fact of life and continues to be strengthened. It is primarily at the official levels that the recognition of the centrality of culture still lacks cogency. And in Trinidad and Tobago, Guyana, and Suriname, cultural policy and integration is also hindered in varying degree by ethnic tension.

In an era of openness, governments are under considerable pressure to manage effectively a variety of societal demands. The capacity of governments is taxed by the wide and increasing range of drug-related criminal activity (drug production, consumption and abuse, trafficking, and money laundering). Both locally and internationally, demands have increased for more equitable treatment of women both in the workforce and in the home. And global recognition of the urgency of sustaining the physical environment as a key component of development has led to the growth of regional and national environmental pressure groups as well as external pressures on governments from the international aid agencies.

Partly because of the well-established Caribbean tradition of metropole-directed migration, public sector capabilities remain limited in many countries. One result is that strategic policy decisions for the development of the Caribbean, for example in the telecom sector, continue to be made by foreign companies: in this case, Cable and Wireless in London, France-Telecom in France, Telefónica de España in Spain, Dutch PTT in Holland, and Atlantic Telenetwork, as well as AT&T in the United States. In the haste to liberalize, Caribbean governments have tended to pay little attention to this phenomenon which erodes their decision-making and bargaining powers and can only be countered by adequate regulatory policies.

In sum, the work of the contributors to this volume implies that if the Caribbean is to successfully meet the challenges of the twenty-first century, various policy changes are needed at the regional and national levels. The articulation and broad acceptance of a common Caribbean identity is not an exogenous factor, but rather a central element in the process of future regional development. At another level, in order to have effective economic growth, it is necessary to inculcate new attitudes to productivity and profitability among Caribbean workers as well as managers. In turn, development requires that regional countries build upon either established or emerging traditions of democracy, so as to establish civil societies where inter-ethnic tolerance, concern for the quality of life, and efficient environmental management are consensually regarded as equivalent in importance to expansion of the Gross National Product. These domestic challenges are both intensified and facilitated by the concurrent need to continue the process of regional integration, so as to generate appropriate economies of scale and scope. The Caribbean Community has now committed itself to deepening its internal market while also attempting to coordinate its trade regime with the Central American Integration System, the Andean Group, the Group of Three, and NAFTA.

Meeting the challenges outlined is not an inconsiderable task. However, it becomes imaginable to the extent to which policy is driven by the interests and aspirations of the "man in the street," not just the politician; by dynamic non-governmental and intergovernmental organizations rather than by government ministries; by the creation of regional private enterprises rather than by enterprise regime agreements; and most of all, by an inclusive approach to dialogue between the region's ethnic, cultural, social, and political groups, in the formulation and implementation of Caribbean public policy during the remainder of the 1990s and the dawn of the succeeding decade.

Appendix 1:
A Policy Vision for the Region

Patrick A. M. Manning

Extract of Speech of Prime Minister Manning of Trinidad and Tobago to the Caribbean Studies Association 18th Convention, Kingston, Jamaica, May 24 1993.

The Impact of Afro-Asian Nationalism

In 1955, a number of academically-oriented political leaders met in Indonesia, in the city of Bandung. They came from all over the world, meeting for the express purpose of discussing some of the current trends of political thought that were sweeping the world at the time. Many of them had attended some of the world's most recognized universities. What united them was the spirit of nationalism and the determination to free their countries from the shackles of colonialism. At Bandung they talked about the nationalist movement that was sweeping the world and that manifested itself in 1947 in India becoming independent, and subsequently led to Bandung, after which Ghana became independent in 1955, followed by Guinea in 1958. Closer home in the Caribbean, a West Indian Federation was formed in 1958, impelled by nationalism, a decision by countries that were subjected initially to that yoke of colonialism to move to a status where they could determine their own destiny.

Caribbean Nationalism

The West Indian Federation came to a sorry pass. Jamaica became independent in August 1962; so too Trinidad and Tobago, and later, Barbados, Guyana, and several other territories. At the same time territories in Africa and the Pacific were gaining their independence, all part of a sweeping nationalist movement. And as these countries became independent, and as those new leaders gained political control of their countries and, therefore, the right to determine the economic system by which these countries would be governed, they recognized that the economic systems that they met in place, systems dominated by large international firms, were geared to satisfying the requirements of the colonial power, and were by no means geared to the aspirations of the countries in respect of which these companies were clients and guests. One good example of this is what we in

223

Trinidad and Tobago found in Caroni (Sugar) Limited in 1974 when the company passed into state hands. Personnel from Tate and Lyle, the British company, were using "jeeps" to oversee the estates and were buying these vehicles from the United Kingdom. At a time when the Japanese had on the market a Toyota jeep that was more powerful and far less costly than the British Land Rover jeep, Tate and Lyle was purchasing vehicles from the United Kingdom as part of the policy of satisfying a requirement of the metropolis. They remained completely oblivious to the realities of the day in terms of cost-effective technology for the developing countries.

This nationalist movement, vision, and view by the leaders in a number of emerging third world countries led to a pattern of economic development that was by and large inward-looking. That was naturally a consequence of the political and economic trends of the day. One of the consequences of this inward-looking policy was a pattern of economic development that was based on the domestic market of the individual countries.

In the case of Trinidad and Tobago, this domestic market comprised about one million people. In Jamaica, there were about 1.6 million people. Jamaica was pursuing precisely the same policies as Trinidad, as indeed were Barbados, Guyana, Grenada, Saint Vincent, Saint Lucia, and almost all the Caribbean. The strategy was to seek to develop industries in the country, using the domestic market as a springboard. The idea was that the domestic market would guarantee the viability of these industries. To achieve that, you have to close your borders, and of course, the borders were closed essentially by the imposition of a negative list, and by tariff barriers. If an investor came to the government wishing to invest in a particular commodity, what the government would immediately do was to put the item on the negative list so that this investor had the guarantee of a domestic market free of competition, and therefore a domestic market that could be used to justify the financial outlay that would have been made and ensure some kind of return on that investment. That is a simplified form of the basic economic strategy that was pursued by countries like Trinidad and Tobago and Jamaica. It worked in many countries. In Trinidad and Tobago, for example, the manufacturing sector was developed on the basis of this approach. However, some of the unintended consequences were that the domestic market was the recipient of shoddy goods. For example, in Trinidad and Tobago, the story goes that even before you came off the ladder after screwing in the light bulb, the bulb blew. There were dangers associated with using a locally-made razor blade. I have no reason to believe that Jamaica was any different in that respect or that Trinidad and Jamaica were different from any other Caribbean country.

In the case of Trinidad and Tobago, there was another important factor and that was the availability of oil and gas. Revenues were enhanced by high oil prices from 1973 onward, especially 1979 and 1980, and by rising oil production from 1972, picking up in 1978 and declining thereafter. These revenues led the government of the day to invest in such a way as to give greater effect to a policy based on nationalism, that is, the policy of seeking to gain control of the engine of economic growth, the commanding heights of the economy, as it was described at that particular point in time. By 1983, not only had oil prices fallen but oil production also had declined. The combination of reduced price and reduced production led to reduced revenues, and therefore the need for some kind of change.

A New Economic Order

There had been discussion taking place around the world about a new international economic order, and, emerging from the developed countries, was the point of view that we all needed to make adjustments to the order as it existed. Looking at the changes in very broad outline, what was being said was that if you have access to my market, I must have access to yours. Immediately, a number of countries, especially developing countries, had to re-think the course of action that they were pursuing by closing their borders, because if the changes were not made, sooner or later you would find yourself isolated, not being able to trade with anyone. And the consequence of that would have been high levels of unemployment and undoubtedly social dislocation, perhaps on a scale that had never been anticipated by any of us. And so these decision-makers in developed countries have set the pattern for a new international order affecting developing countries in such a way that structural adjustment of economies has been required.

One of the consequences of the inward-looking policy had been inefficiency in production, not just directly in the production of goods but also a general inefficiency in the public sector manifested, for example, in high prices for some of the public utilities (water, electricity, port charges, and so on). These are essential inputs into the manufacturing process, and they contributed to prices that were higher than they should have been had the methods of organization been otherwise, had they been methods that had led to high levels of efficiency. In sum, the world today is in a situation where structural adjustment is the order of the day, and there are few countries that will escape that. In some countries, the requirements will be greater than in others, but in nearly all developing countries, there is now a general agreement on the need for structural adjustment.

Competition and Efficiency

What I consider critical is not so much the policies that you pursue in structural adjustment, because many of these policies suggest themselves. What in my view now emerges as a critical consideration in public policy formulation as we go on from here—and in fact it has been so for some time—is not so much what policy you pursue but how you do it. At what rate is it to be done? If all the developing countries are taking the position that economic activities must be stimulated on the basis of export-led growth, I ask the question: Will everyone succeed? Does the world have the capacity to absorb the result of export-led growth policies in all developing countries and in many developed countries also? The answer, to my mind, is no, it does not. I believe that some countries will succeed and others will not. What determines who succeeds and who does not is the simple factor of timing: The early bird is likely to catch the fattest worm. For example, when Jamaica floated its currency, Trinidad and Tobago was in a similar financial position and we took very careful note of it. Subsequently, Guyana adjusted its currency. We knew in Trinidad and Tobago that if we delayed too long in taking this course of action, the fattest worm might go elsewhere. So we successfully floated our own dollar.

If we do not compete effectively, what will happen to the Caribbean? If some are going to survive and some are not, if some are going to succeed and some are not, who will succeed and who will not? I certainly am not in the position to say. What I can say however is this: If the countries in the Caribbean get together and pursue a course of action that is based on a collaborative effort, then the likelihood is that all will succeed. And therein lies a very strong and very powerful case for Caribbean integration, not just economic, but a strong and powerful case for Caribbean political integration.

Organization of Government

Now, what are the methods of organization of your government that will put you in a position to move at the fastest possible rate to enable you to compete against the rest of the world? We must be aware that there is no flock of investors lining up to come into Trinidad and Tobago, or Jamaica, or Barbados, or Guyana. They will come, based on the conditions that they need and based on the circumstances that will give them the best returns and the most stable atmosphere, and not necessarily the cheapest value. Therefore, who will organize the government to do the best in these circumstances?

I use the example of Trinidad and Tobago to note that in most governments you will find only a handful of ministers, perhaps five at most, in whom prime ministers have complete confidence, and therefore who are allowed to run on their own. That is a fact of political life. And in many instances the competence of the cabinet determines the rate at which the government progresses. It follows therefore that if a government wishes to maximize the rate at which it moves, the prime minister (or president) has an important responsibility in the selection of the members of government. Most important, the more competent the ministers are, the faster the country progresses.

There is another aspect: Prime ministers and presidents are human beings, not supermen or women. Our experience in the English-speaking Caribbean is that the Westminster system, as it is operated in Trinidad and Tobago and in the rest of the Caribbean, is very dissimilar to the way it operates in the United Kingdom. In its classical manifestation, politicians are responsible for devising policies and the public servants are responsible for the execution of those policies. In the Caribbean it is not so, nor can it be so. Politicians are responsible for implementation, more often than not. The population does not ask the permanent secretary [head of the appropriate civil service department] any questions. The population votes for the politician and people think: I elected you to do certain things, and therefore you are accountable to me. Ministers therefore must see their responsibility as going beyond mere policy formulation, getting involved to a greater or lesser extent, in the actual execution of policy if they are to properly discharge their responsibilities to the population. It means therefore that ministers must have certain qualities, and in the existing economic circumstances, it is an advantage if ministers can demonstrate managerial competence.

This has been my experience. In this scenario, then, what is the role of the prime minister? In Trinidad and Tobago, the prime minister is minister of nothing else. (There is a minor portfolio in the prime minister's office called "Ecclesiastical Affairs.") This arrangement frees the prime minister from being bogged down in the day-to-day micro-management of a particular ministry, leaving him to coordinate the activities of a large number of competent ministers, assuming that the general direction of the government is a direction that is clearly set and adhered to. The role of the prime minister is to manage the government as a whole. That is how we do it in Trinidad and Tobago, and I have every reason to believe that more and more this will be the norm.

I do not subscribe to the view that, as a result of what I just noted, it follows that a cabinet has of necessity to be large. The reason is that ministers must be given a level of workload that they can properly discharge. If the workload is too heavy, then of course, you know you will get poor results. Therefore the workload has to be worked out in such a way that the ministers are able to properly discharge their duties. That is another reason why in Trinidad and Tobago we have moved away from the double portfolio.

International Agencies

I referred earlier to structural adjustment policies. The minute you talk about structural adjustment, you talk about the international agencies: the International Monetary Fund (IMF), World Bank, the Inter-American Development Bank (IDB). You can take the point of view, as many have done, that these institutions are subversive of good order and subversive of peace and stability in your country. But if you take that position, that is highly theoretical. Saying that the institutions are subversive is fine, and in some respects they are because they are trying to change what exists now, but the reality is that you have to live with them. Actually, in Trinidad and Tobago, we have carefully worked out our position and we find that if you go to the international agencies with a carefully worked-out program and policy, you are in a better position to argue it than they are in a position to argue against it. That has been our experience, and so the government of Trinidad and Tobago has an excellent relationship with the World Bank, an excellent relationship with the IMF, an excellent relationship with the Inter-American Development Bank. When we floated our currency, the most surprised persons were those in the World Bank, the IMF, and the IDB because they did not know. It was a decision of the government of Trinidad and Tobago. If you prepare properly, then you will find that they tend to go along with you. Of course, trust is the basis of all good relationships. As long as those agencies are convinced that you know what you are about, our experience has been that they tend to support you, even if not entirely.

Social Problems

I just want to raise two other concerns very briefly. Again, the moment you talk about structural adjustment, you have to accept that there are going to be high levels of crime in your country. Some social dislocation clearly results from structural adjustment which adversely affects the unemployed and those who are least able to help themselves. Both academics and policy-makers need to ask: What set of social measures must be put in place that will constitute an adequate safety net? And how should we organize the dispensation of social services in our countries to ensure that as responsible societies, discharging our responsibility to a population, we take care of those among us who are least able to take care of themselves?

These, then, are some policy concerns geared towards expeditious actions. If we are to achieve the objectives that we set for ourselves as a country and a society, we need to address these issues urgently.

Appendix 2:
The Future of CARICOM

Edwin Carrington

Excerpts from a set of speeches by Edwin Carrington, Secretary General of the Caribbean Community (CARICOM).

Can CARICOM survive, with just five million people? Yes, if the people of CARICOM want to survive and prosper. Despite the region's small size, it has produced two Nobel prize winners in one decade, the Caribbean team has been world cricket champions for almost two decades, and the region has produced the only new musical instrument the world has seen in the twentieth century. In sum, the Caribbean has contributed much more to the world, in areas such as music, culture, applied democracy, and economic experience, than could have been expected, given population size.

Yet the pace of integration within CARICOM is not fast enough to respond to the changes taking place in the world today. To be sure, trade liberalization has been essentially achieved. When this process began, inter-regional trade amounted to about 5 percent of total member-state trade, a reduction from the 1981 zenith of 13 percent, attributable to the region's declining economic fortunes. Trade amounted to 10 percent in 1993. But it must be admitted that the CARICOM treaty is weak. It provides for regulated movement of capital, and not at all for the movement of labor. The pressure of the people of the region for freer movement within the CARICOM space for work and pleasure will be a critical factor in breaking down internal barriers to economic and social development.*

CARICOM represents an important sub-group of the Caribbean Basin Initiative (CBI) countries, which enjoy significant trade concessions in the United States. Between 1983 and 1990, U.S. exports to the Caribbean surged by 65 percent to almost $10 billion. This contributed to the $1.6 billion trade surplus that the United States enjoyed in its trade with CARICOM during the 1980s. Both U.S. exports to and imports from CARICOM have generated significant job creation and

---

Editors' Note: Since this was written, CARICOM members have agreed to allow freedom of movement for university graduates and certain skilled workers.

maintenance in the United States. It is estimated that CBI imports from the United States in 1990 sustained some 110,000 trade-related jobs. CARICOM had contributed some 36 percent of this, although representing only 13 percent of the CBI population.

Further, every dollar of income received by the CBI countries is estimated to generate 60 cents of imports from the United States, compared to 10 cents of imports from Asia. In addition, U.S. policy-makers and senior corporate officials may wish to consider CARICOM's significant locational and other strategic investment advantages. Language, a skilled labor force, an open investment climate based upon new company, copyright, and intellectual property laws, together with fiscal incentives and a civil democratic society, are factors which add qualitatively to the U.S. returns gained from every investment dollar spent in the region.

The Caribbean has been described as the last playground of imperial influences. These influences generally act as a separating force among the various groups of English, French, Dutch, and Spanish-speaking territories, reinforcing the insularity that is exerted by the sea. The twenty-first century seems set to witness an ever closer knitting together of Caribbean societies. The proposal to form an Association of Caribbean States, initiated by CARICOM heads of government in October 1992, was driven by the Report of the West Indian Commission which recommended that CARICOM should advance economic integration as well as functional cooperation with all countries washed by the Caribbean sea. This initiative—ignoring differences of language and historical imperial affinity—represents a critical challenge to adopt a perspective which sees the Caribbean Sea as a common patrimony, rather than a separating force. This Association [now established] constitutes a market of some 200 million, with a total GNP of approximately $500 billion, ranking fourth in market size after the European Union, NAFTA, and the Asian bloc.

The key difference between the ACS and any earlier such initiative in our history lies in its objective of pursuing, on behalf of all members, a common approach to major international challenges, such as the North American Free Trade Area (NAFTA) and the Single European Market. One of the first difficulties [faced by] the ACS [was] the problem of membership, particularly that of the non-independent territories. In this case, a category of "Associate Member" [was] inevitable. Another difficulty arises from the reaction of the United States to the inclusion of Castro's Cuba in the association, both with respect to permitting the involvement of Puerto Rico and the U.S. Virgin Islands and the treatment of the ACS as a valid interlocutor for its members. A third difficulty concerns the financing of the ACS secretariat, given that resources are scarce for virtually all member-states, many of which are already financing other regional and subregional bodies.

Another question concerns the role of the ACS in relation to national and other group decision-making functions. If, for example, ACS decisions are merely recommendations, would the association not soon be ignored, and lapse into irrelevance? On the other hand, if the ACS were to be given binding decision-making powers, would it ever be able to arrive at effective and timely decisions? The final question relates to the preservation of CARICOM's integrity in the face of a dynamic ACS. Despite CARICOM's decision to implement a single market, the required process of widening and deepening has yet to be vigorously pursued. Yet CARICOM's future as an institution remains dependent upon the extent to which we are able to deepen our own integration. If the establishment of the single market and economy proceeds as planned, then the ACS, a much looser body, could provide the vital supporting framework within which our closer sub-regional integration process can flourish. If, on the other hand, CARICOM stagnates and flounders, the Association of Caribbean States can well become a competing body, as its decisions, recommendatory to CARICOM, become more meaningful than those of CARICOM, either because we continually defer decisions or fail to implement decisions once taken.

Yes, CARICOM can survive if it can function more effectively within a vital ACS framework. There are already positive signs that the business and academic sectors are taking the lead in the process of creating a vigorous Association of Caribbean States. For example, in December 1993, a roundtable for Caribbean and Central American businessmen was convened, and there is increasing cooperation between the Caribbean Association of Industry and Commerce and the Central American Private Sector Organization, FEDEPRICAP. Individual CARICOM entrepreneurs are expanding into the Central and Latin American markets. The Andean Finance Corporation is assuming an increasing role in supporting business enterprises operating in many countries of the ACS grouping.

In addition, the Caribbean Development Bank and the Caribbean Tourism Organization already embrace a number of members from the wider ACS. The University of the West Indies itself is taking preliminary steps to cooperate with sister institutions across the wider Caribbean, within the framework of the Caribbean Forum of African-Caribbean-Pacific States (CARIFORUM). Two critical steps remain: the upgrading of diplomatic relations among the ACS member states, and the removal of visa requirements for travel among them. In sum, the Association of Caribbean States might just be able to provide the supporting framework within which CARICOM can work to ensure its survival.

Appendix 3:
Sustainable Development
of Small Island States (U.N.)

Preamble, Programme of Action for the Sustainable Development of Small Island States, United Nations Global Conference on the Sustainable Development of Small Island Developing States, Barbados, April 25-May 6, 1995.

1. In 1992, at the United Nations Conference on Environment and Development (UNCED), the world community adopted Agenda 21. Agenda 21 reflects a global consensus and political commitment at the highest level on development and environment cooperation. The cooperation of all states is a prerequisite for the fulfillment of the objectives of Agenda 21. Such cooperation must also respond to the special circumstances and particular vulnerabilities of countries through adequate and specific approaches.

2. The Global Conference on the Sustainable Development of Small Island Developing States is the first global conference on sustainable development and the implementation of Agenda 21. Agenda 21 represents a comprehensive document, carefully negotiated, and wherever referred to in the programme of action should be looked to as a whole.

3. The Rio Declaration on Environment and Development identifies human beings as being at the center of concerns for sustainable development. Development initiatives in small island developing states should be seen in relation to the needs and aspirations of human beings, and their responsibility towards present and future generations. Small island developing states have valuable resources, including oceans, coastal environments, biodiversity and, most importantly, their human resources. Their potential is recognized, but the challenge for small island developing states is to ensure that they are used in a sustainable way for the well-being of present and future generations. Although they are afflicted by economic difficulties and confronted by development imperatives similar to those of developing countries generally, small island developing states also have their own peculiar vulnerabilities and characteristics, so that the difficulties they face in the pursuit of sustainable development are particularly severe and complex.

4. There are many disadvantages which derive from small size. These are magnified by the fact that many island states are not only small but are themselves made up of a number of small islands. Disadvantages include a narrow range of resources, which forces undue specialization; excessive dependence on

international trade and hence vulnerability to global developments; high population density, which increases the pressure on already limited resources; overuse of resources and premature depletion; relatively small watersheds and threatened supplies of fresh water; costly public administration and infrastructure, including transportation and communication; and limited institutional capacities and domestic markets which are too small to provide significant scale economies, while their limited export volumes, sometimes from remote locations, lead to high freight costs and reduced competitiveness. Small islands tend to have high degrees of endemism and levels of biodiversity, but the relatively small numbers of the various species impose high risks of extinction and create a need for protection.

5. The small size of small island developing states means that development and environment are closely interrelated and interdependent. Recent human history contains examples of entire islands rendered uninhabitable through environmental destruction owing to external causes; small island developing states are fully aware that the environmental consequences of ill-conceived development can have catastrophic effects. Unsustainable development threatens not only the livelihood of people but also the islands themselves and the cultures they nurture. Climate change, climate variability and sealevel rise are issues of grave concern. Similarly, the biological resources on which small island developing states depend are threatened by the large-scale exploitation of marine and terrestrial living resources.

6. Many small island developing states are entirely or predominantly coastal entities. Due to the small size, isolation and fragility of island ecosystems, their renowned biological diversity is among the most threatened in the world. This requires that in pursuing development, special attention be paid to protecting the environment and people's livelihoods. It also requires the integrated management of resources.

7. In some small island developing states, the rate of population growth exceeds the rate of economic growth, placing serious and increasing pressure on the capacity of those countries to provide basic services to their peoples, and placing a high burden on women in particular as heads of households. Although their population density may be high, many small island developing states have small populations in absolute terms, insufficient to generate economies of scale in several areas, and thus limited scope for the full utilization of certain types of high specialized expertise. They experience high levels of migration, particularly of skilled human resources, which not only places undue burden on training facilities but forces small island developing states to import high-cost foreign expertise.

8. The lack of opportunities for achieving economies of scale, together with their narrow resource base, tends to limit the total production of small island developing states to a narrow range of crops, minerals and industries, both manufacturing and services. Any adverse development concerning these productive sectors, whether arising from market factors, natural or environmental constraints, is likely to lead to significant reductions in output, a fall in foreign exchange earnings and increased unemployment.

9. Partly because of their small size and partly because of their vulnerability to natural and environmental disasters, most small island developing states are classified as high-risk entities, which has led to insurance and reinsurance being either unavailable or exorbitantly expensive, with adverse consequences for investment, production costs, government finances and infrastructure.

10. Because the per capita income of many small island developing states tends to be higher than that of developing countries as a group, they tend to have limited access to concessionary resources. Analysis of the economic performance of small island developing states, however, suggests that current incomes are often facilitated by migrant remittances, preferential market access for some major exports and assistance from the international community. These sources are neither endogenous nor secure. Furthermore, incomes of small island developing states have generally been unstable over time; natural and man-made disasters, difficulties in the international market for particular commodities and recession in some developed economies often reduce incomes in small island developing states dramatically, sometimes by as much as 20 to 30 percent of gross domestic product (GDP) in a single year.

11. Because small island development options are limited, they present special challenges to planning for and implementing sustainable development. To meet that challenge, the most valuable asset of small island developing states is their human resources, which need to be given every opportunity to fulfill their potential and contribute meaningfully to national, regional and international development consistent with the Rio Declaration and Agenda 21. Small island developing states will be constrained in meeting those challenges without the cooperation and assistance of the international community. The sustainable development of small island developing states requires actions that address the above constraints to development. Those actions should integrate environmental considerations and natural resource conservation objectives and gender considerations constant with the Rio Declaration and Agenda 21, into the development of social and economic development policies in international, regional, sub-regional and/or bilateral cooperative programmes related to islands.

12. Within small island developing states the critical contribution of women to sustainable development and the involvement of youth to the long term success of Agenda 21 should be fully recognized. Accordingly, youth should be encouraged to contribute to the decision-making process and all obstacles to the equal participation of women in this process should be eliminated to allow both youth and women to participate in, and benefit from the sustainable development of their particular societies.

13. Sharing a common aspiration for economic development and improved living standards, small island developing states are determined that the pursuit of material benefits should not undermine social, religious and cultural values nor cause any permanent harm to their people or to the land and marine resources which have sustained island life for many centuries. In Agenda 21, the international community committed itself to:

(a) Adopt and implement plans and programmes to support the sustainable development and utilization of their marine and coastal resources, including meeting essential human needs, maintaining biodiversity and improving the quality of life for island people;

(b) Adopt measures which will enable small island developing states to cope effectively, creatively and sustainably with environmental change and to mitigate impacts and reduce threats posed to marine and coastal resources.

Those commitments were later incorporated into General Assembly resolution 47/189 of 22 December 1992, which called for a Global Conference on the Sustainable Development of Small Island Developing states.

14. In establishing the basis for a new global partnership for sustainable development, states have acknowledged their common but differentiated responsibilities in respect of global environmental degradation as stated in Principle 7 of the Rio Declaration. Principle 6 states that the special situation and needs of developing counties, particularly the least developed and those most environmentally vulnerable, shall be given special priority. Under chapter 17G of Agenda 21, small island developing states and islands supporting small communities are recognized as a special case for both environment and development, because they are ecologically fragile and vulnerable and their small size, limited resources, geographic dispersion and isolation from markets all place them at a disadvantage economically and prevent economies of scale.

15. It is in that context that the following programme of action addresses the special challenges and constraints facing small island developing states. Because sustainable development is a process, not a phenomenon, the programme of action focuses on the next steps that can be taken along the comprehensive path to sustainable development which will follow the principles endorsed by Governments at UNCED. The programme of action contains a synopsis of actions and policies that should be implemented over the short, medium and long term. The reports of the regional technical meetings, held in preparation for this Conference, remain an important point of reference since they contain a broad collection of recommended actions for the pursuit of sustainable development in small island developing states.

16. The programme of action presents a basis for action in 14 agreed priority areas and defines a number of actions and policies related to environmental and development planning that should be undertaken by small island developing states with the cooperation and assistance of the international community. In general, financing for the implementation of the programme of action will come from countries' own public and private sectors. Elements for inclusion in the medium- and long-term sustainable development plans of small island developing states are recommended, along with the necessary measures for enhancing their endogenous capacity. Regional approaches to sustainable development/environment problems and technical cooperation for endogenous capacity-building are proposed; and the role of the international community is outlined, including access to adequate, predictable, new and additional financial resources and optimal use of existing resources and mechanisms in accordance with chapter 33 of Agenda 21, and measures for endogenous capacity-building, in particular for developing human resources and promoting access by small island developing states to environmentally sound and energy-efficient technology for their sus-

tainable development. In that context, non-governmental organizations and other major groups should be fully involved.

17. The Programme of Action identifies priority areas with specific actions necessary to address the special challenges faced by small island developing states. In fulfilling those actions several cross-sectorial areas are identified, for example, capacity-building, including human resource development; institutional development at the national, regional and international levels; cooperation in the transfer of environmentally sound technologies; trade and economic diversifications; and finance.

About the Editors and Contributors

Jacqueline Anne Braveboy-Wagner is professor of political science at The City College of New York, and at The Graduate School and University Center of The City University of New York. A former editor of the *Caribbean Studies Newsletter,* she served as president of the Carribean Studies Association in 1992–1993, and is currently on the executive of the International Studies Association. She has published many articles and books, including *Interpreting the Third World, The Caribbean in World Affairs,* and *The Caribbean in the Pacific Century* (with W. Marvin Will, Dennis J. Gayle, and Ivelaw L. Griffith.)

Stella Maris Arnaíz Burne holds a doctorate in anthropology from Laval University, Quebec, Canada. She is a lawyer at the Universidad Nacional del Litoral, Argentina, and a professor and researcher at the Benemerita Universidad Autónoma de Puebla, Mexico.

Denis Benn holds a Ph.D. in economics and is currently United Nations Development Program resident representative for the Caribbean. He has lectured widely, and served as a consultant on international development issues. He is the author of *Ideology and Political Development: The Growth and Development of Political Ideas in the Caribbean 1774–1983.*

Edwin Carrington is Secretary-General of the Caribbean Community (Caricom). Before taking up this appointment, he served as Trinidad and Tobago's ambassador to a number of countries and as head of the African-Caribbean-Pacific Group to the European Community in Brussels.

Alfredo César Dachary earned his master's degree in sociology at the Facultad Latinoamericana de Ciencias Sociales, Chile, and his doctorate in social sciences at the University of Leiden, Holland. He is a lawyer for the Universidad Nacional del Litoral, Argentina, and a professor and researcher at the Universidad de las Américas, Puebla, Mexico.

Jean-Pierre Chardon, a former fellow at École Normale Supérieure of Saint-Cloud, France, taught for twenty-seven years at the Université des Antilles et de la Guyane, Martinique. He is currently professor of geography at La Rochelle University, France.

Cora L. E. Christian holds an M.D. from Thomas Jefferson University and a masters in public health from Johns Hopkins University. She was assistant commissioner of health in the U.S. Virgin Islands from 1977 to

1991, and currently is the medical director of Hess Oil Virgin Islands Corporation as well as medical director and principal clinical coordinator of the Virgin Islands Medical Institute (PRO). She was the first recipient of the U.S. Virgin Islands Public Health Award.

Fred Constant is professor of political science at the Institute d'Études Politiques, Strasbourg, France and visiting professor at Université des Antilles et de la Guyane, Martinique. He has authored and co-authored a number of studies about race, ethnicity, and citizenship in the Caribbean, including *Les démocraties antillaises en crise* (with Denis Martin). He was a Forum fellow in 1995 at the European University Institute in Firenze, Italy.

Damián Fernández is associate professor and chair of the department of international relations at Florida International University. He is the author and editor of several books on Cuba's domestic and foreign policy, and is currently working on a book about informal politics and civil society in Cuba.

Dennis J. Gayle is director of Asian Studies and professor of international business environment at Florida International University. He is managing editor of the Caribbean Studies Newsletter and serves on the executive committee of the Caribbean Studies Association and the Association of International Education Administrators. He is the author of several books, including *Privatization and Deregulation in Global Perspective, Tourism Management and Marketing in the Caribbean* (with Jonathan Goodrich), and *The Caribbean in the Pacific Century* (with Jacqueline Braveboy-Wagner, W. Marvin Will, and Ivelaw L. Griffith).

Rita Giacalone is director of the School of Political Science, Universidad de Los Andes, Mérida, Venezuela. She served as president of the Caribbean Studies Association from 1994 to 1995. Among her recent publications are: "Institutional Development in the Caribbean," *21st Century Policy Review;* "Bureaucracy and Agricultural Policy Implementation in Venezuela, 1958–1991" in A. Farazmand, ed., *Handbook of Bureaucracy;* and "La Asociación de Estados del Caribe: Una institución para un proyecto político de región," *Mundo Nuevo* (Caracas).

Monica Gordon holds a Ph.D. in sociology from the City University of New York and is Adjunct Associate Professor at Medgar Evers College, CUNY. Her research interest and publications are in the areas of international migration and Caribbean migrant experiences, Caribbean studies, and women's issues.

Ivelaw L. Griffith is associate professor of political science at Florida International University. A specialist in Caribbean and hemispheric security, he has published many journal articles and has authored or edited several books, including *The Quest for Security in the Caribbean, Democracy* *and Human Rights in the Caribbean* (co-edited with Betty Sedoc-Dahlberg), and *Sovereignty under Siege* (forthcoming).

Rosemarijn van Hoefte earned her doctorate in sociology from the University of Florida and is currently associate professor, Royal Institute of Anthropology and Sociology, Leisden. Her interests include Caribbean social development and cross-cultural interaction, with a focus on the relationship between the Dutch Caribbean and the other Caribbean sub-regions.

Patrick A. M. Manning is the leader of the Opposition in the Parliament of Trinidad and Tobago. He served as the country's prime minister from 1991 to 1995.

Olga Nazarío, Ph.D., is a senior foreign policy research analyst at the Radio Martí program of the International Broadcasting Bureau in Washington, D.C.

Rex Nettleford is deputy vice-chancellor and professor of Continuing Studies at the University of the West Indies, Jamaica. A former Rhodes scholar, Professor Nettleford is also the founder, artistic director, and principal choreographer of Jamaica's National Dance Theater Company. He is the author of a number of books, including *Rastafarians in Kingston, Jamaica* (with F. R. Augier and M. G. Smith), *Manley and the New Jamaica, Dance Jamaica: Self-Definition and Artistic Discovery,* and *The University of the West Indies: A Caribbean Response to the Challenge of Change.* He is the editor of *Caribbean Quarterly.*

Felipe Noguera holds degrees from Harvard University, The School of Advanced International Studies, and The Fletcher School of Law and Diplomacy. He has published numerous articles on telecommunications and culture. He served as advisor to the Venezuelan government on satellite technology development policy and as manager of strategic planning for the Trinidad and Tobago Telephone Company. He is currently chief executive officer of the Caribbean Association of Industry and Commerce. He is a former secretary-general of the Caribbean Association of National Telecommunications Associations (CANTO).

Ransford W. Palmer is graduate professor of economics at Howard University. He is a former president of the Caribbean Studies Association, and is a specialist in international economic development. His books include *Problems of Development in Beautiful Countries, In Search of a Better Life: Perspectives on Migration from the Caribbean,* and *Pilgrims from the Sun: West Indian Migration to America.*

LaVerne E. Ragster is director of the East Caribbean Center, and professor of marine biology at the University of the Virgin Islands. She is also coordinator of the Caribbean Universities for Natural Resource Management and a former president of the Caribbean Studies Association. Her publications have focused on resource management, and training of resource managers in the Caribbean.

Roderick Rainford is advisor to the executive director for Canada, Caribbean Community countries, and Ireland at the International Monetary Fund. He was secretary-general of the Caribbean Community (Caricom) from 1983 to 1992, and Governor of the Bank of Jamaica from 1992 to 1993. He was a member of the West Indian Commission which prepared the report *Time for Action* concerning the future of Caribbean integration.

Andrés Serbín is special advisor to the deputy director of the Sistemo Latinamericano Económico (SELA), director of the Venezuelan Institute of Social and Political Studies (INVESP), and professor of sociology and international relations at the Universidad Central de Venezuela. He is the author/editor of numerous articles and books on the Caribbean, including *Caribbean Geopolitics, Distant Cousins: The Caribbean-Latin American Relationship* (co-edited with Anthony T. Bryan), and *El Grupo de los Tres: evolución y perspectiva*. He is a former president of the Caribbean Studies Association.

Ewart Skinner holds a Ph.D. from Michigan State University, and is assistant professor in the department of telecommunications, Bowling Green State University, Ohio. He has also taught at Purdue University and the University of Evansville, Indiana. He has done research at the American University in Cairo, and has worked for UNESCO as a development consultant. His publications are in the areas of Caribbean media issues, third world development, Caribbean literature and culture and the political economy of communication.

Bhoendradatt Tewarie is executive director of the University of the West Indies Institute of Business in Trinidad. He was previously minister of industry, enterprise, and tourism in the Trinidad and Tobago government. He holds a Ph.D. from Pennsylvania State University. He has been a lecturer at the University of the West Indies, Trinidad, and currently teaches in the MBA program at the Institute of Business.

Mario Trajtenberg was a journalist and freelance broadcaster in Uruguay before joining the International Labor Office (ILO) in 1969. He held the positions of acting public information officer and spokesman for the director-general, and, before retiring in 1995, he served as director if the ILO offices in Trinidad and Buenos Aires. He has been a frequent lecturer and writer on the ILO and international labor standards.

Index

Printed in the United States
by Baker & Taylor Publisher Services